Great Garden Fix-Its

Great Garden Fix-Its

Organic Remedies for Everything from Aphids to Weeds

Christine Bucks, Editor

RODALE

RODALE

WE INSPIRE AND ENABLE PEOPLE TO IMPROVE
THEIR LIVES AND THE WORLD AROUND THEM

LIBRARY OF CONGRESS CATALOGING-IN-PUBLICATION DATA

    Great garden fix-its : organic remedies for everything from aphids to weeds / Christine Bucks, editor.
        p.   cm.
    Includes bibliographical references and index.
    ISBN 0–87596–997–6 (pbk : alk. paper)
    1. Garden pests—Biological control. 2. Plant diseases. 3. Plants, Protection of. 4. Organic gardening. I. Bucks, Christine.
    SB974 .G74 2001
    635'.0484—dc21   2001000793

Distributed in the book trade by St. Martin's Press

2 4 6 8 10 9 7 5 3 1   paperback

Editor: Christine Bucks
Contributing Editor: Erana Bumbardatore
Cover and Interior Book Designer: Marta Mitchell Strait
Contributing Designer: Dale Mack
Cover and Interior Illustrator: Jason Schneider
Layout Designer: Jennifer H. Giandomenico
Researchers: Claudia Curran, Diana Erney, Sarah Wolfgang Heffner
Copy Editors: Stacey Ann Follin, Candace Levy
Manufacturing Coordinator: Patrick T. Smith
Indexer: Lina Burton
Editorial Assistance: Kerrie A. Cadden

RODALE ORGANIC GARDENING BOOKS

Executive Editor: Kathleen DeVanna Fish
Managing Editor: Fern Marshall Bradley
Executive Creative Director: Christin Gangi
Art Director: Patricia Field
Production Manager: Robert V. Anderson Jr.
Studio Manager: Leslie M. Keefe
Copy Manager: Nancy N. Bailey
Book Manufacturing Director: Helen Clogston

We're always happy to hear from you. For questions or comments concerning the editorial content of this book, please write to:

    Rodale Book Readers' Service
    33 East Minor Street
    Emmaus, PA 18098

Look for other Rodale books wherever books are sold. Or call us at (800) 848-4735.

For more information about Rodale Organic Gardening magazine and books, visit us at

www.organicgardening.com

Rodale

ORGANIC GARDENING STARTS HERE!

Here at Rodale, we've been gardening organically for more than 50 years—ever since my grandfather J. I. Rodale learned about composting and decided that healthy living starts with healthy soil. In 1940 J. I. started the Rodale Organic Farm to test his theories, and today the nonprofit Rodale Institute Experimental Farm is still at the forefront of organic gardening and farming research. In 1942 J. I. founded *Organic Gardening* magazine to share his discoveries with gardeners everywhere. His son, my father, Robert Rodale, headed *Organic Gardening* until 1990, and today a fourth generation of Rodales is growing up with the magazine. Over the years we've shown millions of readers how to grow bountiful crops and beautiful flowers using nature's own techniques.

In this book, you'll find the latest organic methods and the best gardening advice. We know—because all our authors and editors are passionate about gardening! We feel strongly that our gardens should be safe for our children, pets, and the birds and butterflies that add beauty and delight to our lives and landscapes. Our gardens should provide us with fresh, flavorful vegetables, delightful herbs, and gorgeous flowers. And they should be a pleasure to work in as well as to view.

Sharing the secrets of safe, successful gardening is why we publish books. So come visit us at the Rodale Institute Experimental Farm, where you can tour the gardens every day—we're open year-round. And use this book to create your best garden ever.

Happy gardening!

Maria Rodale

Maria Rodale
Rodale Organic Gardening Books

Contents

Contributors

George DeVault is the editor of Rodale's Russian-language gardening and farming magazine. He operates a certified organic vegetable farm in Emmaus, Pennsylvania.

Melanie DeVault, a frequent contributor to Rodale garden books, raises vegetables and flowers on a certified organic farm in Emmaus, Pennsylvania.

Nancy Engel tends a half-acre garden in Putnam County, New York, where she faces the daily challenges of deer, rocks, and roving cats and dogs.

Veronica Lorson Fowler is a freelance garden writer and editor based in Ames, Iowa. She has contributed to various national publications, including *Better Homes and Gardens*, and is also a Master Gardener.

Linda Harris is a horticultural writer, desktop designer of Web sites and catalogs, marketing consultant, Master Gardener, and speaker. She's currently working on a book about birds and butterflies.

Cass Peterson is an editor and garden writer. For 17 years, she operated a Pennsylvania farm, growing vegetables, berries, and cutting flowers.

Barbara Pleasant lives and gardens in Huntsville, Alabama. She is the author of a dozen gardening books and more magazine articles and newspaper columns than she can remember.

Melinda Rizzo is a freelance writer living and gardening in Upper Bucks County, Pennsylvania.

Vicki Webster is the author of numerous books and magazine articles and also has written extensively for electronic media. She's a former editor at *Country Home* and *Better Homes and Gardens* magazines and is currently a book editor at Storey Books.

Fixing Problems from A to Z

The secrets to successful gardening include practice, patience, luck—and a talent for solving problems when they creep up on you. That's because no matter how green your gardening thumb is, you can't control Mother Nature and the potential bugaboos she may unleash in the form of disease, insect, and animal pests and less than stellar weather. But you *can* make the best out of the situation.

That's where this book comes in. We've gathered tips from gardeners across the country who have to deal with the same problems you do—and who have come up with remarkably resourceful, all-organic solutions for fixing those problems. Within these pages you'll find out the fastest way to deadhead perennials, how to hide an ugly heating oil tank in your landscape—and a ton of other practical hints and tips.

FINDING THE ANSWERS

We've arranged this book in alphabetical order by subject; that way, if you have a particular problem that needs your attention, you can easily turn to the chapter about that topic to find an answer. For example, do you love beans but don't have enough room to grow them? Then turn to "Bean Problems" on page 9 to find out how Weldon Burge from Newark, Delaware, grows up to eight different bean varieties in a small bed. Or, maybe you have birds helping themselves to your cherries? In this case, you could turn to "Fruit Tree Problems" on page 69 or to "Animal Problems" on page 1 to learn some simple solutions. (If you glance at the table of contents, you'll discover that our contributing gardeners have covered just about every subject that applies to gardening.)

Of course, you can also browse through this book to get ideas for *preventing* problems in the first place. You'll find out how to use drinking straws to protect your young seedlings from cutworms and how to make a slug motel to trap those slimers before they snack on your plants.

You'll notice that within each chapter we've called out fast fixes, titled "Solutions at a Glance." These are quick solutions that you can do with a snap of your fingers; they don't require a lot of instruction, supplies—or a lot of your time. Also watch for "Pest Detective" charts that help you figure out what disease or bad bug is at work in your garden—and how you can control it organically.

SMART SOLUTIONS START HERE

Ultimately, no matter where you live or how long you've been planting and growing things, *Great Garden Fix-Its* will give you reader-tested information you can use. So the next time you're faced with a broken fence or too much shade, don't despair—you'll find all the practical, organic solutions you'll need right here. And the less time you have to spend on solving problems, the more time you'll have to enjoy your beautiful, bountiful garden.

Animal
Problems

All those lovely vegetables and flowers might constitute a garden to you, but to the two- and four-legged creatures that live nearby, your garden looks like free lunch. Short of growing everything in a greenhouse (and even *that* isn't guaranteed free from furry or feathered beasts), how do you persuade wildlife to look elsewhere for food? Read on for some clever strategies that have worked for other gardeners. Keep in mind that some animals learn quickly, so you may have to switch tactics from time to time to stay ahead of the game.

OUTSMARTING BAMBI

For most gardeners, deer are the biggest challenge. The low fences that dissuade rabbits and groundhogs are an easy leap for these bounding creatures. And the permanent deer fencing that commercial nurseries and market gardeners use only works if it remains powered all the time. The solution: temporary fencing—which is what Hiu Newcomb, a market gardener in Vienna, Virginia, uses.

The most common kind of temporary fencing has two strands of "hot tape" (ribbon-like material with wire woven into it to carry an electric charge) strung on easily installed fiberglass poles. Temporary fencing works best if you bait it because you want the deer to learn that the fence means business. Peanut butter, which deer adore, is a great bait. Smear some directly on the hot tape every 6 feet or so, or make little peanut butter "sandwiches" by putting a teaspoon of it inside a folded strip of athletic tape, wrapping some foil around the tape, and attaching it to the fence. The deer will stay out, and your garden will stay safe.

BAIT YOUR ELECTRIC FENCE WITH PEANUT BUTTER TO TRAIN DEER TO STAY AWAY.

UNDERCOVER DEER DETERRENT

Deer laugh at chicken-wire fencing when it's upright (so easy to jump!)—so lay it flat on the ground around the garden instead. The deer can't see it, and as they approach, they get their hooves entangled in the woven wires. It's easy to install and easy to maintain: Just flip the fence aside occasionally to mow under it so it doesn't become caught in tall grass, and roll it up for storage when the season is over.

THE NOT-SO-SWEET SMELL OF SUCCESS

Hanging out stuff that smells nasty is another way of keeping deer out of where they don't belong. Deer are naturally mistrustful of unusual or threatening scents, so hanging out cheesecloth bags of human hair, dirty socks, or empty detergent boxes may help deter them. Switching from one aromatic repellent to another every few days keeps the deer off guard.

Commercial deer repellents are available, but they don't always deliver the "antibuck" bang for the buck. Connecticut researchers tested several common deer repellents on nursery trees and shrubs. Their results are in the chart below.

TRICKS OF THE TRELLIS

If store-bought fencing isn't an option for keeping deer at bay, why not let trellised vegetables do the job for you? Grow cucumbers, peas, or pole beans on trellises around the perimeter of the garden to protect the veggies within. Deer, being opportunists, will dine on the trellised veggies and leave the produce that they can't get to alone.

SHINE AND SHAKE

When tricks aimed at the deer's nose fail to keep the critter out of your garden, try gambits aimed at the eyes and ears. If there's power nearby,

---

Unwelcome Odors

Surrounding your garden beds with scents deer don't like is one way to pull the welcome mat out from under them. Here's a quick look at five products you can try, their effectiveness, and approximately how much they'll cost.

Repellent	Effectiveness	Cost per Acre
Deer Away (rotten eggs)	46 percent	$990
Hinder Deer and Rabbit Repellent (ammonium soaps)	43 percent	$75
Human hair	34 percent	$24
Magic Circle Deer Repellent (bone tar oil)	18 percent	$74
Miller Hot Sauce (extract of hot peppers)	15 percent	$26

Note: *Always check the labels of deer repellents to see if they're intended for landscape plants only or for vegetable plants as well.*

---

spotlight the deer with motion sensor lights. (The lights will discourage raccoons, too.) Deer are also easily spooked by moving shapes—floating row covers on a moonlit night are sometimes enough to send them packing. Or staple plastic trash bags to tomato stakes: The bags look like people and flap in the slightest breeze.

CROWS OUT, SEEDS IN

Birds, especially crows, love to pull seeds and seedlings out of the ground. Here are two ways to keep your young charges safe.

- Protect newly sprouted corn and beans and freshly planted transplants by tying twine to a double row of short bamboo stakes (like miniature telephone wires) and attaching strips of aluminum foil every few feet. The flapping foil will send crows packing.
- Keep crows from dining on newly planted seeds by covering beds with floating row cover or chicken-wire fencing.

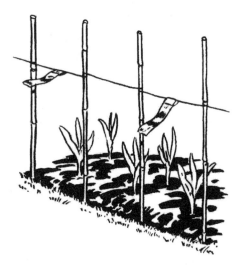

SCARE CROWS AWAY FROM SEEDLINGS AND TRANSPLANTS WITH FLAPPING FOIL.

Solutions at a Glance

PROBLEM: Something is eating all your carrot tops.

CULPRIT: Rabbits

SOLVE IT! Scare them away with plastic snakes. Cut an old garden hose into serpentlike lengths and place the pieces throughout your garden.

BAG 'EM

When crows moved in on her new transplants and wild turkeys took a liking to her strawberries, market gardener Sylvia Ehrhardt of Knoxville, Maryland, decided to bag them. "We filled plastic grocery bags with air and tied them shut, and then we put them on top of stakes throughout the garden, every 10 to 15 feet, up and down the row," says Ehrhardt. "The bags move in the breeze and look like people leaning over."

The multicolored bags are more effective than the aluminum pie plates she tried first, Ehrhardt says. "They work well for new transplants, too, which the crows pull up. We take them down when the plants get bigger."

BLOODMEAL CONTAINED

Bloodmeal is an effective repellent for small rodents, but if you simply sprinkle it around your plants, you'll have to reapply it every time it rains. Here's a way to keep it working all season: Put the bloodmeal into empty margarine or yogurt containers (a tablespoon or so per container is plenty). Add a little water and a rock weight so the container doesn't blow away or tip over. Dis-

PROBLEM: Something is eating your corn.

CULPRIT: Raccoons

SOLVE IT! Plant pumpkins or winter squash among the corn. As the squash plants trellis up the cornstalks, they reduce visibility, which makes the raccoons uncomfortable because they like to stand up and look around while they eat.

---

tribute the containers around your garden. But keep the lids handy so you can cover the containers when you want to work in the garden. Wet bloodmeal puts out a powerful odor.

DISCO DETERRENT

Raccoons love sweet corn, but they don't care much for rock music. Put a transistor radio in the corn patch when the corn is ripening, and turn it on each night to your favorite station. (Cover the radio with a plastic bag to protect it from the elements and keep plenty of batteries on hand.) To add to the disco deterrent, string twinkling Christmas lights through the corn. Your garden will be festive, and the lights will keep the raccoons at bay.

DON'T LET RODENTS BITE THE BARK

Mice, rabbits, and voles love to munch on young trees, but that can mean death for the tree. To protect trees wrap their trunks with commercial tree guards (metal or plastic) or window screen (the openings in chicken wire are too large to keep mice from reaching the bark—they'll slip right through).

If you live in a mild-winter area, a foot or so of trunk protection will be enough to deter mice, rabbits, and voles. If you live in an area where heavy snow is common, make sure the guard extends at least a foot higher than the usual snow depth. Mice and voles will tunnel under the snow to do their nibbling, but rabbits will hop on the top of crusted snow to get at the tender bark higher up.

WRAP TREE TRUNKS HIGH ENOUGH TO KEEP RABBITS FROM USING SNOW AS A LIFT TO THE TENDER BARK.

ALTERNATIVE EATS

Rabbits have to eat, and if your yard and garden look like their favorite restaurant, it may simply be that there isn't much else available in the neighborhood. Letting a few patches of your yard grow up in clovers and wildflowers can help satisfy their hunger and keep them away from your garden. To encourage other wildlife to eat what you want them to, spray the vegetation with a concoction of 1 cup of molasses and 1 tablespoon of salt to 1 gallon of water.

GROW UNPALATABLE FARE

One of the tricks to keeping animal pests out of your garden is to grow things they don't like to eat. Some edibles and ornamentals, like rhubarb and foxgloves (*Digitalis* spp.), are repulsive or even toxic to wildlife. Creating a living fence of these plants around your yard can help deter even large animals like deer. See below for some of the things you can grow to keep wildlife at bay.

Solutions at a Glance

PROBLEM: Your lawn is full of tunnels.

CULPRIT: Moles

SOLVE IT! Discourage them by shoving prickly twigs of multiflora rose (*Rosa multiflora*) or raspberry canes into their tunnels.

FOR THE BIRDS

Birds love fruit, especially berries and cherries. Turn the page for a couple of tips to save these sweet treats from the nibbling beaks.

Plants Pests Will Pass On

If you grow these, they won't come. That's right, a few plants, like foxglove and daffodils, are just as vile to some critters as lima beans are to kids.

What to Grow	What Doesn't Like It
Alliums (*Allium* spp., including ornamental alliums as well as onions and garlic)	Birds, deer, mice, moles, rabbits, voles
Artemisias (*Artemisia* spp.)	Deer, mice, moles, rabbits, voles
Foxgloves (*Digitalis* spp.)	Deer, mice, rabbits, voles
Euphorbias (*Euphorbia* spp.)	Mice, moles
Lavenders (*Lavendula* spp.)	Mice, voles
Mints (*Mentha* spp.)	Mice, rats
Daffodils (*Narcissus* hybrids)	Moles, squirrels
Castor beans (*Ricinus communis*)	Moles
Siberian squill bulbs (*Scilla siberica*)	Gophers
Rhubarbs	Deer, rabbits

Solutions at a Glance

PROBLEM: Something is eating your shrubs.

CULPRIT: Rabbits? Or deer?

SOLVE IT! First you need positive ID on the perpetrator. Has the shrubbery been nibbled off cleanly, as if nipped with pruning shears? That's rabbit damage. Does the damage look ragged? That's the sign of deer munching. Bloodmeal will discourage the rabbit; try hanging soap bars on the shrub if the problem is deer.

PROBLEM: Your storage shed has squatters.

CULPRIT: Mice

SOLVE IT! Traps are your best bet. Bait them with peanut butter, and set a mirror behind each one. Mice are social animals and will approach a trap more readily if they think another mouse is already there.

● When cherries start to ripen, hang cut onions in the trees. You can slice the onions into rings, which are easy to hang on branches, but they'll dry out quickly and need to be replaced more often. It's best to cut the onions into halves or quarters, pierce them with a piece of wire, and hang them on the tree like ornaments.

● Birds like chokecherries (*Prunus virginiana*), elderberries (*Sambucus* spp.), and mulberries (*Morus* spp.) as much or more than they like cultivated fruits, so a slightly unkempt fence row may be the best protection for your cultivated fruits. If your fruit is the only game in town, however, you may need netting to keep some of it for yourself. You don't need to use a tight mesh—most birds won't fly into situations that might impede their wings when they're trying to get out. But make sure you aren't inadvertently keeping a mother bird from her nest! Drape the netting loosely over the tree. If the tree is too large to net completely, cover as many of the lower branches as you can.

Aphids

Aphids are living proof that bad things can come in very small packages. Also known as plant lice or greenbugs, aphids rarely appear in small groups. Instead, you may go to gather some kale that looked perfect only 3 days before and find the leaves nearly covered by swarms of $\frac{1}{8}$-inch-long, green-gray, oblong lumps—aphids! Look on the underside of a leaf, and you'll probably find several hundred more.

But you don't have to let aphids set up camp in your garden. Read on to find out how to repel these bad bugs with citrus, soap, and water as well as how to help plants with aphid damage.

LICK 'EM WITH LEMON "AID"

Aphids are repelled by limonene and linalool, the two compounds that give lemon, orange, and grapefruit rind their pungent scent. To make an effective aphid remedy that smells good too, mix 1 tablespoon of freshly grated citrus rind with 1 pint of boiling water. Let it steep overnight, strain the mixture through cheesecloth or a coffee filter, and pour the resulting "tea" into a pump spray bottle. Add 3 drops of insecticidal soap or dish-washing liquid to help the lemony mixture stick to plants' leaves and aphids' bodies, then give affected plants a thorough spritz with the spray.

WHEN LIFE HANDS YOU APHIDS, MAKE LEMON "AID." STEEP GRATED CITRUS PEEL IN BOILING WATER TO MAKE A LEMON-SCENTED TEA THAT WILL SEND APHIDS PACKING.

YOUR PEST DEFENSE

Although they're small, aphids can do big damage if they go unchecked for too long. When aphids get out of hand, try these tips to help rid your plants of these pests.

START WITH A STREAM. For starters, simply knock the pests from your plants with a strong spray of water from a hose or pressure sprayer. You can repeat this treatment as often as needed to get aphids under control, but don't spray so hard that you harm your plants.

CUT IT OUT. Remove plant parts that aren't likely to recover from aphid injury. Pinch off or prune away severely damaged parts of an infested plant. When you find aphids so densely packed on a stem or leaf that they completely cover its surface, get rid of them by picking or pruning off the affected plant part and dropping it into a pail of hot soapy water.

SCRUB UP WITH (INSECTICIDAL) SOAP. Treat severe aphid problems by spraying insecticidal soap on infested plants and on plants growing nearby. (Test the spray first to make sure it doesn't do more damage than the aphids. Apply the soap to a few leaves and wait 3 days. If you don't see any signs of damage—leaf browning, spotting, or curling—proceed with the spray.) Make sure you completely cover leaf undersides and other sheltered places. Repeat the application every 5 to 7 days until the aphids are gone. The soap also helps remove deposits of unsightly sooty mold, which commonly forms on the aphids' honeydew. Remember that insecticidal soap also harms beneficial insects, so be sure to use it only when absolutely necessary.

TAKE A PREVENTIVE APPROACH. For trees or shrubs that have recurring aphid problems, alternate applications of insecticidal soap and light horticultural oil at weekly intervals beginning in early spring. (Again, test the soap or oil on a few leaves first.) Spray injury becomes more likely at higher temperatures, so be extra careful as spring turns to summer.

THE APHID-ANT ALLIANCE

The sticky honeydew that aphids excrete is a sugary protein substance that's pure candy for ants. Ants have even been seen protecting aphid colonies from predators to safeguard their treats! If you notice ants lurking near clusters of aphids, douse the affected plant with water to knock the ants to the ground. Then encircle the main stems or trunks with a 1-inch-wide band of a sticky material such as Tanglefoot or Stickem to trap the ants as they try to crawl back up the plants. Without their ant bodyguards, aphids are easier prey for hungry predators.

ANTS ACTUALLY TEND COLONIES OF APHIDS SO THEY CAN FEED ON THE STICKY SWEET HONEYDEW THE APHIDS EXCRETE. KNOCK THE ANTS OFF YOUR PLANTS WITH WATER, AND THEN USE A BAND OF STICKY STUFF TO KEEP THEM FROM COMING BACK.

Bean Problems

Beans are some of the easiest and most reliable vegetables to grow, so it's no surprise that they're some of the most popular garden vegetables today. But nothing is foolproof, not even these "easy" vegetables. Coaxing seeds to germinate in cool, spring soil can be tough as can getting seedlings past the tender baby stage when they're so attractive to deer and rabbits. But help is at hand—read on for the secrets to a hearty, healthy bean crop.

Rx for Healthy Beans

A bumper crop of beans will be easy pickin' if you follow these tips for making beans feel right at home in your garden.

GET THEM OFF TO A WARM START. Most veteran gardeners agree that this means waiting until all danger of frost has past—so wait for warm soil and air (both at least 60°F) to plant the beans. If you jump the gun and plant them in cold soil, they'll germinate slowly, and they'll be more vulnerable to rot and soil-borne diseases.

But if you have to have the earliest beans in the neighborhood and the soil temperature is still below 60°F, try these tips: First, for at least 2 weeks before your early target date (slightly before the last expected frost), warm the soil by tightly covering the planting area with black plastic. Second, think purple. Purple varieties tend to be more agreeable to cool soil. (Or check seed catalogs for other early varieties.) Once seedlings emerge, you can use a floating row cover to help protect them from cold temperatures and pests.

PREPARE THE SOIL. Beans don't usually need fertilizer if you enrich the soil with a healthy dose of compost before planting. (Also, the microorganisms in compost help suppress diseases.) However, the beans do like a loose soil that encourages germination and root growth, so dig down 8 to 12 inches.

PREPARE THE BEST SEEDS YOU CAN. Many expert gardeners soak their bean seeds in water for 30 minutes before planting, or they pregerminate seeds by placing them between two damp paper towels overnight. Whether or not you pregerminate, it's a good idea to inoculate the seed to ensure that beneficial bacteria are present. Some seed companies claim a yield boost of 20 percent with inoculant. (Inoculants help beans, which are legumes, fix nitrogen in their root nodules. Inoculants are available at garden centers and through mail-order catalogs.)

Additionally, Dr. Steve Reiners, associate professor of horticulture at Cornell University, Ithaca, New York, says to check seed packets for the germination percentage (catalogs don't give you this information). "You can learn which seed companies tend to offer higher germination," he says. "If you have a 70 percent germination (weak seed), and plant in 55°F soil, you're setting yourself up for trouble. If you have a choice, go for higher germination (85 percent or more)!"

PLANT 'EM SNUG. The biggest disagreement among bean experts is in regard to planting. Traditional wisdom suggests planting seeds 1 inch deep, 2 to 3 inches apart, and then thinning seedlings to 6 inches apart. This strategy is said to increase air circulation and help ward off the spread of disease by removing the weakest plants.

But Reiners says that they've done some amazing studies on bean spacing—and the bottom line is it doesn't really matter whether they're spaced closely or not. You can really crowd those bush bean seeds in there and still get a good crop. "Data collected over a couple of years show it didn't make a difference whether the beans were spaced 2, 3, or even 4 inches apart," he says. And home gardeners can space rows 1½ to 2 feet apart. This denser planting essentially causes the leaves of the plants to grow into a shade-producing canopy that cools the soil and inhibits weeds. So what does this information mean for your garden? Experiment and see what works best for you!

PROVIDE ADEQUATE MOISTURE AND MULCH. Beans have shallow root systems, so they'll suffer badly during a drought. Water plants until they're established, and then keep the soil evenly moist. They need at least 1 inch of water a week once they're up and running, but you should let the soil dry out between waterings. Beans don't like to have perpetually wet feet. Mulch can be a big helper, especially if you live where summers are hot and dry. Grass clippings, shredded newspaper, and straw all have their advocates. These mulches don't just keep the soil moist, they keep weeds at bay, which means your beans won't be competing with them for moisture and nutrition.

PICK, PICK, PICK! Beans need to be picked often—that is, every 2 to 3 days. If the pods are allowed to mature (to get big and tough), your plants will get Mother Nature's signal that it's fine to slack off on pod production. Picking is the number one way to keep 'em coming.

STAY OUT OF THE BEAN PATCH WHEN IT'S WET. If you go trudging through the beans when vines are wet, you're just asking to spread bean diseases like anthracnose or rust.

ROTATE! If you have the space to rotate crops, avoid growing beans in the same spot 2 years in a row (some experts even recommend a 3-year rotation). That's because beans are susceptible to a host of diseases that live in the soil, and rotating your bean plantings helps to prevent a buildup of those diseases. If you have a small space garden (which makes

Pest Detective

Have a problem with your bean plants but aren't sure who the culprit is? This quick reference chart can help you identify the bad guys and give you organic ways to beat them at their own game.

Symptom	Cause	What to Do
Dark streaks on leaves; sunken spots on pods	Anthracnose	Plant tolerant varieties and destroy infected plants. Don't touch plants when wet, or you may spread the disease. Preventive measures include keeping a clean garden (removing spent plants, weeds, and infected plants regularly) and rotating crops.
Mottled, curled leaves; rough spots on pods	Bean mosaic	Avoid touching the plants when wet, or you may spread the disease, and control sucking insects, such as aphids. Destroy infected plants, and plant mosaic-tolerant cultivars.
Skeletonized leaves, holes in beans	Mexican bean beetle (yellow larvae, brownish bugs with black spots)	Destroy yellow egg clusters and adults on undersides of leaves, and encourage beneficial insects, such as adult soldier bugs and parasitic wasps. You can purchase the parasitic wasp (*Pediobus foveolatus*) and release it when the first generation of Mexican bean beetle larvae are about half grown. You can also try planting resistant varieties, such as 'Black Valentine'.
Reddish brown, orange, or yellow bumps on leaves and pods	Rust	Keep the leaves dry. Destroy any infected leaves, and try planting resistant varieties.
Leaves drop or have pale speckles	Spider mites	Use garlic and soap sprays.
Warty bumps on pods	Stink bugs	Remove these brown, shield-shape bugs from the plants by shaking them over trays of soapy water; you can also counter them with beneficial insects, such as parasitic wasps and tachinid flies. Spray plants with insecticidal soap, and control weeds around your beans.

rotating crops difficult), add some compost to your soil before planting—compost helps suppress disease organisms.

IF YOU WANT THE EARLIEST BEANS ON YOUR BLOCK, WARM UP THE SOIL BY COVERING YOUR PLANTING BED WITH BLACK PLASTIC.

SHORT ON SPACE?

No problem, says Weldon Burge, an organic gardener from Newark, Delaware. Probably the biggest myth about beans, he believes, is that you need a lot of garden to grow them. Burge grows all of his beans in a 4 × 8-foot raised bed. He grows six to eight different varieties and supplies his family with ample beans from early summer through late fall. Here's how Burge does it.

He divides his raised beds into 1 × 4-foot-long sections, which he works well to a depth of 8 inches and then mixes in compost and coarse sand. He sows bean seeds in these wide swaths because he believes this not only uses space more efficiently but also boosts bean production by increasing soil moisture and smothering weeds.

He starts planting his early-variety snap beans after the last expected frost in a block at one end of the raised bed. He scatters the seeds so they fall about 1 inch apart, and then he pokes them in about 1 inch deep (he plants them twice that deep in summer). Once plants are established, he makes sure they have adequate water, and he mulches with clean straw to conserve moisture. He does successive plantings every 2 to 3 weeks, moving down the bed, starting with early-season purple varieties ('Royal Burgundy' and 'Purple Teepee' are his favorites), and moving on to mid- and late-season varieties. He sows his final fall crop in August. (Watch the timing in your area to make sure you allow enough time before the first fall frost.)

As each crop finishes heavy production, he cleans the plants out of the foot-wide strip. After he has planted the length of the bed, he returns to these now-empty plots for successive plantings. By removing spent plants, Burge makes room for later plantings and keeps bugs in check. (Despite growing a feast of beans, he reports that he has little problem with Mexican bean beetles.)

SUCCESSIVE PLANTING IN A RAISED BED CAN GIVE YOU AN AMPLE SUPPLY OF TASTY BEANS WHEN YOU'RE SHORT ON GARDEN SPACE.

Berry Problems

Bountiful, beautiful berries are the supreme garden treat, whether you're growing your own perfectly ripened strawberries, luscious raspberries, or plump blueberries. But if you want your share, you'll need to be prepared for freeloaders, especially birds, although many insect pests adore berries as well. Because berries are juicy, sweet, and often soft, they're also prone to mold and mildew problems. Forewarned is forearmed, so read on for solutions.

STRAWBERRY WEED WOES

Strawberries throw out runners hither and yon, making them difficult to hoe, and they're in the ground for several years—perfect conditions to create a serious problem with perennial weeds. How to prevent weed woes? "You have to start with a clean bed," says market gardener Tony Ricci from Three Springs, Pennsylvania. "Cover-crop the bed you want to grow strawberries in for a year or so. If the weeds start out ahead of you, you'll never catch up."

In established beds, a companion crop that's compatible with the strawberries can help control weeds. Ricci sows oats (*Avena sativa*) between his spring-planted strawberry beds in mid-September, which creates a thick mat between the strawberry plants. This cover crop grows 6 to 8 inches tall and dies in the winter. The next spring the debris from the spent oats suppresses early weeds until about May—then the oats break down completely.

Sylvia Ehrhardt, who specializes in berries at her Knoxville, Maryland, farm, uses straw mulch atop four layers of newspaper between the rows of strawberries and mulches between the plants in the rows with compost or old sawdust. "That keeps weeds down and feeds the plants, too," she says.

Ehrhardt also keeps perennial weeds to a minimum—and renovates her strawberry beds at the same time—by tilling the rows of strawberries to about 1 foot wide every year after harvest. The tilling wipes out weeds between the rows and allows the plants to set new runners every year for maximum yields.

A Hilly Advantage

If weeding between strawberry runners isn't your cup of tea, try growing strawberries in a hill system. Under this system, the plants aren't allowed to set runners; you snip those off and direct all the plant's energy into the mother plant. The advantage is that the plants are easier to hoe, and you can eliminate weeds entirely by setting the plants into plastic mulch or landscape fabric.

Say good-bye to strawberry weed woes using the hill system.

Saggy Trellis Solution

Keep your blackberry and raspberry trellises from sagging when wet by using *plastic* baling twine between the stakes. One or two strands are all you need, and you can save the twine to use again year after year.

Outfox Your Feathered Friends

Birds in your blueberries? Here are three ways to put an end to their feast.

USE SCARE TACTICS. When the first berries appear on the early ripening varieties at Melanie DeVault's farm in Emmaus, Pennsylvania, she puts up bird scare balloons and bird scare tape. The balloons (many of them metallic with giant eyes printed on them) and Mylar tape (it hums and flutters in the breeze) are readily available in stores, but you can put together your own bird scare arsenal for less money. Just visit your local florist or party-goods store for Mylar balloons, and cut out strips of aluminum foil for bird scare tape.

PUT UP PLASTIC NETTING. Plastic bird netting (the holes are about a half-inch in diameter) is available in various sizes at garden centers. You can make the whole job of putting up the netting easier if you erect a permanent wooden frame around your bushes. Then just attach the netting to the frame during berry season. (Staple the top of the netting to the frame, run inexpensive twine through some of the bottom holes in the netting, and tie the twine in a bow. That way, it's easy to untie the twine, lift the netting, and pick the berries.)

PLANT OTHER BERRIES. If you have enough space, planting alternative food sources works great for deterring birds. In fact, they prefer mulberries (*Morus* spp.), chokecherry (*Prunus virginiana*), and elderberries (*Sambucus* spp.) to cultivated berries.

Create a party atmosphere in your garden and keep birds out of the berries at the same time.

Solutions at a Glance

PROBLEM: Your berries are rotting.

CULPRIT: Fungal diseases

SOLVE IT! Take a look at your watering practices. Wet berries invite fungal diseases, so drip irrigation or soaker hoses are better than overhead watering.

PROBLEM: Something's eating your grapes and raspberries.

CULPRIT: Japanese beetles

SOLVE IT! Handpick the beetles before 7 A.M., when they're still sluggish.

PROBLEM: Your strawberries are deformed and seedy.

CULPRIT: Tarnished plant bugs

SOLVE IT! Rotate the strawberries every 3 years to prevent pests from building up (potatoes are a great rotation crop). Mow the bed and remove debris each year, and cover the berries with a floating row cover until they're in full flower, to prevent adults from laying eggs on the foliage (it's the nymphs that do the damage). Plant fennel or dill nearby to attract beneficial insects, and don't weed out the Queen-Anne's lace.

PROBLEM: Your blueberry clusters have unwelcome visitors.

CULPRIT: Earwigs

SOLVE IT! Catch earwigs with a shallow container of vegetable oil, or use toilet-paper tubes coated inside with oil and squashed almost flat. The oiliness and the darkness of the tube will attract the earwigs. Check the traps each morning and dispose of any you've caught.

PROBLEM: The blueberry foliage is yellowing.

CULPRIT: Nutritional deficiency

SOLVE IT! Check the soil pH. If it's above 5.2, the problem may be iron deficiency. Add sulfur to acidify the soil. If it's below 5.2, your problem may be calcium deficiency. Add gypsum to provide calcium without raising the pH.

Sulfur Solutions

Blueberries love acidic soil, so it's your job to see that their acid requirements are satisfied. After checking your soil's pH, look at the handy chart below to see how much sulfur you need to add to your soil, if any.

Current pH	Sandy Soil	Loamy Soil	Clay Soil
4.5	0	0	0
5.0	0.4 lb. per 100 sq. ft.	1.2 lb. per 100 sq. ft.	1.8 lb. per 100 sq. ft.
5.5	0.8 lb. per 100 sq. ft.	2.3 lb. per 100 sq. ft.	3.5 lb. per 100 sq. ft.
6.0	1.2 lb. per 100 sq. ft.	3.4 lb. per 100 sq. ft.	5.1 lb. per 100 sq. ft.
6.5	1.5 lb. per 100 sq. ft.	4.5 lb. per 100 sq. ft.	6.7 lb. per 100 sq. ft.
7.0	1.9 lb. per 100 sq. ft.	5.7 lb. per 100 sq. ft.	8.5 lb. per 100 sq. ft.
7.5	2.2 lb. per 100 sq. ft.	6.8 lb. per 100 sq. ft.	10 lb. per 100 sq. ft.

SPACE-SAVING STRAWBERRIES

Coming up short on garden space? Try growing strawberries with asparagus. "My asparagus bed is a single row along a long end of the vegetable garden," says Lisa Krall, a soil scientist with the USDA's Natural Resources Conservation Service. "Weeding this 3-foot-wide bed for one row seemed like a pain, so I put in the strawberries."

Krall plants berries in rows on either side of the asparagus in her garden in Belgrade, Maine, and directs strawberry runners away from the asparagus.

"I think they're quite compatible," she says. "They occupy different parts of the root zone and seem to like the same treatment. This bed is the only one I water regularly, since both crops seem to respond to an inch a week."

Bulb Problems

Bulbs . . . just plunk them in the ground, wait a little while, and watch them burst forth into color, right? Well, yes—as long as pesky critters don't gnaw them, viruses don't zap them, the temperatures are just right, and you've planted them correctly.

But you aren't far off. Plant bulbs correctly and foil the pests, and you'll have a dazzling display of color for years to come. And best of all, many bulbs provide color just when you need it the most—early spring. Here's how to make sure you get the most bang from your bulbs.

DIVIDE AND CONQUER

Love daffodils and want even more? You can propagate your own by dividing the bulbs.

Daffodil gardener Gene Bauer of Running Springs, California, explains that unlike many perennials, daffodils are capable of multi-plying. But they don't necessarily spread on their own—they need a little help.

After a daffodil planting becomes established (say, 7 or 8 years), dig it up in the spring after the flowers have faded and the foliage is browning. Gently break off the little 1-inch or so side bulbs, called the daughters, and set them aside.

Replant the larger bulbs in the regular garden. Then plant the small bulbs in well-marked rows in a nursery bed or in a corner of the vegetable garden. Keep them well watered and fertilize regularly. Don't expect flowers from these small bulbs for at least 2 or 3 years, though. In 3 or 4 years, the bulbs will have grown to about 3 inches, large enough to plant out in the garden where they can fend for themselves.

PROPAGATE DAFFODILS BY BREAKING OFF AND TRANSPLANTING "DAUGHTER" BULBS.

Solutions at a Glance

PROBLEM: Critters are destroying all your flower bulbs.

CULPRIT: Voles, moles, and other burrowing animals

SOLVE IT! Toss several handfuls of sharp gravel into the planting hole, place your bulbs in the hole and cover with more gravel, then fill in with soil, suggests Connie Cross of Connie Cross Garden Design in Catchogue, New York.

COMPANION COVER-UPS

You welcome the color of spring bloomers—daffodils, hyacinths, and tulips. And then you can't stand looking at their unsightly foliage once it starts to fade, right?

Try planting perennials or annuals right on top of them to disguise all of that yellowing and browning. Here's a list of good bulb companion plants that have helpful foliage and modest root systems that won't bother the bulbs.

Plant on Top of Bulbs

- Common lady's-mantle (*Alchemilla vulgaris*)
- Columbines (*Aquilegia* spp.)
- Astilbes (*Astilbe* spp.)
- Fringed bleeding heart (*Dicentra eximia*)
- Heucheras (*Heuchera* spp.)
- Ostrich ferns* (*Matteuccia* spp.)
- Tall marigolds, such as the Inca series (*Tagetes* cultivars)
- Pansies (*Viola* × *wittrockiana* cultivars)
- Common periwinkle (*Vinca minor*)

Plant near Bulbs

- Flowering spurge (*Euphorbia corollata*)
- Broom (*Genista* spp.)
- English ivy (*Hedera helix*)
- Daylilies (*Hemerocallis* spp.)
- Hostas* (*Hosta* spp.)
- Siberian iris (*Iris sibirica*)
- Prostrate speedwell (*Veronica prostrata*)

* Plant with daffodils or other early-spring-blooming bulbs that will grow under deciduous trees. The area is sunny in early spring, before the trees leaf out, and becomes shady later in the season.

USE PERENNIALS TO COVER UP DYING BULB FOLIAGE.

BUY IN BULK

One of the prettiest ways to plant spring-blooming bulbs is in large drifts, but that can be expensive. Avid daffodil gardener Gene Bauer of Running Springs, California, plants thousands each spring and has found ways to trim her bulb bill.

Bauer discovered that the more you order, the more you save, so seek out catalogs that offer discounts according to quantity. Some companies, for example, might offer substantial savings for ordering 50 or more bulbs of one type and even better savings for ordering 100 bulbs at a time. If you're ordering 100 or more, talk to your local greenhouse or bulb supplier. They may cut a deal. (Beware, however, of too-good-to-be-true-prices. The bulbs may be undersized and poor bloomers.)

Buying in bulk really pays off for bulbs that naturalize well, such as daffodils, grape hyacinths (*Muscari* spp.), crocuses, and snowdrops (*Galanthus* spp.). And because these tough bulbs are going to be around for decades, it's easy to buy many of one variety, adding a new variety each year.

Rx for Healthy Tulips

Tulips, unlike many of their spring-blooming bulb counterparts, aren't reliably perennial. The first spring they come on strong, the second they perform less well, and by the third they may be nothing but a few weak leaves and piddly blooms. Keep your tulips going years longer by doing the following:

CHOOSE LONG-LASTING SPECIES AND CULTIVARS. Bulbs that are described as species or botanical tulips tend to come back better year after year. So do Darwin hybrids. Look for label and catalog descriptions that use the word *perennialize.*

GIVE THEM EXCELLENT DRAINAGE. Tulip bulbs need excellent, freely draining soil and benefit from being planted on a slope or in raised beds. "Tossing a little sharp sand directly into the bottom of a tulip planting hole also helps to improve drainage," says gardener Patsy Sadler of Pella, Iowa. "Working plenty of sand into the soil helps too," she notes.

DEADHEAD SPENT BLOOMS. Each spring, cut off fading flowers so that energy can be di-

Solutions at a Glance

PROBLEM: Daffodils aren't blooming but their foliage looks great.

CULPRIT: Fertilizer

SOLVE IT! Go easy on the fertilizer. Daffodils don't respond well to too much nitrogen. Instead, if it's spring and your daffodils aren't blooming, give them a shot of a low-nitrogen organic fertilizer made for stimulating root development. Or scratch in a little wood ash from the fireplace. These generous amounts of potash will help the bulb replenish itself and come back strong next spring—with plenty of flowers.

verted from flower and seed production into rejuvenating for next year.

LEAVE ON THE FOLIAGE. Even though it looks awful, bulbs need that ripening foliage left on until it's thoroughly brown and can be removed only with the gentlest of tugs.

PLANT DEEPLY. Plant tulips 9 inches or deeper. Shallow planting encourages bulbs to split into smaller, nonflowering daughter bulbs earlier, leaving you with bare spots.

Color Coordinated

Do your spring bulb plantings have a hodge-podge look to them? That willy-nilly appearance might be from the colors you're choosing. Too many people order bulbs randomly, giving

Pest Detective

*A*re your tulips less than perfect? Something nibbling them? The blooms looking piddly? Check out these common tulip problems and how you can help.

Symptom	Cause	What to Do
Edges or tops of leaves have been nibbled	Rabbits	Let your cat (or a neighbor's) have free range of the garden, especially at night, until the tulips start blooming.
Bulbs are missing or lying on top of ground	Squirrels or rodents	Plant deep. Even crocuses should be at least 4 inches deep if you have rodent and squirrel problems. Then water well to settle the soil, making it less attractive to these pests. Also, you can temporarily lay a piece of hardware cloth or chicken wire on top of the soil to deter squirrels. And if all else fails, plant rodent-resistant bulbs, such as daffodils, netted iris (*Iris reticulata*), Siberian squill (*Scilla siberica*), ornamental onions (*Allium* spp.), or hyacinths. Also, check out "Solutions at a Glance" on page 18 on planting with gravel.
Light and dark spots or extensive gray blotches on leaves and flowers	Botrytis blight	If bulbs are heavily disfigured, dig up to prevent spread of blight to other bulbs. In the fall, prevent blight by planting only healthy bulbs in well-drained soil. If blight recurs a second spring, as a last resort, try treating with an organic fungicide, such as wettable sulfur.

little thought to how the colors will work together, says Tim Schipper, bulb guru at Color-blends, the color-coordinated Dutch bulb supplier. Just as you would never put together an outfit without considering color, you should never order bulbs without thinking through color schemes.

Schipper suggests using an existing spring-blooming landscape feature—such as a flowering crabapple, redbuds (*Cercis* spp.), or rhododendron—as an inspiration for a color theme. Also, keep in mind not only the color but also the intensity of the color. Most brights, for example, work well with other brights, and most pastels work best with other pastels.

SPEED PLANTING

Have hundreds of tiny crocus bulbs that you need to get in the ground in a hurry? Use a spading fork. Simply insert the fork about 4 inches into the soil, wiggle it around a bit, remove—and, voilà, four perfect planting holes!

Cabbage Problems

Everyone, especially gardeners, should get to know and love cabbage. It's low in calories and rich in vitamins A, B, and C; and it's an Easy (yes, *Easy* with a capital E) vegetable for you to grow. Some people don't like "that cabbage smell" while it's cooking, but other than that, this veggie really won't give you many reasons to complain. And we have some nifty new ideas to share with you for fighting off those few common cabbage pests that you may encounter in your garden.

Rx for Healthy Cabbage

So many varieties of cabbage are available today, it's a wonder cabbage hasn't brought on a gourmet trend like that enjoyed by heirloom tomatoes and baby eggplant. Follow these six tips and you're sure to have success growing early-, mid-, and late-season varieties in a multitude of flavors, shapes, and colors.

START FROM SEED. Cabbage is easy to start from seed. Sow seeds ¼ inch deep and 2 inches apart about 2 weeks before the last frost date or in 1 or 1½-inch plug trays about 8 weeks before the last frost date. Transplant them out a month later. (Remember to harden off the seedlings, exposing them to the outdoors gradually for a week before putting them in the garden.) Cabbage seeds aren't fussy about germination temperature—whether it's 50° or 85°F, they're up in a few days. So if you have a small home garden and have had too much of a good thing in the past (like 12 heads of cabbage at once from a nursery pack), why not purchase several packets of seed and try just a few heads of two or three varieties? You can plant more of them in 2 weeks, or save some of the seed for a fall crop (start them in May and transplant them to the garden in July). But don't worry: If you don't want to plant it now, the seed will keep for years in a dark, dry place.

SPACE FOR SIZE. When you transplant cabbages outdoors, space them 12 to 18 inches apart in rows 18 to 24 inches apart. Wide spacing produces bigger heads; closer spacing produces smaller heads, which are usually tastier.

KEEP CABBAGES COVERED. A simple floating row cover is an easy way to fight some of the worst cabbage pests. Row covers help keep moths away—which keeps them from laying the eggs that give way to several types of worms who love to eat cabbage as much as you do!

KEEP MOISTURE CONSTANT. Cabbage doesn't like to be really thirsty one minute and drenched the next. Uneven watering can cause heads to split, and constantly wet leaves, especially in cool weather or high humidity, can encourage disease. Drip irrigation is one solution, and mulch can help keep moisture in the soil. If you don't have an automatic watering system, be vigilant about watering evenly during dry spells.

COMPOST, PLEASE. Cabbage plants like a side-dressing of compost a couple of weeks after planting. If leaves start to yellow, try a midseason boost with liquid seaweed fertilizer or compost tea. If plants don't bounce back within 2 weeks, pull and burn them so they don't spread disease.

ROTATE TO KEEP CABBAGE HEALTHY. Cabbage crops need to be rotated with noncruciferous crops to fight disease in the garden. They especially like to follow peas, which fix nitrogen in the soil. If you have a small garden and can't rotate crops, add some compost to your bed every year to help suppress disease.

CABBAGE AND CLOVER, OVER AND OVER

An easy way to ensure cabbage health, according to entomologist Geoff Zehnder from Auburn University in Auburn, Alabama, is to seed white clover in fall where you plan to plant cabbage in spring. Then in spring, cultivate strips in the clover and plant your cabbage within those strips. What you'll end up with is cabbage growing in between the flowering clover—which is bringing with it beneficial insects that attack cabbageworms. "We found worms were lower in the areas with the clover all season long. And the clover adds nitrogen to the soil, which benefits the cabbage," Zehnder says.

TURN UP THE HEAT ON PESTS

Science has put an official stamp of approval on what many organic gardeners have known for years: Hot pepper sprays are an effective control for cabbageworms. "We did two seasons of work with it and had good results both times," says entomologist Geoff Zehnder from Auburn University in Auburn, Alabama.

For the study, researchers added 1 tablespoon of ground red pepper (they used McCormick, available in the spice section of the supermarket) to 2 liters of water, plus 6 drops of Ivory dish-washing detergent. They let this mixture sit overnight, stirred to dissolve as much of the pepper as possible, and then sprayed plants once a week. The results showed that the spray was effective in reducing caterpillar populations and insect-feeding damage on cabbage. And damage that did occur was on outer wrapper leaves and didn't affect the head as a whole.

"My feeling is the spray repels the moths. They don't like to lay eggs on the pepper-sprayed leaves. And if you aren't getting the eggs, you aren't getting the worms and the damage," says Zehnder, adding that the spray should be applied early in the season and regularly throughout it.

Cabbage, Cabbage Everywhere

But what do you do when you don't want to harvest all your cabbage just yet? Here's a great way to delay harvest and keep cabbage from splitting when it's mature. Take a sharp spade and drive it straight into the ground, cutting a semicircle around the plant and severing half of its roots. The remaining roots will pull in just enough moisture to keep the cabbage alive and fresh, but not enough to encourage growth and splitting.

By severing just half of a mature cabbage's roots with a spade, you can keep the cabbage fresh without splitting.

Home Brews Keep Your Cabbage Clean

Entomologist Geoff Zehnder from Auburn University in Auburn, Alabama, says gardeners have a couple of scientifically proven options when it comes to mixing something up to wipe out cabbageworms. He believes BT (*Bacillus thuringiensis*) is very effective for the organic home gardener, as long as the plant is well covered with the spray. Also, a garlic spray—made up of 1 part commercial garlic spray (99 percent garlic concentrate), 1 part fish oil, and 98 parts water—was successful at reducing the number of cabbage pests. (And no, the garlic smell didn't linger or flavor the cabbage.) So brew up a batch and take back the cabbage patch!

Keep Cool with Chinese Cabbage

Chinese cabbage is finicky: It likes cool weather and has a reputation for bolting in warmer weather (it does better as a fall crop than as a spring crop), plus it doesn't like its roots to be disturbed for transplanting. So try sowing the seeds for fall Chinese cabbage in July. Chinese cabbage that grows under steadily shortening days won't bolt.

Be warned, though: Flea beetles love Chinese cabbage, so you should use row covers if you want to harvest any crop at all. If you can keep your plants from succumbing to the beetle damage, the cabbage will shape up nicely when the weather turns colder and the beetles disappear.

Cabbageworm Warfare

In her Tennessee Valley garden, Barbara Pleasant, author of *The Gardener's Bug Book*, uses six methods to battle the cabbageworms that come to feed on her favorite cool-season crops. Try any or all of her techniques to keep cabbages and their cousins caterpillar-free in your own garden.

INTERPLANT RADISHES. "In spring I stud my cabbage patch with radishes, and allow the radishes to grow tall and flower," Pleasant says. "Don't ask me how this works," she adds, "it just does!"

EGG PATROL. "As soon as I see white butterflies, I check leaf undersides for their tiny yel-

Pest Detective

Don't let the bad guys get the best of your cabbage crop. Refer to this chart of simple solutions, and you can send pests and diseases packing, leaving heads and heads of cabbage for you and you alone.

Symptom	Cause	What to Do
Holes in leaves make them look like Swiss cheese	Imported cabbageworms	You'll know you have this velvety, pale green, yellow-striped pest if you see dark green pellets of excrement or their yellow eggs. Hand-pick and destroy the worms, and apply hot pepper spray, garlic spray, or BT to the plants. Use row covers and encourage beneficial insects.
Round holes in leaves, looks similar to cabbageworm damage	Cabbage looper	Hand-pick and destroy eggs (which are round and greenish white) and adults (which are green with pale stripes down their backs). Apply hot pepper spray, garlic spray, or BT. Use row covers and encourage beneficial insects.
Damage similar to cabbageworm and cabbage looper damage, but holes in leaves are smaller	Diamondback moth larvae	Hand-pick these very small worms, use hot pepper or garlic spray, or use BT. Use row covers and encourage beneficial insects.
Plants wilt on hot days, or just keel over and die	Cabbage maggot	Prevention is your best bet with these small, blunt-ended, white maggots, so lay a square of tar paper or screening flat on the ground around the stem and dust it with rock phosphate or diatomaceous earth to prevent flies from laying eggs near the cabbage stems. You can also use row covers. And, you can encourage the cabbage maggot's insect predator, the rove beetle.
Many tiny holes in leaves	Flea beetle	Cover seedlings with row covers to protect against these black, shiny, striped pests. Plant white clover as a cover crop, or dust with diatomaceous earth.
Light-colored, distorted patches on leaves	Cabbage aphids	Protect against these powdery gray insects with row covers, or knock them off with a stream of water. Encourage beneficial insects like lacewings, aphid midges, lady beetles, and parasitic wasps; or apply hot pepper spray, garlic spray, or insecticidal soap.
Dark cankers at base of stem; round, brown spots on leaves	Black leg	Rotate crops each season and pull out and destroy diseased plants.

lowish, bullet-shaped eggs. I scrape them off with my fingernail, or I use a wet cotton swab, if I remember to bring one with me to the garden."

HAND-PICKING. "On small seedlings, the little worms like to hide in the new curled leaves of the plants' growing tips," Pleasant explains. "Older cabbageworms often stretch out along the main leaf vein to hide themselves from view. Wherever I find them, I pluck them off and then smash them underfoot."

GET RED. "Cabbageworms are easy to spot on red varieties of cabbage or kohlrabi. Hungry birds often find them before I do!"

FLOATING ROW COVERS. "When I set out brussels sprouts and broccoli in late summer for harvest in fall and winter, I immediately cover them with a very lightweight row cover, held up over the plants with arches made of white PVC pipe. Otherwise, the seedlings would surely be devoured."

BTK (*BACILLUS THURINGIENSIS* VAR. *KURSTAKI*). "In especially bad cabbageworm seasons," Pleasant concludes, "I douse plants with liquid BTK to get rid of small cabbageworms, especially if they're wedged into the ripening heads of broccoli. This biological pesticide is a potent stomach poison when eaten by caterpillars, but it's harmless to beneficial insects." (Because

BTK also kills all kinds of butterfly caterpillars, be careful not to get any on flowers or herbs that attract butterflies.)

RADISHES INTERPLANTED BETWEEN CABBAGE AND ALLOWED TO FLOWER WILL HELP KEEP YOUR PATCH CABBAGEWORM FREE.

HARVEST HINTS

You can begin harvesting cabbage as soon as the heads are firm and glossy. If you're not sure if the heads are firm, you can test them by pressing the back of your hand on them. When you harvest early-season cabbage, leave the lower leaves on the plant and small heads will develop for a tasty and tender second harvest. Your fall plantings will taste best if you wait to pick until after a few frosts but before a hard freeze. Late-season cabbage varieties will keep for a long time (up to 3 months!) if you store the heads in plastic wrap at near freezing temperatures in your refrigerator.

Colorado Potato Beetles

Until Europeans brought vegetables such as eggplant to the New World, Colorado potato beetles had to get by on a diet of weeds. These days only an unlucky few of these striking striped pests are forced to live on horse nettle. The rest find ample dining opportunities in gardens or on farms across most of North America.

A little bit of damage from Colorado potato beetles won't cut into your harvest of potatoes or eggplant, but a few beetles and larvae can quickly grow into a population large enough to strip every leaf off your plants. So here are a few things you can do to help protect your plants—including blocking them out and giving them a little shake, rattle, 'n' roll.

THREE BASIC BEETLE BLOCKERS

Preventing damage from Colorado potato beetles is as easy as keeping the adult beetles off your plants. And that's not as hard as it might seem. Try any or all of these defensive strategies to block out the beetles before they take their first bites from your precious potato plants:

MULCH. As soon as the soil warms up in late spring, place at least 3 inches of mulch around your potato plants. The mulch makes it more difficult and hazardous for adult beetles to make the trip from their underground hiding places to the surface. Ground beetles and other beneficial insects that live under deep mulch may turn the tired beetles into their breakfast.

COVER. Use lightweight floating row covers to keep beetles off of your potatoes and eggplant. Check often under the covers to make sure none of these troublemakers has been trapped underneath. Remove the covers by midseason.

TRENCH. Dig a trench that's at least 45 degrees steep around your potato (or eggplant) patch and line the trench with plastic. Beetles that emerge from the soil in the spring are too weak to fly to your plants, so they have to walk. When they reach the trench, they fall in and the plastic makes it too slippery for them to escape. Hungry birds will clean out the trenches for you.

NATURAL CONTROL

A special strain of BTSD (*Bacillus thuringiensis* var. *san diego*) provides excellent control of potato beetle larvae if you apply it to plants when the critters are young. If you grow a lot of potatoes or eggplants, check the undersides of the leaves often, and apply BTSD at the first sign that eggs have hatched. This handy biological control doesn't harm birds, bees, or other beneficial insects or wildlife. Reapply BTSD after heavy rains to keep beetles at bay.

SHAKE THEM OUT

If an outbreak of beetles catches you by surprise, shake them off of plants into a shallow box. Or, place old sheets over the ground beneath plants, and gently stir the foliage with a broom to send the bugs rolling. You can crush the eggs and larvae or hand-pick the larvae and drown them in a pail of soapy water or dump them on any paved surface far from your garden (where birds will enjoy the beetle larvae buffet).

Colorado Potato Beetles

COMBAT COLORADO POTATO BEETLES BY STIRRING THINGS UP A LITTLE WITH A BROOM. JUST MAKE SURE YOU PLACE AN OLD SHEET BENEATH THE PLANTS, TO CATCH THE BEETLES WHEN THEY FALL.

Compost Problems

Composting is all about building the soil—the foundation of any garden—so that your plants get off to a great start in life. And turning kitchen and garden wastes into black gold doesn't seem very difficult, does it? After all, you just throw everything on a pile, turn it once in a while, make sure it has adequate moisture—and, voilà, compost. Oh, but what about a slimy pile or a smelly pile or a pile that's just too darn hard to turn? Take the following advice from some great decomposers, and you should have no trouble mastering the technique.

Rx for Healthy Compost

Patrice Kleinberg, who's the compost project director for the Queens Botanical Garden in New York, believes that although there's a science to composting, most gardeners should consider it an art. Here, she shares her tips for creating a compost masterpiece.

FOR PERFECT COMPOST, SHOOT FOR A CARBON-TO-NITROGEN RATIO OF 30:1. See "The Compost Construction Crew" on the opposite page for examples of carbon- and nitrogen-providing ingredients. Kleinberg realizes, however, that most home gardeners have an abundance of greens all spring and summer, then an abundance of browns (leaves) in the fall, and hardly any greens in the fall and winter. She suggests stockpiling leaves in the fall and adding them to your pile a layer at a time in spring and summer—and using kitchen scraps for greens in the fall and winter.

COMPOST FRUIT AND VEGETABLES SCRAPS, PLANT MATERIAL, COFFEE GROUNDS, tea bags, eggshells, paper towels, cardboard, and newspaper. Avoid composting meat, fish, chicken, bones, oils, fats, dairy products, and waste from Fido or Kitty.

CHIP, CHOP, OR SHRED BIG PIECES of stuff into smaller pieces to help them decompose faster.

GET MICROBES INTO THE PILE WHEN STARTING A NEW ONE FROM SCRATCH. You can do this, Kleinberg says, by digging a hole and building the pile in the hole. Or, if you're using a bin with a bottom, add a few shovelfuls of earth along with the material you're composting.

TURN YOUR PILE. Turning adds oxygen to the pile, stoking it, making it hotter, and helping things break down. You don't have to turn the pile every day; once a week is plenty.

ADD WATER WHEN NEEDED. A compost pile shouldn't be dripping wet or bone dry; it should be slightly damp.

KEEP COMPOSTING DURING THE WINTER. If you live where it gets really cold and your compost pile freezes, simply add kitchen scraps to bags of leaves you collected in the fall. "Bury the scraps in the middle," says Kleinberg, "and add the whole thing to your compost pile in the spring."

THE COMPOST CONSTRUCTION CREW

A carbon-to-nitrogen ratio of 30:1 works best for making compost. Here are some examples of each:

Carbon	Nitrogen
Cardboard bits	Alfalfa
Cornstalks	Bloodmeal
Dry leaves	Coffee grounds
Sawdust	Fresh weeds
Shredded paper	Grass clippings
Straw	Human hair
Wood chips	Kelp meal
	Kitchen scraps
	Manure

TIP THE SCALES IN YOUR FAVOR WHEN CREATING BLACK GOLD BY USING A CARBON-TO-NITROGEN RATIO OF 30:1.

QUICK COMPOST

Impatient? Want compost now, not tomorrow, but don't know the road to the fast track? Take a lesson from Renée Beaulieu, who gardens in Waterbury, Connecticut. Here's how she had a pile of hot compost brewing in a mere 2 days.

WATER IS KEY FOR HOT COMPOST. SO KEEP YOUR PILE COOKING BY ADDING H_2O IF THE INGREDIENTS GET TOO DRY.

"I bought a bale of straw (not hay, because it contains seeds, which can sprout) and built a pile," says Beaulieu. "The secret, besides layering straw with all the fresh green stuff (spent pea vines, bolted lettuce, coffee grounds, banana peels) was water. I'd read about piles being too wet, but in retrospect, I think mine were always too dry. I kept the hose nearby as I constructed the pile, and watered the debris as I layered it in, so there was plenty of moisture available. I topped off the whole thing with a covering of straw, and the pile was very hot within 2 days."

A HELPING HAND

If you're having trouble turning your pile, take a look at the tool you're using. You might be better off using a manure fork. "The manure fork, with its long handle and much narrower

PROBLEM: Your compost smells like ammonia.

CULPRIT: Too much nitrogen

SOLVE IT! Add dry, carbon-rich material like cornstalks, leaves, and wood chips.

PROBLEM: Your compost pile is really dry.

CULPRIT: Drought

SOLVE IT! Sprinkle the pile with a watering can or hose nozzle, turning the pile as you water to moisten the whole thing, even the center. When you squeeze a handful of compost, it should feel like a wrung-out sponge, damp but not soggy.

PROBLEM: Your pile is slimy.

CULPRIT: Too much moisture

SOLVE IT! Add more dry, carbon-rich material like cornstalks, leaves, and wood chips. Turn the pile as you add the dry stuff so it sops up the excess moisture.

PROBLEM: Something's picking at your pile.

CULPRIT: Rodents

SOLVE IT! Make your compost bin rodent resistant by installing ¼-inch wire mesh on the bottom, top, and sides, or consider purchasing a metal barrel compost tumbler. Also, avoid throwing dairy or meat scraps in your pile.

PROBLEM: Winged insects are flitting around your pile.

CULPRIT: Vinegar flies

SOLVE IT! Vinegar flies may be a nuisance around piles that have too much fermenting fruits and vegetables. If they bother you, add carbon-rich material like cornstalks, leaves, and wood chips.

tines and bigger head, does a better job lifting and spreading compost than the spading fork I had been using," says gardener Renée Beaulieu from Waterbury, Connecticut. "Hey, I grew up in the city, so what did I know about farm tools?" she adds.

THE LONG HANDLE AND NARROW TINES OF THIS MANURE FORK TAKE THE TROUBLE OUT OF TURNING A COMPOST PILE.

MANURE HOT AND COLD

Well-aged manure goes a long way toward improving the health and draining power of any soil. Curing your own supply, says Master Gardener Jane Anders from Portland, Oregon, can be easier—and neater—than you might think. Here's how she handles the truckloads she gets from a nearby horse farm.

1. Spread a heavy tarpaulin on the ground.
2. Dump the manure onto the tarp.
3. Fold the tarp up and around the pile.
4. Lay another tarp on top, fold it down around the first one, weight it down, and cut a few slits in the tarps to let some heat escape. The high temperatures generated by the manure will kill most weeds.
5. Let the pile sit for 6 months or so and it'll be cool, weed-free, and ready to add to your garden beds.

"If you have the space," Anders advises, "keep two or three piles going at different stages of cooling. That way you'll always have a ready supply on hand."

A LITTLE GOES A LONG WAY

You don't need to bury your garden under truckloads of compost to have bountiful harvests and beautiful flower borders. In most areas of the country, an annual application of a half-inch-thick layer of compost is all you'll need for established garden beds. (In the longer growing seasons of the South and in areas with very high rainfall, double the annual rate to 1 inch.) This will provide enough organic matter and ample nutrients for excellent plant growth. For one-time applications to new garden beds, you can double or triple the annual rate.

Container Garden Problems

A lack of land shouldn't limit your gardening! If you don't have much in-ground gardening space, move your garden into containers instead. With containers, your deck, patio, rooftop— even your houseboat—can become a great place to grow vegetables, flowers, and more. To succeed with container gardens, the most important steps you can take are to start with the right-size containers and a good soil mix and to be ever mindful of the top problem that container gardeners face: saving plants from dehydration.

Rx for Luscious Container Gardens

"Anything you can grow in the ground you can grow in a container," says Julie Willimott, whose Portland, Oregon, garden thrives in pots. "I've even raised corn in containers," she says. Here are some of Willimott's tips for container garden success with vegetables.

1. Gather some 15- to 20-gallon pots and wash the pots in a mild bleach solution (1 part bleach to 5 parts water) to kill disease organisms. (If you buy new pots you don't need to wash them out with the bleach solution.) Willimott says she favors black plastic nursery pots. "They attract and hold the sun's heat—and most veggies like warm soil."

2. Add a handful of washed rocks or pot shards for drainage.

3. Stir together a 3:1 mixture of sterilized potting soil and compost (which will help suppress disease), and fill the pot.

4. Plant seeds or transplants in the container. You can plant a single crop or combine crops that are beneficial companions, like tomatoes and basil. (For more ideas, see "Recommended Reading" on page 206 for books on companion planting.) Then, put the container in full sun.

5. Water regularly (when the top couple of inches of soil have dried out). "Moisture is the key," Willimott says. "In pots, roots can't go deep for moisture like they can in the ground."

6. Feed your crops two or three times during the growing season with an organic fertilizer to keep them lush.

DEEPLY DOES IT

To make sure water reaches the whole rootball when you plant a tree or shrub in a pot, container gardener Julie Willimott from Portland, Oregon, offers this advice: "Plant a piece of bamboo or PVC pipe with 1/8-inch holes in it with the tree or shrub. Each time you water, soak the soil *and* fill that reservoir."

DRILL 1/8-INCH HOLES IN A PIECE OF PVC PIPE, PLACE THE PIPE IN YOUR CONTAINER, AND YOU'LL HAVE AN INSTANT WATER RESERVOIR THAT WILL KEEP THIRSTY ROOTS HAPPY.

A LONG SOAK SAVES STRESSED PLANTS

You forgot to water your container plants, and now they're so dry they won't even take up water. Don't despair—your plants may not be gone for good. When a pot dries out thoroughly, "the soil will form crevices under the surface, where you can't see them," says container specialist Linda Waller, owner of Seattle's Doolittle Gardens. "After that, whenever you water, the water will run right through those little tunnels and out the bottom of the pot." If your plants look stressed even though you water frequently, they're probably the victim of those hidden tunnels. Waller's advice: Soak the soil well. Allow 5 minutes of gentle hosing for a pot 20 inches in diameter and 20 inches deep. Never fear that you'll overwater. Says Waller, "Outdoors in the summer that's all but impossible to do."

SOME LIKE IT DRY

Because the soil in containers dries out faster than the soil in your garden beds, you might opt for drought-tolerant plants for container gardens (especially if you tend to pot things up and then forget about them!). Drought-tolerant ornamental grasses; annuals such as geraniums and marigolds; and perennials like daylilies, sedums, and hardy cacti (*Opuntia* spp.) are good choices. Many herbs are native to hot, dry climates and are also easy to care for—perennials like chives, oregano, sage, and thyme will grow for several years in a large container. And annual herbs like basil and dill are also drought-tolerant.

Container Garden Problems

Corn Problems

Young, old. Rich, poor. Everyone, it seems, *loves* garden-fresh sweet corn. In fact, some of us can't even wait to get it into the kitchen. We eat it right off the cob—raw—in the middle of the garden. The trouble is, we humans aren't alone in our love of corn. A whole host of pests—deer, raccoons, crows, possums, and insects—get a craving for corn, too. You won't need to go hungry while the garden pests feast, though. Here are some resourceful ways (including using newspaper and soap) to make sure your corn crop is everything you want it to be.

Rx for Healthy Corn

You're sure to have a high-yield harvest of oh-so-sweet ears if you follow these great tips from market gardener George DeVault, from Emmaus, Pennsylvania. They'll help you choose, grow, and gather corn with ease.

USE A QUICK-MATURING VARIETY. At 65 days, 'Kandy Kwik' is the leader of the pack, followed closely by 'Trinity', at 68 days. Scout the seed catalogs for other early or short-season varieties, especially if you garden in the far north.

PLANT NO CORN BEFORE ITS TIME. As much as you want to get a jump on the season, you have to wait until soil temperature is warm—at least 65°F— before you plant corn. Waiting until the soil has sufficiently warmed guarantees good, uniform germination and also helps reduce insect and weed problems. Warm soil is especially important when using super-sweet varieties.

DON'T SKIMP ON THE SEEDS. You'll need to plant a minimum of two rows of corn (four short rows are better than two long rows) in order to have good pollination and well-filled ears.

FEED THE SOIL. Corn is a heavy feeder, particularly when it comes to nitrogen, so make sure your soil has plenty of organic matter. For an early nitrogen boost, work some fish meal into the soil. And add rock phosphate to provide phosphorus, and compost, plant residues, manure, greensand, or granite dust to provide potassium.

Overseeding a nitrogen-fixing legume (like hairy vetch or red clover) between your corn rows in July or August will keep your soil in top condition and provide ample nutrition for future crops. Remove cornstalks as soon as you harvest all the ears to give your cover crop full sun and room to grow. (The cover crop will protect your soil through winter.) Till it into the soil a few weeks before you start your garden the following spring.

PICK IT WHEN IT'S RIPE. To get the highest sugar levels and the most old-fashioned corn taste, you absolutely must pick sweet corn on time. Watch for tasseling, and jot down the date when about half of your plants have tassels. Depending on the weather, your corn will be ready for picking 18 to 22 days later. Look for clues like drying and browning silks to help you zero in on the exact date, or pop a few kernels with your thumbnail to make sure they're full and milky. Better yet, pick an ear off the stalk and take a big bite out of it! (If corn is too young to eat, the kernels won't be filled out and it won't have full flavor. If it's past it's prime, the kernels will be tough and chewy and will taste starchy.)

FIND OUT IF YOUR CORN IS RIGHT FOR THE PICKIN' BY POPPING A FEW KERNELS WITH YOUR THUMBNAIL TO MAKE SURE THEY'RE MILKY.

GIVE IT LOTS OF WATER. Corn is a heavy drinker, too. It needs adequate moisture throughout the season, but especially when setting ears. Super-sweet varieties need twice as much moisture to germinate as regular corn does. For best germination of all varieties, avoid planting corn when the soil is extremely dry, and water the corn regularly during dry spells.

PEST-FREE CORN

Humans aren't the only creatures that think corn on the cob makes a sweet meal on a summer night. Plenty of pests that creep, crawl, and fly like it, too. But here are some super-effective tips to make sure that the only one eating your corn is *you*.

The task of keeping worms out of your corn has been made easy by researchers at the University of Massachusetts and Hampshire College. They reduced earworm damage to corn by 90 to 100 percent by using a mixture of vegetable oil and BTK (*Bacillus thuringiensis* var. *kurstaki*). Just use an oil can or eyedropper to apply 5 drops of an oil and BTK mix to each ear when the silks begin to turn brown.

Birds are another big problem. They'll pluck young corn plants out of the ground as well as pick kernels or corn and damage ears.

You can successfully camouflage your young corn plants by interplanting them with garlic or by mulching around them with fresh grass clippings. "Scare-eye" balloons—15-inch inflatable plastic balls that resemble beach balls—help mimic the eyes of predator birds and can also keep your crop safe.

Raccoons can be crafty little pests, but you can keep them out of ripening corn by spreading newspaper on the ground around the stalks. Raccoons are reluctant to walk across the dry, rustling material, so your young ears will be safe. You can also use netting on the ground to repel these furry foes.

And to keep deer out of your growing corn, hit 'em right in the nose—with a strong scent, that is. Try hanging deodorant soap in net bags from stakes scattered around your corn patch. Fencing helps repel a wide variety of animal pests but must be 8 to 10 feet tall to block deer.

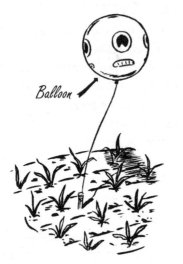

Balloon

Keep your corn crop safe from critters with "Scare-eye" balloons.

Beat the Winter Corn Blues

Ever get a craving for an ear of sweet, buttered corn right around the end of January? Well, if you plan ahead, you can have the very taste of summer itself. Just stash a few ears in the freezer at the peak of summer's harvest, and you can enjoy delicious corn on the cob year-round. All you need to do is husk the ears, clean off the silk, and blanch the ears in a pot of boiling water for 6 to 8 minutes. Cool the ears quickly (stick them in a sink of cold water), and then pack them in freezer bags and stick them in the freezer.

Baby Your Corn

You don't have to wait for ears to fully mature to enjoy garden-fresh corn. Any early-maturing variety can be harvested as "baby corn," the tiny ears popular in stir-fries and salads or pickled.

Plant your seeds as close as 6 to 8 inches apart. Harvest just as soon as you feel a small bulge inside the little ears, usually about 5 days after silk appears. You can harvest any corn as baby corn, but some varieties (such as 'How Sweet It Is', 'Bodacious', and 'Bonus') are especially tasty.

Invite the Three Sisters to Your Garden

If you find that your corn is getting snacked on by the local wildlife, try growing the three sisters—a traditional Native American intercropping. This veggie combo of beans, corn, and squash repels critters, naturally!

Beans use the cornstalks as a trellis (make sure you plant a pole bean—and use a corn variety with a strong stalk, such as 'Texas Honey June' or 'Stowell's Evergreen'). The squash vines form a living mulch that conserves soil moisture and helps prevent weeds. But best of all, the prickly squash vines help keep raccoons and deer from snacking on the sisters.

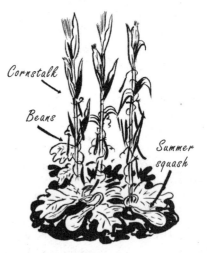

Cornstalk

Beans

Summer squash

The prickly squash vines in the three sisters combination helps keep raccoons and deer away from your corn.

Crop Rotation Problems

Growing the same crop in the same spot every year may lead to problems with pests and diseases. And different veggies use different nutrients, too, so growing the same ones in the same soil year after year may produce malnutrition problems. Although rotating crops in large farm fields isn't too challenging, it can be tough in small backyard gardens. So here are some ways to make the most of crop rotation in smaller spaces and at the same time help to solve some of your other garden problems—like those pesky weeds in the carrots.

10 TIPS FOR SUCCESSFUL ROTATIONS

SEPARATE FEUDING FAMILIES. Vegetables that belong to the same botanical family—like tomatoes, potatoes, and eggplant (all from the Solanaceae, or nightshade family), or broccoli, cabbage, and cauliflower (all from the Cruciferae, or mustard family)—will attract the same pests and suffer from the same diseases. Minimize contagion by planting them away from each other.

KEEP FRIENDS TOGETHER. Some plants grow well together, and should be rotated together. Carrots and tomatoes get along because both dislike too much nitrogen, and they don't share common insect pests or diseases. Cabbage and dill are happy together because when dill flowers, it attracts beneficial insects that feed on aphids and cabbageworms that are attracted to the cabbage plants.

ROTATE ROOTS, FRUITS, AND GREENS. Plants that produce edible roots, like carrots and beets, take different nutrients out of the soil than plants that produce fruits (like tomatoes and peppers) or edible greens (like lettuce and spinach). Grow a different edible in the same section of the garden each year to make efficient use of the soil's fertility.

FERTILIZE WITH ROTATIONS. Follow a crop that uses a lot of nitrogen, like sweet corn, with a crop that makes its own nitrogen, like peas or beans. Why buy fertilizer if nature will fertilize for you? And you can save your precious compost for the plants that really need it.

PLOW WITH ROTATIONS. Market gardener Tony Ricci likes to follow potatoes with garlic on his Three Springs, Pennsylvania, farm because digging the potatoes creates a clean bed for the fall-planted garlic. "When you dig the potatoes, you're really getting the late-germinating weeds out," he says. "The ground is all broken up and just needs to be raked smooth for the garlic." (*Note:*

This method works best when the potatoes are growing in hills that you have weeded on a regular basis during the growing season.)

WEED WITH ROTATIONS. Have a problem with perennial weeds? Plant a vine crop, like winter squash, to smother them.

POLLINATE WITH ROTATIONS. Don't forget flowers or flowering vegetable crops as part of the rotation. For example, plant early-blooming annuals like snapdragons and calendula (*Calendula officinalis*) near summer-

Starting Up

If you want to rotate crops but aren't sure what crop should follow what, use this handy chart to help get you started.

Crop	Follows	Why?
Cabbage family crops	Garlic, leeks, onions	Onion family crops thwart parasites and pests that trouble cabbage.
Carrots, onions, other root crops	Winter squash or pumpkins	Vining crops smother weeds, making it easier to keep root crops clean.
Eggplant, potatoes, tomatoes	Mustard, rape, turnips	Cruciferae crops help cleanse the soil of pathogens that attack Solanaceae crops.
Garlic, shallots	Potatoes	Potato harvest results in a clean planting bed for fall-planted crops.
Lettuce	Root crops	Roots loosen soil, making penetration easier for shallow-rooted lettuce.
Okra	Marigolds	Marigolds exude substances from their roots that deter nematodes, to which okra is sensitive.
Peas and beans	Cabbage family crops or corn	Nitrogen-fixing legumes replace nutrients used by heavy-feeding crops.
Potatoes	Corn	Corn as a preceding crop increases potato yield.

bearing cucumbers and squash to attract pollinating insects.

FIGHT PESTS WITH ROTATIONS. Farmers have followed onion-family crops with cabbage-family crops for years because the skin of onions exudes a substance that suppresses certain plant parasites. Onions don't attract flea beetles, either, so soil that held onions won't be filled with overwintering flea beetles, which love to feed on cabbage-family plants.

KEEP THE GARDEN DEBRIS-FREE. Rotations are tough in small gardens. "I wouldn't worry about it much, as long as you aren't having disease problems," says Ricci. "If you can't rotate your crops, taking out plant debris will help." This means yanking out fusarium-prone plants like basil and tomatoes, roots and all, at the end of the season.

KEEP RECORDS. Try this creative method. Draw the garden to scale on a piece of poster board, and permanently ink in perennial crops. Lay a piece of onion-skin paper over the drawing and pencil in where you want to plant

annual crops. Next year, lay a new piece of onion-skin paper over last year's—and, voilà, you'll know where not to plant what.

PRACTICE THE BUDDY SYSTEM WHEN ROTATING CROPS BY KEEPING FRIENDS LIKE CARROTS AND TOMATOES TOGETHER.

Cutworms

Dressed in camouflage colors that help them blend in with the soil, cutworms are moth larvae that hide in soil and mulch during the day, and come out at night to taste the tender stems of young plants. Most of these nocturnal nibblers feed by wrapping around a plant's stem at soil level and taking a bite—or several bites.

A few cutworm species climb up onto plants and eat the leaves, but the big heartbreakers are "surface" cutworms that girdle seedling stems and leave behind sad little stumps and felled plants where your garden used to be. Because cutworms work at night, you probably won't spot the culprits that toppled your tender transplants. So use these ideas for providing protective armor, along with tilling hints, to cut off cutworms from their next meal.

FOIL CUTWORMS WITH TILLING

You can help cut down on cutworms in your beds by planting a cover crop in the fall, and then, tilling it under in the spring, as soon as you can work the ground. Turning over the top layer of soil will expose cutworms to predators such as birds. Tilling also helps eliminate young weed seedlings, which wipes out easy meals for cutworms.

DRESS YOUNG PLANTS FOR SUCCESS

To outwit the cutworms that continue to hang around in your garden soil, clothe young plants in armor that protects the lowest 2 inches of stem from cutworm attack. Because seedlings come in different shapes and sizes, tailor your choices from the following list to get a good fit. And don't wait to go on the defensive–install cutworm deterrents when you set out transplants or as soon as seedlings are up. It only takes one night for cutworms to wreak their awful havoc on unprotected plants.

CIRCULAR COLLARS. Make collars from cans or paper cups with their bottoms removed, or cut the cardboard rolls from toilet paper or paper towels into 2-inch-long pieces. Place the collars around seedlings, and push them into the soil about 1 inch deep.

STEM SHEATHS. Cut plastic drinking straws into 2-inch-long pieces, slit them down the side, and pop them around plant stems. Or, loosely wrap plant stems with small pieces of aluminum foil or double folds of waxed paper.

PROTECT YOUR YOUNG PLANTS FROM NASTY CUTWORMS WITH AN ARMOR MADE OUT OF PLASTIC DRINKING STRAWS.

PROBLEM: Something's damaging your spring garden bed-to-be.

CULPRIT: Cutworms

SOLVE IT! Mix moistened bran with molasses and BTK (*Bacillus thuringiensis* var. *kurstaki*) and sprinkle it over the soil in your garden about a week before you plan to plant. BTK is a biological control for moth larvae. Cutworms that dine on this sweet treat won't be around in the future to snip off your seedlings and transplants.

INVITE THE "GOOD GUYS" IN

A number of beneficial insects parasitize cutworm larvae, including many parasitic wasps (Braconid and Ichnuemonid families, and tachinid flies). You can invite them into your garden by providing plants rich in pollen and nectar such as dill, alyssum, yarrow, and cosmos. (Make sure you protect beneficial insects by avoiding the use of any toxic sprays or dust in your garden.)

Damping-Off

Starting seeds can be a lot of fun and is a great way to grow the varieties you really want to grow, rather than having to choose plants from what might be a limited selection at your local garden center. But how often have seeds that you've started indoors germinated just fine and looked healthy and robust until— yikes!—they started keeling over and dying? The culprit is a fungus that causes a disease called damping-off. A few precautions will keep damping-off from doing in your seedlings.

Lighter Is Better

Don't be tempted to use garden soil to start your seedlings. Use a sterile seed-starting mix instead, which is not only fungus-free but also lighter in texture. If you use a standard potting soil, it's a good idea to lighten it up with some vermiculite or perlite to improve aeration so those tender roots don't become waterlogged.

Don't Get Bogged Down

Keep your seed-starting soil moist but not wet because fungus thrives in boggy conditions. Spread a thin layer of milled sphagnum moss on the top of the flat after you've sown the seeds. Because the moss is resistant to moisture, it helps keep the stems and leaves of your fragile seedlings dry. Also, try watering seedling flats from the bottom, rather than sprinkling water over the top. The easiest way to do that is to set the seed pots into a flat that has no holes; then pour the water directly into the flat. The roots get the moisture they need, but the foliage stays dry and is less susceptible to damping-off.

WATER FROM THE BOTTOM TO PUT A DAMPER ON DAMPING-OFF.

Foil the Fungus

Got a spot of damping-off anyway? Mix hydrogen peroxide half and half with water, and soak the affected area to kill the damping-off fungus and prevent it from spreading to healthy seedlings.

Deer Problems

Although they're beautiful animals, deer are a problem for gardeners almost everywhere—except perhaps rooftop gardeners! The growth of the suburbs has left less land for deer to roam and fewer predators to keep their population in check. In most parts of the country, deer drive gardeners crazy by eating their favorite plants, including perennials, annuals, trees, shrubs, and bulbs. In fact, sometimes they nibble so much new growth off of young trees and shrubs that there's nothing left on the plant to grow back—and you're stuck with a bare spot in your yard. You've probably tried a multitude of deterrents, including fencing and deer-resistant plants. Well, we don't want deer to get the best of your garden and landscape, so we've put together some new twists on old solutions, like fencing, in an effort to thwart deer dining tactics.

KNOW THEIR EATING HABITS

Try as you might, you can't always predict when deer are going to be chowing down and what they're going to be eating. Seems as if they eat one type of plant in spring and a different type in fall. That's true, says John Van Etten, grounds superintendent of the Mohonk Mountain House in New Paltz, New York. His strategy for foiling hungry deer? Know how deer operate.

Deer eat more herbaceous plants in spring and summer. Toward fall, their digestive systems change and they start gearing up for woody plants. Just knowing this bit of information can help you protect the right plants at the right time. For example, you may want to set up temporary deer fencing or netting around your foundation shrubs after the second killing frost, and leave it in place over the winter until midspring.

CHANGE THE MENU

If you garden in an area that's home to lots of deer and don't have the money or time to put up a fence or to keep replanting the plants they nibble on, all isn't lost. You can still grow a garden—you just have to outsmart the deer by planting things they don't like to eat. John Van Etten came up with a list of plants that deer don't eat, based on his 12 years at the Mohonk Mountain House in New Paltz, New York. So take a look at what they're eating, and then make substitutions where you can based on this list.

Annuals

Common snapdragon (*Antirrhinum majus*)

Wax begonias (*Begonia* Semperflorens-Cultorum hybrids)

Strawflower (*Bracteantha bracteata,* also called *Helichrysum bracteatum*)

Snow-on-the-mountain (*Euphorbia marginata*)

Sweet alyssum (*Lobularia maritima*)

Stock (*Matthiola incana*)

Flowering tobacco (*Nicotiana* spp.)

Scented geraniums (*Pelargonium* spp.)

Dusty miller (*Senecio cineraria*)

Marigolds (*Tagetes* spp.)

Nasturtium (*Tropaeolum majus*)

Common zinnia (*Zinnia elegans*)

Herbaceous Perennials and Bulbs

Common yarrow (*Achillea millefolium*)

Common monkshood (*Aconitum napellus*)

Stars of Persia (*Allium christophii*)

Meadow saffron (*Colchium autumnale*)

Common bleeding heart (*Dicentra spectabilis*)

Common foxglove (*Digitalis purpurea*)

Coneflower (*Echinacea purpurea*)

Globe thistle (*Echinops* spp.)

Iris (*Iris* spp.)

Lavender (*Lavandula* spp.)

Daffodils (*Narcissus* spp.)

Common peony (*Paoenia lactiflora*)

Trees and Shrubs

Bottlebrush buckeye (*Aesculus parviflora*)

Shadblow (*Amelanchier canadensis*)

Red osier dogwood (*Cornus sericea*)

Spruce (*Picea* spp.)

Pine (*Pinus* spp.)

Northern red oak (*Quercus rubra*)

Rugosa rose (*Rosa rugosa*)

DEER DON'T EAT EVERYTHING, EVEN THOUGH IT SEEMS THAT WAY. YOU CAN PLANT SOME ANNUALS (SUCH AS WAX BEGONIAS) AND HERBACEOUS PERENNIALS (SUCH AS PEONIES), AND DEER WILL LEAVE THEM ALONE.

PROTECT TRUNKS WITH PLASTIC

In the beginning of September, bucks rub their antlers on bark to peel off the velvet on their antlers and mark their territory. If they rub hard enough, though, the rubbing can girdle and eventually kill young trees. And any tree with a straight trunk is a prime target.

Don't let potential deer damage discourage you from planting new trees on your property, however. You can protect young trees by wrapping a plastic spiral tree protector around the trunk, from the ground up to about 5 feet. "This plastic expands when the trees grow," says John Van Etten, grounds superintendent of the Mohonk Mountain House in New Paltz, New York. "I make sure to wrap the trunks by the end of August," he adds.

Hardware cloth also works well for protecting tree trunks, says Tim Steinhoff, who has been gardening for 20 years in New York State. "For a 4½-foot-tall stewartia (*Stewartia* sp.), I use hardware cloth that's 40 inches across, along with a hood of fruit tree netting over the top of the tree," says Steinhoff.

PROTECT THE TRUNKS OF YOUNG TREES FROM THE ANTLERS OF BUCKS BY WRAPPING A PORTION OF THE TRUNK IN HARDWARE CLOTH.

CHANGE OF SCREENERY

You love your "green screens" of arborvitaes (*Thuja* spp.), rhododendrons, and hemlocks (*Tsuga* spp.). Problem is, deer love them, too. The solution may be as simple, however, as planting different evergreens. Here are some suggestions for evergreen shrubs that deer aren't fond of nibbling.

BOXWOODS (*BUXUS* SPP.). Commonly used in formal gardens, this evergreen can also be attractive in natural landscapes.

SAWARA FALSE CYPRESS (*CHAMAECYPARIS PISIFERA*). This handsome evergreen tree has a pyramidal form; its cultivars vary in size.

CAUCASIAN DAPHNE (*DAPHNE CAUCASICA*). This semievergreen holds its leaves late, finally dropping them in winter before the snow season. (*Note:* This plant is toxic, so you might want to avoid using it if you have small children.)

AMERICAN HOLLY (*ILEX OPACA*). Deer leave this evergreen alone because of its spiny leaves.

JAPANESE PIERIS (*PIERIS JAPONICA*). This 6- to 8-foot-tall evergreen shrub has fragrant white flowers in spring and should be planted in well-drained soil.

THWART DEER BY SUBSTITUTING JAPANESE PIERIS WHEN PLANTING AN EVERGREEN SCREEN.

Solutions at a Glance

PROBLEM: Four-footed foes are eating all your tulips.

CULPRIT: Deer

SOLVE IT! Try a smell repellent. Spray Hinder, an organic product made out of fatty acid soaps, on tulips as soon as the foliage emerges and again 2 weeks later. Hinder is safe for both ornamental and food plants and doesn't burn their foliage. (See "Resources" on page 196.)

MAKE YOUR GARDEN ENTRÉES LESS APPETIZING FOR DEER (AND CUT DOWN ON WATER USE AT THE SAME TIME) BY XERISCAPING AND INCORPORATING ARID-CLIMATE PLANTS SUCH AS YUCCAS.

BRING IN THE DESERT

If your landscape is a veritable lunch counter for deer, one way you can make the entrées less appetizing is by changing the offering—that is, changing the style of your landscape. That's what Eve Marx, who gardens in Katonah, New York, did when she decided to xeriscape her property.

"Over the years we've decided to get into xeriscaping, partly because a certain amount of our property closely resembles a high desert, and partly because the deer don't much like yuccas (*Yucca* spp.), ornamental fescues (*Festuca* spp.), zebra grass (*Miscanthus sinensis* 'Zebrinus'), or sedums," says Marx. "We really don't have a lot of problems with the deer now that we've come to terms with the fact that if we want tulips, we'll buy them at the florist," Marx adds.

FIGHT BACK WITH FENCING

Deer are creatures of habit and tend to travel the same paths looking for food. But what do you do if the path is through your backyard? Here's some fencing advice that goes against the norm, from Nancy Engel, who gardens in Cold Spring, New York. Engel's property sits at the edge of a community backing up to 700 acres of posted property—home to a large number of deer.

"My neighborhood was originally a summer community, so the deer were quite used to having the whole place to themselves all winter," Engel explains. "When I bought my house, there was a well-traveled path through my backyard to the lake and the woods beyond. Of course, the deer saw this path as a kind of freeway exit to the diner on my property. So I installed a 6-foot-tall black mesh fence. Although many people insist that a fence must be 10 feet high to keep deer from taking a running start and jumping over it, the deer have not tried to jump this fence once in 15 years."

Engel put up the fence (which she bought in 50-foot rolls from Agway) a full year before she started to plant the backyard. "I got the deer out of the habit of browsing in my yard before it was extra-tempting. Besides, I think deer are lazy, and there are much easier pickings in my neighbors' yards, which aren't fenced," she says.

Go Electric

Electric fences, although expensive, are one option for keeping deer out of a prized orchard or vegetable patch. Electric fencing provides a sharp electric jolt that doesn't injure deer but convinces them that whatever is on the other side of the fence isn't worth it. To ensure that deer make contact with the wire and get the "keep out" message, put aluminum foil flaps smeared with peanut butter here and there

Solutions at a Glance

PROBLEM: Something's eating all your hostas.

CULPRIT: Deer

SOLVE IT! Try lining the perimeter of your property with arborvitaes (*Thuja* spp.), three rows deep. Deer love arborvitae and are happy to forgo hostas in favor of it. If your yard is too large to "fence" completely with arborvitaes, try planting a triple-deep hedge along the boundary where deer are most likely to enter your yard.

along the electric fence. A number of commercial deer fence products are available, but be sure you understand and follow all of the manufacturer's safety instructions before installing an electric fence. Or have a professional install it for you.

Diseases

Detective work is the name of the game when it comes to identifying and controlling garden diseases. That's because plant diseases are caused by microorganisms too tiny to see. However, you can easily learn to recognize the symptoms they cause—and once you diagnose a disease, you may be able to intervene and effectively rid your garden of the problem. But preventing diseases is usually simpler than curing them, so use these expert tips (such as mixing things up) to keep your garden disease-free and growing strong.

RX FOR HEALTHY PLANTS

Barbara Pleasant, author of *The Gardener's Guide to Plant Diseases*, suggests four main strategies for preventing disease problems. "They're basic to growing a healthy garden," she says.

MIX THINGS UP. Grow a highly diversified garden that includes a number of different plants, and your garden will be naturally resistant to disease. That's because diseases, like insects, are able to damage only specific plants. And once a plant is infected, the disease can spread to other plants that are of the same species or that are closely related. For example, the main disease that causes dark spots to form on the leaves of tomatoes, early blight (*Alternaria solani*), can spread to potatoes but not to beans, corn, or cucumbers. So preserve the peace in your garden, and don't crowd too many family members into your plot together.

KEEP THINGS MOVING. Most plant diseases persist from year to year in soil or plant debris, so you can make a big impact on disease problems by rotating where you plant, making sure that you don't grow the same plants in the same soil 2 years in a row. Of course, it's impractical to move long-lived shrubs, trees, and perennials, but you can still deal diseases a huge blow just by gathering up diseased leaves and pruning back withered stems every chance you get. Discard these diseased castoffs—don't compost them—and you'll help avoid spreading plant diseases all around your yard and garden.

GROW NATURALLY HEALTHY PLANTS. Seek out disease-resistant varieties whenever you can. Resistant varieties haven't yet been developed for all diseases, but you'll probably find that any variety that shows excellent growth and vigor in your garden will also be a champ at standing up to diseases.

STOP DISEASES BEFORE THEY START. You can prevent many soilborne diseases by gardening only in well-drained areas and by enriching your soil with compost or other forms of organic matter at every opportunity. This will help control disease-causing fungi, which multiply by releasing thousands of spores. And fewer spores mean less disease.

PREVALENT AIRBORNE DISEASES

The most common diseases in any garden arrive on warm spring breezes, find homes on plant leaves, and flourish through summer as pesky parasites. The three biggies—powdery mildew, early blight, and rose black spot—are all fungi, and they're found almost everywhere! But here are some tips to put the kibosh on these diseases before they put the kibosh on the plants in your garden.

POWDERY MILDEW. Your best bet is to grow resistant varieties of the vegetables and flowers known to fall victim to this disease, which makes affected leaves look like they've been lightly dusted with flour. Powdery mildew sucks the life out of leaves and weakens plants, sometimes to the point of death, so you'll need to watch tall garden phlox, monarda, zinnias, and roses closely for early signs of powdery mildew. Early first aid is essential to saving your plants from this disease.

EARLY BLIGHT. Your best defense against this disease truly is a good offense. "A little leaf spot can produce hundreds of spores, so I patrol my tomatoes at least once a week and clip off any leaves that show suspicious black spots," says Alabama gardener Barbara Pleasant. "Besides reducing the number of new spores that can infect other leaves, my light clipping gives the plants a better shot at fresh air and sunshine—the biggest enemies of early blight—and it's a lot less messy than spraying."

You can diagnose this disease on potatoes and tomatoes by looking for irregular dark spots with concentric rings around their edges. The spots begin on lower leaves and need damp conditions to flourish and spread. When you see the signs, get clipping!

Remove blight leaf

USE YOUR OFFENSIVE GAME WHEN IT COMES TO EARLY BLIGHT AND CLIP OFF ANY LEAVES THAT HAVE SUSPICIOUS BLACK SPOTS ON THEM.

ROSE BLACK SPOT. Many new shrub roses show excellent tolerance to this widespread disease, which causes rose leaves to become speckled with black spots that have fringed edges. But even tolerant cultivars may need you to jump in and fight for them when the weather is warm and damp. So pick off badly spotted leaves to limit the number of spores that can infect new ones. Clip off faded blossoms and thin crowded stems so plenty of light and fresh air penetrates the plants. Promote the production of new leaves with regular water and organic fertilizer. By following these steps, you can help keep black spot from weakening or killing your roses.

HELP YOUR ROSES BEAT BLACK SPOT BY WATERING THEM REGULARLY AND APPLYING ORGANIC FERTILIZER.

BE A SMART SHOPPER

Make shopping for disease resistance a priority when you invest in ornamental shrubs or perennials. Recently, the nursery industry has made huge strides in identifying disease-resistant cultivars, but it's up to you to reward these efforts by choosing only the most disease-tolerant plants for your garden. As gardeners show that disease resistance is important to them, more of these varieties will become available, and that means fewer gardening frustrations for us!

FIGHT FUNGI WITH FUNGI

Science has finally confirmed what organic gardeners have known for years: Good compost is a banquet of micro-critters that not only help nurture plants but also may suppress diseases.

Scientists at the USDA's Biocontrol of Plant Diseases Laboratory have helped select and evaluate the disease-fighting punch of a beneficial fungus called *Gliocladium virens,* now sold in granulated form as SoilGard. What did they find? The *Glio* guys actually strangulate some disease-causing fungi, proving that putting good fungus head-to-head with bad fungus is great for your garden—and that compost really is your first line of defense against plant diseases!

"I never plant anything without putting compost into the soil first," adds Barbara Pleasant, author of *The Gardener's Guide to Plant Diseases.* "You never know what kind of bad guys might be lurking in the dirt, but by adding compost I figure the troublemakers will have plenty of company that might take away their lunch, or better yet, eat them for dinner!"

FIRST AID FOR FOLIAR INFECTIONS

The fight against foliar infections isn't hopeless—you can fight them off and reclaim your prize plantings. Just follow this expert advice from Barbara Pleasant, who gardens in Huntsville, Alabama.

1. Prune out affected stems, and rake up any diseased leaves that have fallen to the ground. Don't throw them on the compost pile, though; diseased plant parts need to be destroyed.

2. Top-dress with a thin layer of rotted manure or compost. Mix a handful of any good organic fertilizer into the topdressing.

3. Spray plants thoroughly with one of the disease-deterrent sprays below. Then, 1 week later, spray with the other mixture. (Alternating oil- and soap-based sprays will help keep an oily residue from building up on the leaves.)

Oil and Baking Soda Spray

1 tablespoon light horticultural oil (such as Sunspray)

1 tablespoon baking soda

1 gallon water

Soap and Baking Soda Spray

1 tablespoon insecticidal soap or liquid dishwashing soap

1 tablespoon baking soda

1 gallon water

LOOK OUT FOR YOUR PLANTS

Plants have to work with the conditions we give them, so it's up to us to make sure they're living in a happy, health-promoting environment. To prevent foliar diseases, follow these four guidelines.

1. Keep leaves as dry as possible because most diseases spread only on wet leaves. Use drip irrigation or water early enough in the day so leaves are completely dry by the time temperatures fall at night.

2. Put mulch to work as a barrier to keep muddy water from splashing on leaves. Use a good straw mulch beneath roses to trap black-spot spores that are washed down with rain. When the mulch dries, the spores will be history!

3. Use balanced organic fertilizers that release nutrients slowly. Plants that are underfed or overfed are more susceptible to diseases.

4. Clean up all old plant debris in winter. Replace old mulches with fresh material by the time spring arrives.

ONE OF THE EASIEST WAYS TO PREVENT PLANT DISEASES IN YOUR GARDEN IS TO CLEAN UP OLD PLANT DEBRIS AT THE END OF THE SEASON.

KEEP IT CLEAN

Moving your green babies into dirty containers is just asking for trouble, so make a habit of scrubbing out flower pots between uses.

"I do my pot cleaning on a hot day when playing in water is fun," reports Barbara Pleasant, Alabama gardener and author of *The Gardener's Guide to Plant Diseases*. "I put all my dirty flats and pots in a wheelbarrow and fill it with warm water and a tablespoon of granulated dishwasher detergent. After a 10-minute soak, I scrub them with a stiff brush, rinse them clean, and set them in the sun to dry. Besides avoiding disease problems, I always have clean containers ready to use when I want them," Pleasant says.

A WHEELBARROW MAKES A HANDY SINK IN WHICH TO WASH OUT DIRTY FLATS AND FLOWER POTS.

UNDERGROUND DISEASES

You garden soil contains thousands of different microorganisms—meaning dirt is anything but dead. And while most of these life forms help plants by releasing plant nutrients or by supporting other forms of soil life, a few aren't so nice. These tips will help you handle any disease that attacks your plants at their roots.

DAMPING-OFF. Growing seedlings in sterile soil that contains no fungi is the safest strategy for preventing this disease that causes young seedlings to suddenly collapse and shrivel. That's why most gardeners used bagged products known as "soilless mixes" to start seedlings. Damping-off is caused by several strains of soilborne fungi, so if you use potting soil you've made yourself or bagged soil that's been open for a while, heat up small batches to kill off those fungi. Just place as much soil as you need in an oven-proof container, sprinkle on some water, and cover it with a lid or aluminum foil. Put it in a 250°F oven for an hour, and all those fungi will be steamed off to fungi heaven!

HEATING UP SMALL BATCHES OF HOMEMADE POTTING SOIL CAN HELP KILL OFF FUNGI THAT CAUSE DAMPING-OFF.

FUSARIUM WILT. This pervasive disease is the athlete's foot of the plant world, attacking the roots of a number of vegetables and flowers. Hair-thin feeder roots are the first to go, followed by larger roots and the main stem; plant growth usually screeches to a halt, older leaves droop and turn yellow, and the rest of the plant just sits there looking miserable. But don't despair; these strategies will keep your fusarium frustrations at a minimum.

- Grow only resistant varieties of tomatoes, melons, and cabbages.
- Pull out infected plants and throw some compost down the hole to give the fusarium fungi a fight from friendly fungi.
- Plant only in well-drained soil; these fungi thrive in waterlogged soil.
- Prevent fusarium problems with long-lived asparagus, chrysanthemum, and cyclamen by monitoring your soil's pH and adding small amounts of lime (if needed) to keep the pH between 6.5 and 7.0.

Solutions at a Glance

PROBLEM: Bruised seedling stems are creating an entry point for damping-off fungi.

CULPRIT: Your fingers

SOLVE IT! When transplanting young seedlings, handle them only by the seedling leaves—the first ones that pop out when the seeds germinate.

ONE WAY TO BEAT FUSARIUM WILT ON TOMATOES IS TO GROW VARIETIES THAT ARE SPECIFICALLY RESISTANT TO THE DISEASE.

NUKE THOSE NEMATODES

Nematodes, microscopically small wormlike parasites that infect and clog up plants' roots, can turn any day in the garden sour. But if you know your enemy, there are a few strategies you can try to root these nuisances out.

If you have a plot of soil that you know has nematodes, plant it with French marigolds. Root-knot nematodes—the type gardeners in warm climates tangle with most often—can't abide 'Golden Guardian' and several other French marigold varieties.

You can also cook nematodes to death by harnessing the heat of the summer sun. Cultivate a troubled spot of soil, wet it, and cover it with a sheet of clear plastic for at least a month. Make sure the edges are securely buried so that plenty of heat is trapped under the plastic. Besides killing nematodes, this solarization process will rid the soil of many insects and weed seeds, too. And it'll be ready just in time for fall planting!

Evergreen Problems

Evergreen trees and shrubs, with their year-round interest, form the backbone of home gardens. They take center stage during the winter by adding texture, color, and structure to the otherwise brown landscape. And many evergreens add the sparkle of long-lasting flowers in spring and summer. For the rest of the year, they assume more of the role of a supporting cast member.

Most of the time, evergreens are fairly easy to grow and perform their roles year in, year out without complaints. But, just like other plants, they can have problems. And because these hardworking trees and shrubs are usually the most expensive plants in the garden, we all want to nip any problems in the bud. So here's some advice on heading off evergreen problems from deer, cold weather, insect pests, and more.

RX FOR HEALTHY PRUNING

For many of you, pruning ranks right up there with having a tooth filled—you'd prefer to avoid it. Pruning doesn't have to be a pain, however. Here are some tips to follow from John Van Etten, grounds superintendent of Mohonk Mountain House in New Paltz, New York.

REJUVENATE LEGGY BROAD-LEAVED EVERGREENS (SUCH AS RHODODENDRONS) BY CUTTING THEM BACK about one-third right after they're finished blooming. This will stimulate new growth from the base of the plant. (Make sure not to remove more than one-third of each plant at one time so the plant doesn't lose its natural shape or the ability to produce its own food.)

GIVE YOUR RHODODENDRONS A BOOST BY CUTTING THEM BACK BY ONE-THIRD AFTER THEY'RE FINISHED BLOOMING.

Solutions at a Glance

PROBLEM: Something's eating your evergreens.

CULPRIT: Deer

SOLVE IT! Plant evergreens that don't appeal to deer, such as spruces (*Picea* spp.), Scotch pine (*Pinus sylvestris*), and Douglas fir (*Pseudotsuga menziesii*).

PROBLEM: Evergreens take up a lot of space.

CULPRIT: Limited space

SOLVE IT! Look for trees that won't outgrow their space when they're mature. Check what the full size of the tree will be before you buy it and make sure you have enough room to accommodate it.

PROBLEM: Narrow-leaved evergreens, particularly yews (*Taxus* spp.) and some conifers, are opening up in the middle.

CULPRIT: Snow

SOLVE IT! Gently brush the snow off your trees if they aren't too tall. Use a sweeping motion moving from the center to the outer tips of the branches. Or erect tall stakes around the tree and loosely wrap burlap to the stakes and across the tops of them.

PROBLEM: Your broad-leaved evergreens are rolling up tight.

CULPRIT: Cold weather

SOLVE IT! These curled leaves are the plant's defense against the elements. When the leaves curl, water has less surface from which it can evaporate. You can lessen this leaf curling by continuing to water these shrubs in the fall and early winter until the ground freezes. You can also apply an antidessicant in the late fall, to slow down the rate at which the plant loses water.

Pest Detective

*S*omething's turning your healthy, vigorous evergreens into sad images of their former selves. Not sure who the culprit is? Check out this chart to find out who's doing the damage and how you can stop it.

Symptom	Cause	What to Do
Brown, cone-shaped galls on Colorado blue spruce (*Picea pungens forma glauca*), Engelmann spruce (*P. engelmannii*), oriental spruce (*P. orientalis*), and Sitka spruce (*P. sitchensis*). The galls look like needles that are curled inward. They're found at the tips of branches and sometimes toward the center of the tree.	Cooley spruce gall adelgid	Early identification is the key to eliminating the Cooley spruce gall adelgid population from your trees. In June, examine your trees for the brown, cone-shaped galls. Hand-pick the galls and burn them before the insects emerge in July and August to lay their eggs. The immature females also like to feed and overwinter on Douglas fir (*Pseudotsuga menziesii*), so keeping Douglas fir and spruce trees separate may help weaken the populations. Insecticidal soap is also effective at stopping galls; apply it in mid- to late April just before the buds open.
A dry, woolly substance that looks like white fuzz appears on new hemlock growth (particularly on the undersides of needles)	Woolly adelgid	If woolly adelgids have attacked your hemlocks (*Tsuga* spp.), apply horticultural oil or insecticidal soap in late April or early May, again in late June or late September, and the following year in early June (it's important to thoroughly cover the trees). By improving the tree's overall health and vigor—that is, maintaining good soil, ensuring adequate moisture, and pruning damaged wood—you can help slow down the adelgid.
Round notches on the edges of azalea, rhododendron, and yew (*Taxus* spp.) leaves	Black vine weevil	If you don't have too many plants, hand-pick the larvae and adults as you see them. You can also sink small, tuna-size cans in the ground; some of the weevils will inevitably fall off the plants into the cans and will be trapped. You could also apply nematodes to the soil in late spring or fall to take care of the black vine weevil larvae.
Leaves or needles are stripped from branches. Larvae live in curious baglike, 2½-inch-long cocoons studded with pieces of leaf and plant debris. Larvae are 1-inch-long, dark brown caterpillars.	Bagworm	Hand-pick the bags during winter. Cut bags away with a knife to avoid leaving a band of silk that could girdle the twig. Spray with *Bacillus thuringiensis* var. *kurstaki* (BTK) every 7 to 10 days from early spring to early summer to kill larvae.

GRADUALLY REDUCE THE SURFACE AREA OF NARROW-LEAVED TREES such as Norway spruce (*Picea abies*) so the trees will be less susceptible to ice, snow damage, and wind. You can do this just before new growth begins on the trees. This selective pruning also creates more air circulation through the trees, improving their health. Also, prune to cut out dead wood, crossed branches, or narrow crotches. (You can prune out dead or diseased wood anytime; prune crossing branches and do other corrective pruning after the "plant's bloom sequence is complete," says Van Etten.)

TRIM THE TIPS OF YEWS (*TAXUS* SPP.) AND HEDGE PLANTS ONCE EACH SPRING to encourage bud growth. Take care not to cut more than 2 or 3 inches of foliage during pruning.

WHERE ARE THE BERRIES?

You have some lovely holly bushes in your yard; the problem is they flower, but they never produce berries. What are you doing wrong?

The problem could be that you have either all male or all female holly bushes. Although both sexes will flower, only females will fruit. And the only way you'll get berries is if you have a female plant and a male plant *of the same species* within half a mile of it. With the help of bees, one male plant is sufficient to pollinate several females. If you aren't sure if your holly plants are male or female, look at the flowers. Male holly flowers have pronounced stamen covered with pollen. Female flowers have nubby stamen and a developed pistil, which is the swollen sack inside the plant's flower.

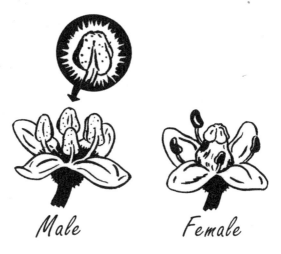

Male   Female

YOU'LL NEED BOTH MALE AND FEMALE HOLLY BUSHES IF YOU WANT BERRIES. SO IF YOU AREN'T SURE OF THE SEX OF YOURS, TAKE A CLOSER LOOK: MALE HOLLY FLOWERS HAVE PRONOUNCED STAMEN COVERED WITH POLLEN; FEMALE FLOWERS HAVE A NUBBY STAMEN AND A DEVELOPED PISTIL.

Eyesores

Every garden has at least one. Maybe the sight that makes you cringe is the stump left behind when a nor'easter felled your 80-year-old oak tree. Perhaps it's the overpowering highway that just a few years ago was a meandering country lane. Or it might be the 20-story building across the street from your third-floor terrace. Don't despair. Here are four terrific techniques that will help banish visual clutter and reclaim your garden as a place of repose and contentment.

GETTING OFF TO A GOOD START

If you take a look around your yard, you're sure to find *something* that needs concealing or enhancing. But before you rush off to the garden center to find a quick fix, heed the advice of Portland, Oregon, landscape architect Julia Lundy: "Think before you plant." Buy trees and shrubs that will be the height you're looking for when they reach maturity. That tidy little tree in its nursery pot might seem just the ticket for the front of your house now, but, Lundy warns, "a few years down the road it could be a monster and chances are it will have to go."

Never plant—or build—a taller screen than you need, Lundy says. "It may block necessary light and air circulation, and you'll have more problems than you started with."

Remember that plants grow out as well as up. Be especially aware of that horizontal dimension if you have a small garden or, says Paul Soniat, director of the New Orleans Botanical Garden, "You could sacrifice half your space to block a view." When space is limited, he says, vines on trellises can be your best friends. Or, try one of these plants for screening views:

- Leyland cyprus (*Cupressocyparis leylandii*). Hardy to Zone 6, leyland cyprus needs little or no water once it's established and thrives on the north side of a house.
- Holly-leaf osmanthus (*Osmanthus heterophyllus*). This plant takes heavy pruning so well that you can keep it skinny enough to suit the smallest yard.
- Mountain ash (*Sorbus aria*). This tree is slim, making it great for small gardens.

HIDE THAT ROAD!

Penny Grist's garden on Washington's Vashon Island overlooks the breathtaking blue waters of Puget Sound. Unfortunately, it also overlooks a two-lane highway that skirts the shoreline. Grist could have planted trees to hide the highway, but eventually they would have grown tall enough to hide the blue water, too. So Grist devised this simple method for figuring out how high a view blocker really needs to be, based on the fact that the eye is a trickster, seeing objects grow smaller as one moves away from them.

For example, let's say you want to block your neighbor's metal shed from view when you're on your patio. First, stand on your patio, looking at the shed. Have a friend stand at the edge of your property in front of the shed, holding against the ground a wooden strip marked at 1-foot increments. At the spot where you no longer see the structure above the strip, note the measurement. Then plant something that will reach that height at maturity. "In our case," Grist says, "a 4-foot hedge banished the road from sight but left the Sound in full view." Good hedges for hiding eyesores include forsythias (*Forsythia* spp.), hollies (*Ilex spp.*), northern bayberry (*Myrica pensylvanica*), azaleas (*Rhododendron* spp.), and yews (*Taxus* spp.).

The Cold Shoulder Treatment

If the object of your discontent is a 10-story building right behind your house, don't try to block it from view. Instead, create a lovely scene that will draw your attention down and away from the monstrosity, says Master Gardener Caroline Wiejek of East Longmeadow, Massachusetts. A tall hedge will create an illusion of separation, says Wiejek, "but it won't begin to cover something that big, and it might even emphasize it." But add a pond, a garden seat, or a sculpture at the base of

the hedge, and your eye will naturally gravitate toward it, rather than the building towering above.

Flowery Makeovers

What do you do with eyesores that are hard to hide, yet important to your creature comfort— such as heating-oil tanks and air-conditioning units? Why not put your creative juices to work and have some fun with them?

Natasha Zahn Pristas of Juneau, Alaska, painted her heating-oil tank blue, perched flower-filled window boxes on its support frame, and erected a picket-fence gate in front for service access. Rosalia Kung, a gardener from Skillman, New Jersey, surrounded her air-conditioning unit with a four-sided lattice box decked with realistically painted vines. The lattice allows plenty of air movement and the painted vines keep their distance from the air vents without the constant clipping real ones demand.

Have some fun turning an eyesore like an oil tank into an eye soother. Flower boxes and a picket fence disguise the bulky tank and its ugly metal frame.

Fencing Problems

Fences can be beautiful or functional, or—ideally—both. But if you're like many gardeners, you may have a fence that has seen better days. So whether your fence is falling down on the job or just not getting any easier on the eyes, we have the secrets to making your fence work for you! Read on for some innovative ways to enliven and secure the perimeter of your yard or garden.

LIVEN UP THAT UGLY FENCE

Whether you have an old split-rail fence with wire, a designer fence that's lost its pizazz, or plain chicken wire, you can bring your tired old fence to life. Literally.

Marzee Etheridge, who gardens in Ider, Alabama, did exactly that when she made a "living fence" around her nearly quarter-acre garden. "I was tired of getting wiped out by deer or rabbits, you name it. They'd eat a whole row of beans like nothing," she says. So she con-structed a barrier fence with nothing more than twine, posts, and a little help from Mother Nature.

Here's Etheridge's method: Pound posts (she used steel, although anything durable and about 5 feet long will do) 1 foot into the ground about every 8 feet. ("They should be close enough so that the heavy-duty twine you'll put between them doesn't sag," she says.) Then she runs twine securely between the posts, starting about 1 foot above the ground and continuing upward, making three or four rows 1 to 1½ feet apart.

She completely plants the spaces between the posts (don't forget to leave an entrance for yourself) with plants that benefit from sup-port—cucumbers, morning glories, melons, pole beans, sunflowers, and more. Then, she further enhances the barrier properties of her living fence by spraying the plants with hot pepper sauce. It has worked beautifully, she says. The 32 kinds of peppers and 15 to 20 tomato varieties, beans, and other veggies growing inside the living fence haven't been bothered since the fence went up, and the fruits and vegetables growing right on the fence do well, too.

"Deer don't like to get tangled in the twine. And the other animals don't like the twine or the hot sauce," she says.

If you already have "a big ugly" you'd like to make more attractive but you don't want to pull it out entirely and go with Etheridge's all-living fence, you can use your fence as a backdrop for flowering vines, clusters of flowers, or climbing roses. Or you could use Etheridge's planting plan of putting veggies and flowers along your fence (add a trellis or string some twine along the inside for those plants that need some climbing handholds)—and enjoy the beauty and the bounty that your former eyesore will bring to your landscape!

BRING AN OLD, UGLY FENCE TO LIFE BY PLANTING FLOWERS AND VEGGIES THAT NEED SUPPORT BETWEEN THE POSTS.

WHAT WEEDS?

Fencing, particularly around a garden's edge, needs to be kept relatively free from weeds to keep its appearance neat and to keep the vole and harmful insect populations down. So here's a great idea that kills two birds with one stone: Build a fence that keeps out weeds as well as garden pests.

Before setting in the fence posts, cut out a 1-foot section of sod around your fence perimeter. You can partially backfill with soil after putting in the fence posts, lay weed barrier fabric on each side of the buried fencing, and then fill in the trench with crushed rock, chipped bark, or another permanent mulch. You may have an occasional stray weed that needs to be pulled, but they'll pull out easily and the perimeter will stay neat—saving you hours of labor!

SAVE THAT BROKEN FENCE POST

You don't have to trash a perfectly good fence just because a post rots or breaks off at the soil line. Such problems can usually be fixed, rather than replaced, relatively easily. Just follow these four simple steps:

1. Get two 3-foot lengths of 1 × 4-inch lumber to brace each faulty post. (If the post is heavy and wide, you may need to go to 1 × 6-inch lumber to make sure the braces are strong enough.)
2. Sharpen one end of each 3-foot piece of lumber into a point and position one brace next to one side of the post, with the pointed end toward the ground.
3. Nail a piece of scrap wood atop the other end of the brace (so it doesn't split), and hammer the brace in for at least 1½ feet—tight against the post.
4. Fasten the top of the brace to the failing post with screws or nails. Then repeat with the other brace on the opposite side of the post in the same manner. Wrap a wire collar around both braces and the post to add more strength.

This system should hold your fence securely for years. If several post sections are broken in a row, however, you'll most likely need to remove the old posts entirely and install new ones.

Flea Beetles

There's no way of knowing whether flea beetle feeding plagues plants in the same way that fleas pester people and pets. But it's clear that these tiny beetles that jump like fleas can do some serious damage in your garden if you let them. A large infestation of flea beetles can kill young plants with heavy feeding early in the growing season, and plants that withstand the injury to their leaves may fall prey to viruses spread by the beetles.

Several flea beetle species are common in gardens, including potato flea beetles, striped flea beetles, spinach flea beetles, and a special species that feeds on corn. All of them chew small, circular gouges in leaves, and they multiply like mad. If you see lots of little holes in leaves and dark jumping beetles the size of sesame seeds, prepare for a flea beetle battle.

STICK 'EM UP

In her organic market garden in southwestern Ohio, Lucy Goodman-Owsley captures thousands of flea beetles with sticky traps made from plastic dish-washing, soda, or water bottles (yellow bottles work best) covered with petroleum jelly or Tanglefoot. "We bought a gallon of Tanglefoot, which turns out to be enough to cover 5 to 6 acres if you spread it out thinly like they tell you to," Goodman-Owsley says. She fills the empty yellow bottles with water to keep them from blowing in the wind, coats each bottle with Tanglefoot, and sets the sticky bottles on the ground between mature eggplants. "Besides being attracted by the yellow color, flea beetles are attracted to the nighttime warmth given off by the water-filled bottles," Goodman-Owsley explains. "They jump right down onto the side closest to the plants. When that bottle gets black with beetles, it's time to put a new bottle in the garden.

(Goodman-Owsley also notes that these sticky traps work well for catching flea beetles under row covers, too.)

SWING A FLEA SWATTER

Aiko Scales, a quick-thinking gardener in Woodinville, Washington, makes her flea beetles hop to a sticky death. "I paint a scrap piece of illustration board with yellow acrylic paint, coat it with Tanglefoot, and staple it onto a stake like a wooden row marker," Scales says. "I stick the traps in the ground around plants that have flea beetle problems. When I'm in the garden, I pull up a trap, hold it just above a leaf where flea beetles are feeding, and gently tap the leaf. They hop right up!" Scales reports.

Captured flea beetles

HOLD A STICKY TRAP OVER FEEDING FLEA BEETLES WHILE DISTURBING THE PLANTS TO MAKE THE BEETLES JUMP UP AND ONTO THE TRAP.

COVERED EGGPLANT CAGES

Eggplant are particularly vulnerable to flea beetle damage. But don't despair! You can shield your eggplants from this pest and encourage

Solutions at a Glance

PROBLEM: Your cabbage, eggplant, and potato foliage have lots of small holes in them.

CULPRIT: Flea beetles

SOLVE IT! Use row covers to keep these pesky critters out and to keep your plants intact.

plant growth by surrounding your plants with tomato cages covered with floating row covers. Set up the cages as soon as you transplant your seedlings to the garden. Wrap the cages with row cover fabric, fold over the seams at the top and sides, then staple them closed. Remove the staples and open the tops for pollination when the plants begin to bloom. (Don't remove the cages because you might damage the plant. Plus, you'll find that your eggplants are so big and vigorous, they'll need the support!)

SEEDLING PROTECTION

Plant the crops most susceptible to flea beetles such as eggplant and cabbage as late as possible in the spring. Flea beetles are the most damaging in early spring when seedlings may be killed by a heavy infestation of overwintering adults. (Larger plants can usually survive the feeding damage.)

Flower Garden Problems

If only they'd look like the pictures in the magazine. But flowers have minds of their own. They grow too small or too big, bloom only a little or not at all, fall prey to nasty pests, or even get stomped out by the kids.

Take heart, however. You can indeed have flowers that are as gorgeous as those glossy photos. All it takes is a little know-how. Read on and you'll be a few steps closer to realizing the beautiful blooming garden of your dreams.

FRESHENING UP

Ugh. It's late summer and your flowerbeds are looking the way you feel in all that heat and humidity. Perk up lackluster late-season beds and borders with reinforcements. Buy large pots or other lush containers of annuals—by late summer they're usually half-price—and plant them in your flowerbed right in their pots. Just pull a little mulch or soil over the rim. Trailing petunias and other hanging basket plants are ideal because they cover a large area.

DIVIDE AND CONQUER

No need to dig up the whole gigantic root ball when you're dividing perennials. As long as there's no dead spot in the center of the plant, simply slice off a piece or two—or three, or four—of the outside portion of the plant with a healthy chunk of roots attached.

DIVIDE PERENNIALS SIMPLY BY DIGGING UP AN OUTSIDE PORTION OF THE PLANT.

KILLING IT SOFTLY

What a quandary. You want to plant a wildflower meadow because it seems like such a wonderful, earth-friendly way to landscape an open area. Then you find out you have to kill the weeds first. Instead of resorting to chemicals, try this no-drug method. In just five steps you'll be well on your way to creating a beautiful, weed-free wildflower meadow.

1. Dig or till under existing weeds and turf.
2. Give the area a good soaking to encourage dormant weed seeds to germinate.
3. Cover the entire area with a tarp or spread it with newspapers, wetting them and weighting with rocks or bricks to prevent them from blowing away.
4. Allow to set at least a couple of weeks, then remove the cover.
5. Water again. Wait another week or two and then till, dig, or hoe up germinating seedlings.

A Summer Place

Summering houseplants outdoors is great, but may take up precious deck and porch space. So instead, summer your houseplants outdoors—in your flowerbed. (And save a little money on not having to buy as many flowers, too.)

The lovely colors and textures of your favorite houseplants are wonderful combined with garden flowers. Simply set the houseplants in their pots right on the soil, or sink the pot and all into the soil, concealing the rim with soil. In the fall, lift the pot and give the plant and the pot a gentle rinse with the garden hose to wash away any pests or problems that might spread indoors.

GIVE YOUR HOUSEPLANTS A NEW SUMMER HOME IN YOUR FLOWERBED.

Solutions at a Glance

PROBLEM: You keep forgetting when you're supposed to fertilize or repeat a pest control application.

CULPRIT: Your memory

SOLVE IT! Put those little white plastic labels to a new use. Write down what you're supposed to do and when you're supposed to do it. Then push the label into the soil by the plant.

FLOWER GARDEN UNDERSTUDIES

The Heath, Massachusetts, acreage of gardener extraordinaire Elsa Bakalar is a mecca for visitors and tour groups, so she has to keep it looking tip-top all season long. She recommends filling in bare spots by first sowing seeds of annual "understudies" between rows in her vegetable garden in the spring. By early summer, when problems become apparent but there are few annuals to be found in local nurseries, Bakalar just digs up her understudies and plants them into troublesome areas, a pretty fill-in for the garden "star" or two that didn't come through. Bakalar uses only those understudies that are shallow-rooted and don't resent transplanting. Her recommendations include

FOR THE BACK OF THE BORDER. Cosmos (*Cosmos bipinnatus*) 'Purity' in white or 'Dazzler' in red and 'Italian White' sunflower (*Helianthus annuus* 'Italian White').

FOR MIDBORDER. 'Marine' heliotrope (*Heliotropium arborescens* 'Marine') and flowering tobacco (*Nicotiana alata*) in white or other colors.

Solutions at a Glance

PROBLEM: Your flowerbeds are being squashed.

CULPRIT: Your kids

SOLVE IT! Visual clues can help keep kids in line. Edging, both flat and raised, clearly delineates which is a stay-off flowerbed and which is walk-on-me lawn. Paths of any sort also are a tremendous help, clearly identifying where kids may walk.

FOR THE FRONT OF THE BORDER. 'Red Plume' blanket flower (*Gaillardia pulchella* 'Red Plume') in deep red; annual candytuft (*Iberis umbellata*) in mixed colors; 'White Rocket' (*Iberis amara* 'White Rocket'); and a white variety of the low, groundcover-like Mexican zinnia (*Zinnia angustifolia*).

LATE BLOOMERS

Late summer into fall tends to be garden downtime for many perennials. But it doesn't have to be, says gardener Elsa Bakalar of Heath, Massachusetts. Here are some of her favorite perennials that burst forth with color as the season starts to wind down.

- Azure monkshood (*Aconitum carmichaelii*)
- White baneberry (*Actaea alba*)
- Garlic chives (*Allium tuberosum*)
- Japanese anemones, particularly 'Honorine Jobert' (*Anemone* cultivars)
- Purple parsnip (*Angelica gigas*)

- White mugwort (*Artemisia lactiflora*)
- New England aster (*Aster novae-angliae*)
- New York aster (*A. novi-belgii*)
- Boltonia (*Boltonia asteroides*)
- Rose turtlehead (*Chelone obliqua*)
- Late-blooming Kamchatka bugbane (*Cimicifuga simplex*)
- Weyrich chrysanthemum (*Dendranthema weyrichii*, also called *Chrysanthemum weyrichii*)
- Joe-pye weed (*Eupatorium purpureum*)
- Bottle gentian (*Gentiana andrewsii*)
- Common sneezeweed (*Helenium autumnale*)
- Late cultivars of obedient plant, such as 'Vivid' (*Physostegia* cultivars)
- Blue sage (*Salvia azurea*)
- Late-blooming goldenrods (*Solidago sphacelata* 'Golden Fleece')

SPEEDY DEADHEADING

Using bypass shears to deadhead long-blooming flowers with many small blooms, such as coreopsis or golden marguerite (*Anthemis tinctoria*) can take forever. To speed things up, get out those hedge clippers or the lawn shears that you use for tall grass along the fence. They'll make quick work of those offending blossoms, and you'll be done in no time.

USE LAWN SHEARS TO MAKE QUICK WORK OF DEADHEADING PERENNIALS WITH MANY SMALL FLOWERS.

No-Brainer Flowers

Need a garden you can't kill and has something in bloom all season long? No, we aren't talking about silk flowers. We're talking about easy-to-grow perennials and bulbs. Plant our baker's dozen here and you'll have something going from early spring to late fall.

Late winter: Crocuses
Very early spring: Daffodils
Early spring: Columbines (*Aquilegia* spp.), fringed bleeding heart (*Dicentra eximia*)
Late spring: Peonies
Early summer: 'Moonbeam' threadleaf coreopsis (*Coreopsis verticillata* 'Moonbeam'), Siberian iris (*Iris sibirica*)
Midsummer: Daylilies, Shasta daisies (*Leucanthemum × superbum*, also called *Chrysanthemum × superbum*)
Late summer: Obedient plant (*Physostegia* spp.), 'Autumn Joy' sedum
Early fall: Chrysanthemums (*Dendranthema × grandiflorum*, also called *Chrysanthemum × morifolium*)
Late fall: Asters

Dry Ideas

Just because you live where rainfall is scant doesn't mean you can't have beds full of lovely annuals and perennials—you just have to know what to look for when buying plants. Usually, if a plant has one or more of the following characteristics, it can go without water longer than most:

● Hairy leaves or stems
● Silver-gray foliage
● Stickers or thorns
● Thick, succulent-type leaves
● Waxy leaves

More Flowers Longer

Do you have a fairly large stand of perennials that bloom in mid- to late summer and then peter out? Here's a way you can prolong the bloom.

Once the plants are several inches high in early or mid-spring, trim back a row in the center of the stand, about a third of its depth. Then, about 1 week later, trim the front third.

You'll create a stair-step effect of bloom. The back "row" will bloom first. Once those have faded, the second "row" will start; at that time, trim the back row to deadhead and to conceal unsightly foliage. Then, when the front row starts blooming—about the time the second row is fading—cut back the second and third rows to remove unsightly spent blooms and foliage.

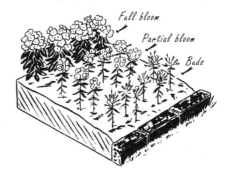

TRIM YOUR PERENNIALS IN STAGES FOR CONTINUOUS WAVES OF BLOOM.

Standing Up for Shrubs

If your flowerbeds and borders look too flat or ragged early and late in the season, tuck in a few shrubs, advises Gloria Seborg of Seattle, Washington. "Shrubs can give a garden a sculptural quality," Seborg says.

Evergreens are especially good choices because they look great year-round. And during the height of the blooming season, evergreens provide a pleasantly neutral backdrop that sets off flowers nicely.

Pest Detective

Flowers are ailing, but you aren't sure why? Check out these three common pests that love annuals and perennials and see if they might be visiting your garden without an invitation.

Symptom	Cause	What to Do
Leaves are curled and yellow. May be coated with a sticky substance.	Aphids	Aphids do little damage in small numbers. For more extensive infestations, spray plant with a garden hose. Follow with an application of insecticidal soap, and reapply as the label directs.
Leaf tissue becoming lacey from insect damage. Flowers are being eaten, too.	Japanese beetles	Flick beetles off plants into a bucket of soapy water; apply milky spore disease to lawn to control grubs.
A small white cloud arises when you brush the plant. Plant may be mottled and yellow.	Whiteflies	If it's the end of the season and your region gets freezing temperatures you don't have to do anything. Whiteflies can't survive the winter. But earlier in the season, spray with an insecticidal soap, and reapply as the label directs.

FLIP THAT FLOP

Your sedum is sprawling, your lilies are lolling, and your asters are all askew. Help them regain their stature without the unsightliness of stakes. Simply take a length of clear monofilament fishing line and tie the plants up into a big, loose bundle. The great thing about using the fishing line is that it's nearly invisible, so it looks as if your plants never flopped in the first place.

RX FOR WONDERFUL WILDFLOWERS

When the call of the wildflowers beckons, follow this advice from native-plant gardener Danielle Green of Chicago.

WORK WITH YOUR SITE; DON'T STRUGGLE TO MAKE IT A HAVEN FOR WHATEVER STRIKES YOUR FANCY IN THE CATALOGS. Discover what your geographic niche offers in the way of hospitality, including soil quality, light level, drainage, and hardiness. Then find plants that naturally flourish in those surroundings.

START WITH PLANTS RATHER THAN SEEDS. Many wildflower seeds take 2 to 3 years to germinate, and that's a long time to spend looking at bare ground and fending off weeds. The price tag will be much higher for plants than seeds (another reason to start small) but your success rate will increase dramatically.

BUY YOUR PLANTS AS CLOSE TO HOME AS POSSIBLE. They'll be better adapted to your microclimate. Buy only from reputable nurseries, and make sure the plants were propagated, not illegally taken from the wild.

STEER CLEAR OF PREPACKAGED MIXES WHEN YOU DO BUY SEED. Instead, look for individual species that are native to your area.

Fruit Tree Problems

Biting into an apple, pear, peach—or any fruit that you've picked from your own tree—is simply divine, isn't it? After all, it's hard to beat the luscious flavor of fruit you've grown yourself. (And desserts taste oh so much better made with fresh-from-the-backyard fruit.) But fruit trees can have an intimidating side to them, too. Lost all your cherries to the birds? Not sure how much you should thin those apples? And how the heck do you know when fruit is ripe for the picking? Luckily, some gardeners out there do have the lowdown on fruit trees—and they were happy to share their wisdom with us.

Rx for Healthy Fruit Trees

Tom Burford, a former Virginia orchardist and nurseryman who's now an orchard designer and fruit tree consultant, has put together five tips to help you keep your fruit trees healthy.

KEEP THE GROUND UNDER YOUR FRUIT TREES CLEAN. Remove grass from the base of the trees (so you can easily inspect the tree for damage from insects and rodents). Make sure any mulch is about 6 inches away from the trunk of the tree to discourage mice from nesting against the trunk and nibbling it. Also, pick all ripe fruit and any branches or leaves up off the ground, and remove all mummies (shriveled fruit) from the tree.

WRAP THE TRUNKS OF NEWLY PLANTED TREES IN LATE FALL WITH A SPIRAL VINYL WRAP. Wide swings in temperature can cause fissures in young trees, and the fissures can be home to insects and diseases. Wrapping the trunk will help protect the tree (remove the wrap in spring when temperatures have stabilized; wrapping will also protect the tree from nibbling animals and mechanical damage).

PLANT NEW FRUIT TREES AWAY FROM COMPETING MATURE TREES. Also, never plant fruit trees near walnut trees; the juglone in the walnut trees is toxic to some members of the rose family.

PRUNE FRUIT TREES ANNUALLY SO SUNLIGHT CAN PENETRATE AND AIR CAN CIRCULATE THROUGHOUT THE TREE. Allowing sun to get in through the branches helps reduce the growth of fungus. "You want to keep a tree open enough so that ideally a robin could fly through without its wing tips touching any branches," says Burford.

FEED YOUR TREES—ESPECIALLY YOUNG ONES.
Fish emulsion is a great fruit tree fertilizer, says Burford. Give your trees a good application in spring, and then follow that up with a monthly feeding. "As long as the leaves remain bright and green, your tree is getting enough nutrition," Burford notes. "If the leaves become dull and overall growth slows down, you should have a soil test done to determine which nutrients your soil needs."

YOU'LL KNOW YOU'VE PRUNED JUST ENOUGH FROM YOUR FRUIT TREES IF A ROBIN CAN FLY THROUGH WITHOUT ITS WINGS TOUCHING THE BRANCHES.

FASTER FRUIT

If you can't wait years to taste your first apples or pears, add a little weight to the tree and you'll get your fruit faster, says Lee Reich, Ph.D., a garden writer from New Paltz, New York. Simply hang weights on the branches to bend the branches down to about a 60-degree angle. (You can fill plastic sandwich bags with sand and use them for the weights.) The bent branches slow down vegetative growth, so the tree has more energy to form fruit buds.

THE SKINNY ON THINNING

Thinning excess fruit from a tree is as important as pruning dormant wood because overbearing is damaging to trees and affects future production, says Tom Burford, a former Virginia orchardist and nurseryman who's now an orchard designer and fruit tree consultant. "If you thin you'll get larger, higher quality fruit," Burford notes, "and the tree will be very appreciative. If you don't thin, especially on a young tree, the fruit will be degraded and the tree will take a number of years to recover."

In an effort to avoid stressing your tree, Burford offers this thinning advice.

"Use your hand as a guide," he says. "Thin fruit so the spread is about the distance between your thumb and index finger—4 to 6 inches. And if you're thinning from a young tree, make sure to remove fruit from the main stem. If you don't, you'll end up with a great crook in the main stem the following year."

(Also keep in mind that you should thin fruit early in the growing season, when the fruit is no larger than a dime.)

THIS HANDY GUIDE TO HELP YOU THIN FRUIT IS RIGHT AT YOUR FINGERTIPS.

Pear-Picking Pointer

Sam Benowitz, owner of Raintree Nursery in Morton, Washington, offers this tip for timely pear picking. "Put the palm of your hand underneath the pear and raise your palm," says Benowitz. "If the pear breaks off the stem then it's ready to be picked, even though it may still be hard. Then simply store it on a counter until it softens."

GIVE A PEAR A HAND TO TELL IF IT'S READY TO BE PICKED.

A Touch of Lime

Here's a way to control fungus and insect problems from Frank Pollock, who runs an organic fruit and vegetable farm in the Pocono Mountains of Pennsylvania. "We follow an old practice of using lime to dust our fruit trees from time to time," says Pollock. "We generally do it in early to late spring. Using lime is cheap, and it's relatively effective."

One-Two Punch

Looking for easy ways to thin out large fruit, like apples and peaches? Try hitting the fruit with a strong stream of water from a hose, advises Lee

Solutions at a Glance

Problem: Your apples are damaged.

Culprit: All kinds of pests

Solve It! Tie paper bags over the fruit as soon as the fruit has set and leave the bags on until 2 to 4 weeks before harvest.

Reich, Ph.D., a garden writer from New Paltz, New York. You can also attach a rubber hose to the end of a stick and bat at the branches.

Wonder of Whitewash

The trunks of many young peach and cherry trees are susceptible to cracking, says Frank Pollock, who runs an organic fruit and vegetable farm in the Pocono Mountains in Pennsylvania. To prevent cracking, Pollock paints the first 3 to 4 feet of the trunk with a whitewash—but he *doesn't* use latex paint, as some people recommend. Instead, he mixes lime with water and an extender and paints the lower trunks in late spring. (Pollock says the lime whitewash also helps to repel insects.)

Beating the Birds I

Lon Rombough, a horticulturist from Aurora, Oregon, offers two suggestions for winning the birds versus your cherries game.

"You can buy bush cherries (a cross of *Prunus japonica* and *P. jacquemontii*); at maturity they're around 6 feet tall, and they look and taste like a pie cherry. They ripen in late Au-

PROBLEM: You hate picking fruit.

CULPRIT: You

SOLVE IT! Pick all the fruit you can easily reach and then shake the rest down and use it for canning and freezing; it's the lazy man's way of harvesting.

gust, so the birds usually leave them alone, plus the bushes are small enough that you can easily throw a net over them."

BEATING THE BIRDS II

Frank Pollock, who runs an organic fruit and vegetable farm in the Pocono Mountains in Pennsylvania, suggests putting up purple martin houses among your cherry trees. "Purple martins are very proprietary," says Pollock, "and they'll chase other birds away from your cherries. And because purple mar-

Pest Detective

A little brown spot here, a hole or crack there—something is turning all that sweet fruit on your trees into sour grapes. But once you know what the troublemaker is, you can fight back. Here are the tools you need to do just that.

Symptom	Cause	What to Do
Thin brown tunnels throughout the apple	Apple maggot larvae	Catch adult apple maggots on red ball traps coated with Tanglefoot. Hang the traps in June—one per dwarf tree and four per semidwarf tree. Hang the traps at eye level and 2 to 3 feet within the tree. Clear the leaves from right around the trap. Clean up dropped apples weekly to help prevent problems next year.
Curled cherry leaves with a sticky coating; small, shiny black insects on leaf undersides	Black cherry aphids	Cherry aphids leave the trees by midsummer, so you may not have to do anything. If the infestation is severe, remove the aphids with a strong spray of water or spray them with insecticidal soap or neem
Tunnels to the core of the apple with perhaps a plumb pink larvae still in the fruit	Codling moth	Pick up dropped fruit; wrap corrugated cardboard wraps around the tree trunk. The cardboard will attract the larvae looking for a protected spot to pupate. Destroy the old wraps and replace the cardboard weekly during the summer.
Tiny red and green insects on pear trees	Pear psylla	Limit fertilization; use thinning cuts when pruning so you don't encourage a lot of succulent new growth that will attract psylla. (Pear psylla are sucking insects that can spread fire blight, a deadly pear bacterial disease). If psylla are on the tree during the growing season, spray insecticidal soap or summer oil to control them.

tins are in the swallow family, they primarily eat insects—meaning they'll leave your cherries alone."

ASHES TO ASHES

Are your peach or cherry trees plagued by borers? If so, do what organic fruit and vegetable farmer Frank Pollock does.

"Every year we put a scoop of wood ashes around the base of all of our peach and cherry trees," explains Pollock. "We put the ashes right up against the tree, and the ashes tend to repel the borers. The ashes also deter ants to some extent, which are often a problem in spring."

FROSTY PROTECTION

Early-blooming fruit trees like apricots and peaches may pay the penalty for their early budding by being hit with frost. You can help prevent frost damage on early bloomers by planting them near the north side of a building, says Lee Reich, Ph.D., a garden writer from New Paltz, New York. That way, the trees won't warm up as quickly as they would in another location.

Symptom	Cause	What to Do
Brown or olive green spots on apples, or knobby apples with corky, cracked areas	Apple scab	Avoid this problem entirely by planting disease-resistant apples like 'Liberty', 'Goldrush', 'Freedom', and 'Enterprise', which are resistant to scab. Spray scab-susceptible trees with sulfur beginning when the tree leafs out in the spring and repeat after a heavy rain or weekly until midsummer. (The scab fungus takes about 12 days to appear on leaves and fruit from when the infection occurs. Once you can see it, you have a problem on your hands.) You can eat the scabby apples.
Dark spots that fall out from plum leaves, leaving holes	Bacterial leaf spot	Prune for good air circulation; remove affected fruit and leaves; spray lime sulfur every 10 to 21 days. If bacterial spot is a serious problem in your growing area, plant disease-resistant cultivars such as 'Au-Amber', 'Au-Rosa', 'Red Heart', and 'Crimson'.
Olive green spots on immature peaches; peaches become distorted	Peach scab	Collect and destroy infected or dropped peaches and fallen leaves. Prune to increase air circulation. You can eat lightly damaged peaches.
Deformed flowers on your apple tree that don't open and whitish velvetlike patches on the flower stems in spring.	Powdery mildew	Prune for good air circulation within the tree—remember a robin should be able to fly through the tree (old-timers used to suggest throwing a cat through the tree but that seems to be a technique your kitty wouldn't care for). Cut off and destroy infected shoots when you see them. Spray the tree with sulfur when the weather is wet or humid and the temperature is above 59°F. Repeat after rain or every 7 to 10 days until midsummer. Plant disease-resistant apple varieties; many are also resistant to mildew.

Garden Design Problems

The pros make it look so easy. A few flowering shrubs here, some perennials there, a lovely brick pathway to tie it all together—the perfect garden. But those of us who have struggled to plan a wonderful garden know better: Good garden design takes practice. It's a lot easier, though, if you know a few tricks of the trade. Armed with a little knowledge, you'll soon find yourself building a beautiful work of art. And unlike the pros, you'll design the garden for yourself they never could—a garden that uniquely reflects your personality.

SAFETY IN NUMBERS

Prevent yourself from digging up or "weeding" newly emerging perennials in early spring by planting at least three—and preferably five—together. One tiny plant all by its lone-some can look very much like a weed. But five, evenly spaced, are less likely to be mis-identified.

ARBOR DOS AND DON'TS

Stumped on where to position one of those pretty walk-through arbors? Here are some rules of thumb to get you started:

Do Place an Arbor
At the beginning or end of a path
As a bridge between two flower borders
Where a gate would naturally go into a
   fence or hedge
At the entrance of a vegetable or cutting
   garden
At the end of a vista

Don't Place an Arbor
In the middle of a lawn
On a steep slope where it would be difficult
   to walk
Under a tree all by itself
By a pond all by itself

DOGGY DESIGN

Take a cue from your pet when laying out your garden—let it go to the dogs. Millie Kiggins and Penny Vogel, owners of Kinzsy Faire Garden in Estacada, Oregon, have 50 acres to deal with, 2 of them flower gardens. When it came time to figure out how to landscape the wide-open spaces, they simply mulched over a network of paths that the dogs had beaten in their daily roamings. Then they started designing beds that fit with the paths.

REPEAT YOURSELF

To avoid ending up with a chaotic jumble of plants when designing flowerbeds, keep in mind that repetition is important, says Eve Davis, owner of the Hawk and Ivy Bed and Breakfast and its accompanying large garden in Barnardsville, North Carolina.

Choose a plant or two that looks terrific all season long and has a distinctive shape, such as an ornamental grass, Siberian iris (*Iris sibirica*), or peony. Then use it at regular intervals throughout the border or garden, to give order to your beds.

ROOKIE TRYOUTS

How often have you given a new plant a whirl in an established bed, only to have its performance be less than stellar? Next time you're unsure how a plant might do in a bed or border, try it in a nursery bed first.

Karen Strohbeen and Bill Luchsinger of Macksburg, Iowa—artists, gardeners, and producers of the PBS television show *The Perennial Gardener with Karen Strohbeen*—use a series of raised beds to experiment with new plants before they add the little newcomers to their main borders.

Not only does this method keep their main garden at its prime, it also saves money. By the time Strohbeen and Luchsinger are ready to put a perennial into the main border, it's usually large enough to divide.

Solutions at a Glance

PROBLEM: Wasted outdoor space; people keep using the wrong door.

CULPRIT: A seldom-used side door

SOLVE IT! Turn it into a container garden. Dennis Ahl of Minneapolis, Minnesota, filled his seldom-used steps and landing with pots large and small, making it clear that this wasn't a door to use. He also gained a little extra planting space and found an excellent staging area for his pots.

Although Strohbeen and Luchsinger have several of these 4 by 4-foot nursery beds in their sprawling country garden, urban gardeners with more limited space could set aside a corner or two of the vegetable garden.

CRACKING UP

When Lenore Chen's seldom-used driveway in Des Moines began to crumble, she turned a major problem into an asset. Here's how she did it.

Because the driveway connects with the entranceway to the house, she left the front portion of the driveway (which was fairly sound) intact and created a curving edge to help it gracefully flow into the front walk.

Then, a jackhammer crew broke up the remaining concrete into rough chunks. Chen salvaged the concrete, using it to create a retaining wall alongside the drive. She placed the rough edges out to give it the look of natural stone.

Over time, the concrete has become weathered, mossy, and the perfect spot for rock garden plants and others that demand excellent drainage.

TURN BITS OF AN OLD DRIVEWAY INTO A USEFUL RETAINING WALL.

THE BIG PICTURE

Having trouble envisioning just where the new beds you want to plant should go? Follow the lead of Linda Corson, a landscape architect in Philadelphia.

Corson photographs gardens she's going to design by standing in one spot and snapping shots as she turns around 360 degrees. After the film is developed, she tapes the pictures together, end to end.

"A landscape is very different when you view it in a photograph, as opposed to when you look at it with the naked eye," Corson says. "Because you're looking at all the elements of the landscape on a much smaller scale in a photo, you tend to see aesthetic detractors such as phone lines."

And even if you don't know a lot about plants, a photo guides you to the right shapes and forms. "It helps you figure out the heights of plants, where the windows are—that sort of thing," Corson says.

Once the landscape is neatly spread out before her, Corson then likes to take tracing paper and lay it over the photos, drawing in her dream landscape and experimenting with different designs.

TAKE YOUR GARDENING TO NEW HEIGHTS

Pete Black of Halstead, Kansas, likes raised beds, but he doesn't like the cost or hassle of building them. So he creates his raised beds with concrete blocks.

Black often finds the blocks for just pennies at garage sales or for free from neighbors. Also try your local landfill, which may be happy to give them away.

To build his concrete block raised beds, Black simply lays the blocks right on the soil surface, holes facing upward. He fills the holes with sand to further weight the blocks down and discourage weeds.

Black's raised beds are just one block high, but you can make them two blocks high without having to use any reinforcement.

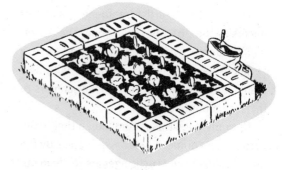

CREATE EASY, INEXPENSIVE RAISED BEDS WITH RECYCLED CONCRETE BLOCKS.

GRAND ILLUSIONS

Herb Kessner of Fairfax, California, likes to create the illusion of space in his small Bay-area garden by putting smaller plants at the far end of the garden. Keeping smaller things off in the distance creates a sort of forced perspective, making the yard look longer than it really is. Old-hand gardeners have been doing a version of this for years—trimming hedges so that they're slightly shorter at the far end to make them look longer and more imposing.

MAKE YOUR GARDEN LOOK BIGGER BY PUTTING SMALLER PLANTS AT THE FAR END, CREATING A FORCED PERSPECTIVE.

MIX & MATCH A GARDEN PATH

Looking for something different in a garden path that isn't too expensive? One way to do it is to combine materials. Dianne Olivieri of Santa Cruz, California, has created wonderful paths doing just that.

She might combine flagstone, brick, and round pavers she has covered in a pottery mosaic, for example. And this mixing of materials makes sense. It lets you better use recycled items, which can be hard to find in large quantities, especially if you're using bits and pieces you have around the house. After all, mixing adds variety and personality to your garden in a way a plain old brick path never could. Here are some more mix-and-match ideas.

- Bark mulch
- Bricks from a landfill
- Plastic bucket lids painted a funky color or with designs
- Clay tiles purchased as remnants or on clearance
- Bits of broken concrete
- Old ceramic or plastic dinner plates and platters
- Flagstones painted with fun designs
- Pea or colored gravel, laid in a pattern divided with edging
- Old iron manhole covers or other flat scrap metal
- "Mini-decks"—lumber cut into 24-inch squares and joined together on the back with lengths of other lumber
- Concrete pavers painted with concrete paint or stained with a concrete stain
- Concrete pavers topped with pottery or tile mosaic
- Homemade concrete pavers, made from concrete mix and poured into a pizza box for a mold and inset with marble, tiles, stones, or anything else
- Wood pavers cut from horizontal lengths of an old tree and coated in deck sealer
- Crushed seashells
- Terra-cotta pot drainage trays, turned upside down
- Leftover bits of marble or slate tile from a demolition project

Don't Get Strung Out

Whenever you're using stake and string to lay out a garden bed, be sure to use mason's line, which you can buy at any hardware store. Unlike regular string, it won't stretch, requiring you to position and reposition your stakes to accommodate sagging.

Stop and Compare

When Gloria Seborg of Seattle, Washington, is mulling over how to move around her perennials and small shrubs so that they combine well, she uses an old trick first espoused by that famous English gardener Vita Sackville-West. She snips a clipping of one plant and takes it over to the other plant to see how well they go together.

Patio Plant Pockets

Need a home for plants that like to grow in tight spots? If you're building a patio, leave a few planting holes here and there in the overall surface. Or how about setting your pavers, stone, or tile in sand instead of concrete to accommodate plants that love to grow in cracks, especially reseeders.

Ann Bauer of Palos Verdes Estates, California, has a tile patio that has a few tiles missing here and there—on purpose. She loves the little holes for planting creeping herbs and other plants that like it tight.

And sometimes, when a plant has reseeded itself in a crack, she pops out the tile to give it a little more room to sprawl. "And when the plant dies, if it looks bad, we just put the tile back in again," Bauer says.

POP A PAVER OR TWO TO CREATE CHARMING PLANTING POCKETS IN YOUR PATIO.

Gnats

Gnats are, in a word, annoying. Not dangerous, not destructive, not particularly painful. (Although some varieties do bite, and if you've ever had a gnat in your eye, you know how uncomfortable that is!) If it weren't for gnats, summer evenings would be the perfect time to garden or relax outside. But a cloud of gnats—sometimes called midges or no-see-ums—can send you fleeing indoors in an effort to keep the tiny creatures out of your eyes, nose, mouth, and ears. But don't try to take out these tiny torturers with a chemical bug spray; we can help you reclaim the night the herbal way.

GIVE GNATS A PINCH

If you grow herbs in your garden, a quick-and-easy gnat repellent may be right at your fingertips. Betzy Bancroft, an herbalist living in Port Murray, New Jersey, says she simply pinches off some peppermint or basil leaves and rubs them on her exposed skin to help repel insects. But be careful if you have sensitive skin, she warns. Test these herbs on a small area, wait at least 15 minutes, and watch for signs of irritation. If no such signs appear, pinch away!

RUB FRESHLY PICKED PEPPERMINT LEAVES ON YOUR SKIN AND SAY GOODBYE TO GNATS.

GNO MORE GNATS!

According to Mindy Green, director of education at the Herb Research Foundation in Boulder, Colorado, and co-author of *Aromatherapy: A*

Solutions at a Glance

Problem: When you're in your yard or maybe even your home, you spend most of your energy swatting tiny bugs away from your face and your ears.

Culprit: Gnats

Solve It! Gnats like standing water and moist places and are attracted to lights, so reduce sources of standing water, and position outdoor lighting away from air-conditioner units or windows where gnats may be able to enter your home.

Complete Guide to the Healing Art, you can make your own natural bug repellent by using some common essential oils.

Combine 1 ounce of carrier oil (a vegetable oil like canola will do) with 4 drops of cedar, 2 drops of eucalyptus, 4 drops of lavender, 2 drops of orange, 1 drop of peppermint, and 2 drops of rosemary. (*Note:* Orange oil heightens sun sensitivity, so if you'll be using this repellent during the day, leave the orange out.) Smooth the mixture on the exposed skin of anyone age 5 or older.

Do a patch test before you apply this concoction (and don't attempt to use it if you have a known allergy to any of the ingredients). Rub a small amount on the inside of your forearm and watch it for 15 minutes to see if you have an allergic reaction.

FISH FOOD

The larval stage of gnats is aquatic and is actually an important food item for fish. If you have a water garden in your home landscape, stock it with sturdy goldfish and these brightly colored beauties will get rid of gnat larvae for you. (A good rule of thumb is to plan for one fish for every 2 or 3 square feet of surface.)

Groundcover Problems

Groundcovers are supposed to solve problems, not cause them, right? After all, a groundcover can turn a hard-to-mow slope into a beautiful flowering bank. It can replace the lawn you're tired of mowing every weekend. And it can cloak the soil under your shade trees where grass won't grow. But if you choose the *wrong* groundcover, you can end up with more problems than you started with. Whether you've already learned that the hard way, or you're about to choose and plant a groundcover and want to get it right the first time, expert help is close at hand.

NATIVES TO THE RESCUE

In the last big rainstorm, your hillside got an itch to travel and took the groundcover with it, much to your dismay. That's not uncommon, especially on sites where developers' bulldozers scraped the plate clean before the houses went up. The solution: Plant a groundcover that grabs the soil—a job at which native plants excel, says Danielle Green, who gardens with native species in Chicago. "Plants that grow on stream banks, on steep hillsides, or in wind-swept areas tend to have fine, dense, and often very deep root systems, and that's what it takes to control erosion." Her suggestion: Replant your slope with deep-rooted trees, shrubs, flowering perennials, or grasses native to your area and your terrain. (See page 196 for sources of native plants.)

WHEN YOU NEED TO COVER A HILLSIDE, CHOOSE PLANTS WITH STRONG ROOTS. TURF GRASS CAN'T PERFORM HALF AS WELL AS NATIVE GRASSES.

INVASION OF THE GROUND SNATCHERS

There's often a fine line between a plant that will neatly carpet that awkward spot by the mailbox and one that will turn into a force worthy of the D-Day invasion. Says Jack Poff, alpine plants curator at the Berry Botanic Garden in Portland, Oregon, "The very thing that makes a plant a good groundcover—its ability to spread quickly—can also make it a menace." So how do you get the curative qualities of a groundcover without the nasty side effects? Here are a few good prescriptions:

- Beware of plants that spread by underground stems called rhizomes, such as *Anemone nemorosa*, says Poff. Some very choice groundcovers do produce rhizomes, "but you have to be careful where you put them. They're much harder to control than plants that increase by above-ground means. Make sure you know what you have before you plant it."
- Master Gardener Judy Wong of Menlo Park, California, takes an aggressive approach to overly energetic groundcovers. "I put two kinds next to each other and let 'em duke it out," she says. "It seems to keep them both under control."
- For Marilyn Dube, owner of Natural Design Plants in Portland, Oregon, the key to curtailing a groundcover's wayward ways is simple: "Put it where it isn't happiest." For instance, she says, "Sweet woodruff will tolerate anything from dense shade to full sun, but its home of homes is a moist site in morning sun. If you put it there it will take over everything. If you plant it in dry shade it will still thrive, but it will be more likely to stay within bounds."

BYE-BYE BACKACHE

If you have a big lawn, replacing some of it with groundcover will save a lot of hassle in the long run. But when you set out to remove turf by hand so you can plant groundcover, even a tiny area of grass looks as big as a golf course. Betsy Becker, horticulturist and propagator at the Berry Botanic Garden in Portland, Oregon, offers this easy alternative to cutting sod by hand:

1. In late summer, cover the grass with a layer of newspapers at least 1 inch thick. Water thoroughly and keep the papers moist enough so they don't blow away. (If winds are fierce where you live, add rocks at strategic spots.)
2. In the fall, spread 6 to 12 inches of leaves across the papers.
3. Let it all decompose through the winter. In the spring, add a foot or so of good soil (Becker uses a sandy loam, sold in many nurseries as three-way planting mix). Then just set in your plants.

GETTING RID OF LAWN TAKES ABOUT 6 MONTHS USING THE NEWSPAPER METHOD, BUT IT'S NOT NEARLY AS DIFFICULT AS CUTTING SOD AND DIGGING THE SOIL UNDERNEATH.

CURE FOR BALDNESS

If you're starting to see bare ground where there used to be a healthy planting of groundcovers, it's time to take action. Here are some possible causes and cures:

TOO LITTLE LIGHT. If you planted a sun-worshiping groundcover several years ago, and since then nearby trees have grown bigger, or a house has been built next door, chances are the shade they spread is your problem. The solution: Limb up the surrounding trees to let in more light, or dig up your site and plant a shade lover like bugleweed (*Ajuga* spp.) or sweet woodruff (*Galium odoratum*).

TIME FOR A HAIRCUT. Many groundcover plants—especially herbs—need shearing now and then. Give your blanket of greenery a pass with the lawn mower, and set the blade at about 2 inches. You'll encourage the groundcover to grow fuller and fill in those bare spots.

TUCKERED OUT. If your groundcover has been in place for several years and nothing in its en- vironment has changed, the plants may be feeling the need for more nourishment. To get them off and running again, remove any dead plants and dig rotted manure or compost into the bare spots. They'll soon disappear under new growth.

PROPER SOIL PREP

When you're trying to grow a good groundcover, thorough soil preparation is essential, especially in difficult sites. Plants will take off and grow faster if you give them a head start, and you'll have less competition from weeds. (If you haven't had your soil tested, consider it; you'll learn a lot about its condition.) Before you plant perennial groundcovers, spread 2 to 3 inches of compost over the area and dig it into the soil. The organic matter and nutrients the compost provides will give your planting a boost.

After planting, cover the soil between plants with a fine mulch like shredded leaves to protect the soil and also to suppress weeds while the groundcover plants establish themselves.

Groundhog Problems

Woodchucks, whistle pigs, groundhogs—whatever you call them, these oversize rodents can do a number on your garden. Their dens are a menace to livestock and machinery (and people, as anyone who has inadvertently stepped in a hidden groundhog hole can attest). Groundhogs hibernate in the winter, but they wake up hungry. They also eat heavily in the fall to store up fat for their long snooze. In between, well, they eat more. Here are some ways to encourage them to do their dining elsewhere.

HOUND GROUNDHOGS OUT OF THE GARDEN

One way to defeat groundhogs is to "Get a dog," says market gardener Tony Ricci from Three Springs, Pennsylvania. The dog doesn't have to be a Jack Russell terrier (renowned for its groundhog-hunting prowess). It doesn't even have to be a large dog. A minimutt, Lily, patrols Ricci's farm. She isn't big enough to kill a groundhog, but she chases the rodents and barks at them. "She worries them to death," Ricci says. "Either that or they get tired of hearing her and move on."

MAKE 'EM THINK YOU HAVE A DOG

If a canine companion isn't an option, borrow the essence of someone else's. Give an old rug, towel, or piece of carpet to a friend to use as bedding for his dog. Then transfer the dog-scented material to your garden. Loan bedding to several dog-owning friends, and rotate the scraps often to keep the scent fresh and varied. The groundhogs will think you have a kennel full of canines.

KITTY CAN HELP, TOO — LITTER-ALLY

Got an indoor cat? Empty the litter box into the groundhog's entrance hole. The rodent will clear away the cat box contents for a while, but persistence pays off. Eventually, the scent of used kitty litter discourages even the toughest groundhog.

When the groundhog departs, fill up the entrance hole and all the exit holes with rocks or soil to keep other animals from moving in. If you aren't sure where all the exit holes are, toss a few Fourth of July smoke bombs into the entrance hole and seal it tightly with a clump of sod. Wait a few minutes, then look around to see where smoke is rising from the ground.

En Garde! Fence Them Out

Although fences are effective against groundhogs, the best are partly buried below ground to foil the burrowing animals. For this, a permanent fence of welded wire works best because it won't rust out as quickly as chicken wire or woven-wire fencing. Here's how to install it:

1. Dig a trench all the way around your garden, about 24 inches deep.
2. Install metal T-stakes at each corner and at least every 8 feet on the sides.
3. Attach a 6-foot-high piece of welded-wire fence to the T-stakes. Bury 2 feet of the fence below ground in the trench you've dug, and bend the top foot over to form a baffle.
4. To disguise the fence in the spring, plant daffodils and Siberian squills (*Scilla siberica*) in the trench before you fill it in.

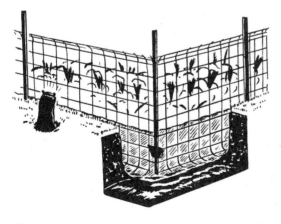

FENCE GROUNDHOGS OUT BELOW GROUND, AS WELL AS ABOVE.

Keep Your Crops under Wraps

If other vegetation is around for groundhogs to eat, simply covering vulnerable garden crops can sometimes be enough to prevent damage. "I put floating row covers over the things they like, and usually they get discouraged," says market gardener Sylvia Ehrhardt, whose Knoxville, Maryland, farm is surrounded by woods.

DISCOURAGE GROUNDHOGS FROM DINING IN YOUR GARDEN WITH OVER-THE-TOP FENCING.

Floating row covers are available in rolls of 25 feet or more. Anchor one to the ground with boards, bricks, or sandbags, instead of burying the edges with soil. The row cover will last longer, and you'll be able to remove and replace it more easily.

Chicken-wire fence or plastic netting installed over wire hoops is also an effective groundhog deterrent. Use 6-inch pieces of heavy 9-mil wire, bent into U-shapes, to pin the fence or netting to the ground and prevent groundhogs from nosing underneath. For extra protection, use bloodmeal as a repellent. Put a tablespoon or so in a margarine container or yogurt cup, add a little water and a rock for weight, and place it among the vegetables to discourage the pests.

No Place to Hide

If you want to control groundhogs on your property, thinking like a groundhog will help. They'd rather take a long detour through a meadow than cross a mowed lawn, and they dart for cover when discovered in the garden. "Animals don't like to be in the open," says market gardener Tony Ricci of Three Springs, Pennsylvania. "So don't put veggies in an area that backs up to the woods or is surrounded by tall weeds."

Groundhogs love to burrow under woodpiles, mulch piles, and hay stacks. If possible, move these piles around every year to keep them from becoming a permanent shelter for groundhogs or other animal pests. Even a slight dip in the ground provides a place for animals to lie low and escape notice. So if you have holes and dips near the garden, fill 'em up to discourage the pests.

Easy Movable Fencing

If you just haven't had the time to install permanent fencing to keep out groundhogs, here's another alternative—a temporary, portable fence to protect individual beds or crops from those munching varmints. Here's what you'll need to do:

Cut several 4- or 5-foot lengths of 1-inch-mesh chicken wire.

Attach a metal or fiberglass post to each end of each chicken-wire panel. Allow an extra foot or so of the post to extend past the bottom of the fencing, so that the posts can be pushed into the ground.

Use the panels to surround susceptible crops such as young broccoli or lettuce plants. Just be sure to put the fence up before the groundhogs start nibbling on your tender plants. When you don't need the fence anymore, take the panels down, and store them flat.

Herb Garden Problems

Herbs rank among the garden's most trouble-free plants. Still, growing them isn't without its challenges. If you've discovered that already—or if you've been seduced by the magic of herbs and want to start your garden on the right foot— read on as some long-time herbalists share their secrets for dealing with aphids, whiteflies, hardpan, powdery mildew, poor drainage, and more.

KEEPING MINT IN CHECK

If you're singin' the "Mint Strangulation" blues because your herb garden is now nothing but mint, here's a workable solution to growing mint in harmony with other herbs, from Linda D. Harris of Fulton, Kentucky. "Use an old, deep, 5-gallon bucket with the handle removed. Drill 8 to 10 ¼-inch holes in the bottom (or punch them in using a large-bore screwdriver). Put a layer of gravel in the bottom of the bucket. Dig out your mint, then plant it in the bucket. Dig a large hole in your garden, set the bucket down in the hole, and fill in soil around it. Keep the lip of the bucket just a little bit above the soil surface," says Harris.

The bucket walls will prevent mint stolons from spreading. (For a while, mint will keep sprouting from any underground pieces you missed when you dug up the plant. Pull those up and toss them—or use them to make iced tea!) Every few years, it's a good idea to lift and divide the mint in the bucket to keep it healthy and full. Give some away (along with the bucket idea) to a friend. This method of taming invasive plants also works well for bee balm (*Monarda* spp.), catnip (*Nepeta cataria*), and other plants that are too rampant for your garden taste.

HOT PEPPER HELPER

You say something's devouring your herbs and there's nary a pest in sight? When Savannah, Georgia, gardener Ashby Angell found herself in that predicament recently, she gave her plants a spritz of a special hot sauce. Here's how she makes it:

Boil together a handful of hot peppers and a handful of southernwood in a half gallon of water. Let the mixture cool, then strain it through a piece of cheesecloth. After straining, add a few drops of dishwashing liquid, and then spray or pour the mixture on your herbs.

Pest Detective

The flavors and aromas that attract us to herbs seem repugnant to most insects. Indeed, some herbs are so abhorrent to multilegged creepers, crawlers, and fliers that you can use them as efficient insect repellents. So if your herb garden seems to be attracting pests, it's probably because conditions on the home front don't measure up to your plants' standards, such as too much or too little light or poor drainage. Whichever the reason, here are a few unwelcome visitors you might see and how you can cut their party time short.

Symptom	Cause	What to Do
Stunted or malformed leaves or stems coated with a clear, sticky substance	Aphids	Wash them off with a spray of water or rub them off between thumb and forefinger and squash them; spray with insecticidal soap.
Chewed leaves or flowers (especially on members of the carrot family, such as angelica, chervil, and dill)	Caterpillars	Unless your whole crop is under attack, identify the critter before you do anything. It may be the larva of a butterfly whose presence will be well worth a little cosmetic damage. But if the invasion is too intense, pick the caterpillars off by hand and destroy them.
Stunted growth; leaves stippled yellow, curling or turning brown; sooty black substance on leaves or stems	Whiteflies	Use yellow sticky traps or insecticidal soap sprays, or spray plants with water, wiping them off if needed. If infestation is severe, dig up plants and destroy them.

WHAT'S THE PROBLEM?

If your herbs fall prey to a fungus disease—such as powdery mildew, rust, or root rot—you might be watering too much, says Menlo Park, California, herb gardener Judee Humburg. If you catch the problem when the plants are just turning yellow—a sure sign of overwatering—you can probably head off further trouble by simply easing up on the hose trigger. Most herbs, says Humburg, especially those of Mediterranean origin (such as thyme, lavender, rosemary, oregano, and marjoram) like their soil on the dry side. Her testing method: "Stick your finger in the ground 1 to 1½ inches. It should feel dry from the tip up."

RAISED BEDS TO THE RESCUE

Another way to help improve drainage for herbs is by planting them in raised beds. In Juneau, Alaska, where Natasha Zahn Pristas gardens, adding some height also helps the soil warm up more quickly in the spring. Here's how she builds her beds: "I dig down about a foot and a half to loosen the soil," she says. "Then I add edging about 1½ feet high. Finally, I throw on commercial potting soil, peat moss, and either chicken or steer manure or mushroom compost and mix it all together." (*Note:* Remember to always use *rotted* manure on food crops.)

RAISED BEDS HELP THE SOIL WARM UP FASTER IN SPRING, HELPING HERBS TO GET OFF TO A GOOD START AFTER A LONG, COLD WINTER.

HARDPAN, HIT THE ROAD

Hardpan equals poor drainage which equals poor herbs (and everything else you're trying to grow). Here's a simple method for getting better drainage and more oomph into the soil, from Jack Talerico, who gardens on Washington's Vashon Island. "What I do is essentially underground composting," he says. "I dig a hole as deep as I can reasonably go. Sometimes that's only a foot or so; sometimes it's 3 to 4 feet. Then I dump everything in and cover it up. I use the shallower holes for leaves and grass clippings, the deeper ones for substantial things like watermelon rind that take longer to decompose. I give it a couple of months to cook, then plant right on top."

TOO DARN HOT

Even heat-tolerant herbs give up the ghost in sweltering southern climes. Gardener Ashby Angell from Savannah, Georgia, has developed a handful of coping mechanisms that let her herbs take the humid heat almost in stride. Here are some of her secrets.

GROW EVERYTHING IN RAISED BEDS. "Raised beds improve not only drainage but also air circulation," she says. "That's crucial in preventing fungus diseases in a humid climate."

ADD PLENTY OF MANURE AND COMPOST TO THE SOIL. They help maintain a healthy nutrient balance and help prevent undue stress.

PROVIDE SOME SHADE. All herbs need shelter from 2 P.M. on, Angell says. Otherwise, "the late afternoon sun just wipes them out." Some plants need even more protection. Angell grows parsley and lemon balm (*Melissa officinalis*) in a bed permanently covered with shade cloth. And chives thrive under a lattice roof.

ADJUST YOUR CALENDAR. Some herbs won't survive a southern summer no matter how much you coddle them. "Chervil and coriander are winter plants here," Angell says.

WHERE SUMMER HEAT IS INTENSE, LOTS OF HERBS PREFER LIFE IN THE SHADE, SUCH AS UNDER THIS LATTICE ROOF.

GETTING A GOOD START

One of the best ways to avoid trouble in the herb garden is to start out with healthy plants. Here are some points to keep in mind when shopping for herbs at a nursery.

CHOOSE HERB PLANTS THAT LOOK HEALTHY AND VIGOROUS, not stressed with brown, shriveled, or insect-damaged leaves. Check the undersides of leaves for any insect pests.

TRY TO BUY YOUR HERBS FROM AN ORGANIC GROWER so your herb seedlings will be free from pesticide residue.

CHOOSE HERBS THAT HAVE WELL-DEVELOPED CROWNS AND ROOTS THAT FILL THE POT. Gently dump the plant out into your hand so you can look at what's going on with its roots. If the roots go right to the bottom of the pot, it's a sign the plant has been growing for a year or so. If there's more soil than roots, it means the nursery has bought the plant as a "seed plug" in the early spring, potted it up, and is selling it a few months later. The top growth might be similar in size to the older plant but in 2 to 3 months the more mature plant will be much bigger and stronger.

YOUR CLUE TO THE BEST PLANT CHOICE IS IN THE ROOTS, NOT THE FOLIAGE. FIND A LOCAL OR MAIL-ORDER NURSERY THAT GROWS ITS HERBS IN THE FIELD FOR A YEAR BEFORE SELLING THEM.

KEEPING FLAVOR IN THE BAG

Bundles of drying herbs hanging from the rafters of a country kitchen might look picturesque, but they tend to lose color and flavor this way. If your herbs are lacking oomph, switch from that romantic but unsatisfactory technique to the practical paper bag system, says Patrick Rogers, a Master Gardener from Portland, Oregon.

PROTECT HERBS WHILE THEY DRY BY SEALING THEM IN PAPER BAGS TO HELP THEM RETAIN COLOR AND FLAVOR.

1. Cut the herbs early in the morning when their volatile oils are still fresh.
2. Gather them into bunches of 5 to 10 sprigs each. The bushier the herbs, the fewer sprigs you need per bundle.
3. Put each bundle stem-side up in a brown paper bag with the stems sticking out about 1 inch. Wrap a rubber band around bag and stems.
4. Tuck the bags away in any moisture-free space (a closet will do) and check them every week till they're dry.

Houseplant Problems

One way to turn a house into more of a home is to add houseplants. After all, houseplants can give a room that extra oomph it needs to make it warm and inviting. And with tons of houseplants to choose from, you can even pick them to go with your decorating style. Maybe you have cactus for a Southwestern feel or African violets for a more Victorian look. No matter what kind of houseplants you have, though, they all may suffer from problems at one time or another, such as whiteflies, spider mites, lack of humidity, and pot-bound roots. So to keep your charges happy in their home, check out the following advice.

Rx for Healthy Houseplants

How often have you had a houseplant start to head downhill, while you fight to keep it from dying? Instead of using energy to keep dying plants alive, head off problems *before* they start by focusing your energy on what you need to do to help healthy houseplants stay that way.

BE CONSISTENT. Once you figure out what a plant needs, deliver it consistently. But don't put all your plants on the same schedule. Each plant is unique. For example, some plants only need to be watered once a month (such as a cactus).

CHECK FOR STRESS. Although Penny Engel, a gardener from Jamaica Bay, New York, doesn't water all of her 100 houseplants every day, she examines each one daily for signs of stress, such as yellowed leaves. With so many plants, she can't allow a pest or disease to spread. If she sees a problem, she isolates the plant and treats it promptly, protecting the other plants.

CUT THE CHLORINE. Engel has municipal water, which is chlorinated and thus is harmful to plants. So she leaves uncovered old soda bottles full of water around the house. That way, the chlorine evaporates before she uses the water on her plants. Plus, the water is always room temperature (ice cold water can shock plant roots, and hot water can scald them), and as the water evaporates, it adds humidity to the air.

GIVE THEM A SUMMER VACATION. Every summer, Engel gives herself and her indoor

Pest Detective

Something's flitting around your houseplants or has made its home on the undersides of their leaves. Don't be so quick to pitch the plant; rather, match the symptoms to those in the following chart, and find out what's causing the problem and what you can do about it.

Symptom	Cause	What to Do
Honeydew on plant leaves; white, waxy insects on undersides of leaves	Mealybugs	Wash plant with soapy water (2 teaspoons of dishwashing soap, not detergent, to 1 gallon of water). A jet of clean water may knock insects off the plant, or remove them with tweezers or a toothpick. You can also use rubbing alcohol on a swab. Dip the swab into the alcohol, and gently touch the insect to remove it. Be careful not to spread alcohol on the plant tissue because you may injure the plant.
Very tiny waxy or hard shells on plants	Scale	Wash plant with soapy water (2 teaspoons of dishwashing soap, not detergent, to 1 gallon of water). A jet of clean water may knock insects off the plant, or remove scale with tweezers or a toothpick. You can also use rubbing alcohol on a swab. Dip the swab into the alcohol, and gently touch the insect to remove it. Be careful not to spread alcohol on the plant tissue because you may injure the plant.
Slow-moving dots on the undersides of leaves; you may be able to see webbing if you hold the plant up to light.	Spider mites	Wash with soapy water; a jet of water will knock mites off plant.
Tiny white flies flitting around your plants; plants may send up white "clouds" when disturbed	Whiteflies	Wash plants, including tops and undersides of leaves, with soapy water and a soft brush. Use 2 teaspoons of a dishwashing soap, not detergent, to 1 gallon of water. A strong jet of water may also knock insects off.

garden a vacation by putting all her houseplants outside. She tries to mimic their natural habitat when she does, by putting some in the shade, some in the sun, and some in the screened porch. The rain and the warm, moist breezes off Jamaica Bay keep the plants watered and happy, and she gets a break to go to the beach. Plants thrive outside because the light conditions in the shadiest place outdoors are better than the brightest place in the house. If you give your houseplants a break outside during warm weather, by the end of the summer they'll have a postvacation glow, looking strong and healthy. (Engel suggests bringing the plants back indoors at least 3 weeks before you turn on the heat. This gives the plants a chance to get acclimated to the decreased light and dry air in the house before they're assaulted by central heat.)

CLEAN OUT THE PESTS. Many of you may fear your plants will be invaded by insects if you put them outside. Engel has a solution for this, too. Before you bring the plants in the house, add a squirt of liquid detergent to a full watering can. Water everything thoroughly. Engel has been doing this for 40 years and hasn't had an insect problem yet. You also might want to wash the leaves, including their undersides, with soap and water.

IF YOUR WATER CONTAINS CHLORINE, FILL EMPTY CONTAINERS, SUCH AS SODA BOTTLES, LEAVE THE TOPS OFF, AND PLACE THEM AROUND YOUR HOME. THE CHLORINE WILL EVAPORATE, ALLOWING YOU TO GIVE YOUR HOUSEPLANTS A CHLORINE-FREE DRINK.

HOME ALONE

How do you keep your houseplants from drying out if you're going to be away from home for a while? Cross your fingers and hope they don't get overly thirsty? Ask a friend to come over for watering duty? Try to teach the dog to do it? Gardeners Harold and Penny Engel of Jamaica Bay, New York, found an easy solution to the problem.

KEEP YOUR HOUSEPLANTS HYDRATED WHILE YOU'RE ON VACATION BY PUTTING THEM ALL IN A SUNNY ROOM, WATERING THOROUGHLY, AND THEN HANGING A HEAVY SHEET OF PLASTIC ACROSS THE DOORWAY TO SEAL IN HUMIDITY.

They move all their plants into the sunroom, water everything thoroughly, and turn the heat down. Then they hang a heavy (3-mil) sheet of plastic across the entrance to the room (they attach the plastic to the doorway with duct tape). The plastic seals in the humidity. And, the Engels say the plants like being crowded together; they collectively add humidity to one another. The Engels always do this before they head off on vacation. They haven't lost a plant yet in all the years they've done this.

Solutions at a Glance

PROBLEM: Long and leggy plants

CULPRIT: Winter—specifically, its decreased light and lack of humidity

SOLVE IT! Bring the plant closer to a natural light source. Raise the humidity by putting the pot in a tray of pebbles and water.

PROBLEM: Roots are potbound.

CULPRIT: Pot too small for plant

SOLVE IT! Take the plant out of the pot. Using a knife, score the roots so they're not circling the plant—then repot the plant in a bigger container. If you don't have a larger container, trim the roots (using a sharp pair of scissors) after scoring until the rootball will fit comfortably back into the pot. (You might also want to trim the foliage to keep the top and bottom of the plant in balance.) Wash the pot and add fresh soil before replanting.

FELINE-DIGGING DISCOURAGEMENT

If you have a cat and also have large houseplants, you know that the two don't always mix. That's because cats love to dig in the soil. Linda D. Harris of Fulton, Kentucky, thwarts her cats' effort to use houseplants as a litter box by filling the area between the soil surface and the top of the container with whatever assortment of rocks or shells she has collected. Rocks can be of any shape or color, and about 3 to 6 inches in size (larger is better). Cats can't move the rocks, the rocks make a great mulch, and the weight of the rocks lends stability to tall foliage plants. Good sources for rocks include your garden, a quarry, a landscaper, or a farmer's field.

Japanese Beetles

At the worst possible time—just as roses approach perfection, raspberries ripen, and hollyhocks stand tall—hoards of 1/2-inch-long beetles appear out of nowhere and munch their way through your garden and landscape. Roses, raspberries, hollyhocks, and grapes are all on the list of favorite Japanese beetle foods, but these voracious pests will eat almost any plant they land on. The shiny copper beetles with green and white markings would be beautiful if they weren't so ravenous. Indeed, the only good thing about Japanese beetles is that they're rarely seen west of the Mississippi River.

In spite of their numbers and the damage they do, Japanese beetles are controllable. Here are a few ways to do it, ranging from engaging in grub warfare to protecting preferred plants.

ENGAGING IN GRUB WARFARE

Two biological weapons can turn Japanese beetle larvae to mush. If you have terrible problems with Japanese beetles, you can use both of these at the same time.

MILKY SPORE DISEASE is a blend of two naturally occurring bacteria that make the grubs get sick and die. Milky spore takes a couple of years to become established in the soil, but then it persists for many seasons. It's sold as a powder; you apply it by placing spoonfuls of the powder on the surface of your grass just before a rain. Any time that the ground isn't frozen is a good time to inoculate your lawn with milky spore.

BENEFICIAL NEMATODES are another natural enemy of beetle grubs, but you'll need to apply them at just the right time, which is in mid- to late spring when the soil is warm enough to be hospitable to beneficial nematodes *and* when the grubs are close to the soil's surface. You apply beneficial nematodes by first mixing them with water and then spraying the solution on your lawn. Be sure to reapply every year as needed, to control Japanese beetle grubs—as well as cutworms, June beetles, and other pests that spend their larval stage in the soil.

PROTECTING PREFERRED PLANTS

Japanese beetles adore roses, and they're crazy for grapes and a dozen other plants, too. While the adults are feeding, take steps to protect the plants they like the most. If you can limit the damage they cause, your plants can usually recover and grow more leaves later in the season when the beetles' food orgy has ended.

So try this trick that Eileen Squitiro in New Milton, West Virginia, uses. "Hot pepper spray works great!" Squitiro says. "I simply boil up a handful of dried cayennes and jalapeños in a gallon of water (make sure you cover the pan because the steam can make your eyes tear) and then strain and spray. Pepper spray has kept Japanese beetles off my roses and grapevines better than anything else I've ever tried. After rain it has to be reapplied, and you should be careful not to breathe the spray—it will bring tears to your eyes."

BOIL UP A POT OF PEPPERS TO MAKE YOUR OWN JAPANESE BEETLE SPRAY.

THE JAPANESE BEETLE DEATH DROP

Everybody who has 'em hand-picks Japanese beetles one way or another, but you'll get more beetles if you take advantage of their tendency to drop from leaves or blossoms when they're disturbed. Don't try to gather them in midday when they usually fly off instead of dropping down. Hunt them in the morning or evening instead.

JAPANESE BEETLES CAN'T SWIM—SO GET RID OF THEM THE EASY WAY BY SHAKING THEM INTO A BOWL FULL OF SOAPY WATER.

"I use a broad bowl filled with water with some soap added to break the surface tension," says Jenny Estes, a Master Gardener in Guntersville, Alabama. "Early in the morning, I go around and hold the bowl under branches with beetles on them, shake gently, and they just drop right in and drown." In addition to roses, Estes battles the beetles on her crape myrtles—a favorite flowering shrub in the South. "I keep my crape myrtles pruned low to make it easier to get the beetles," she says.

Lawn Problems

If you believed everything you saw on TV, you'd think you needed to resort to chemical fertilizers, insecticides, or herbicides to evoke the envy of your turf-crazy neighbors. True, fertilization, pest insects, and weeds are lawn challenges, but that doesn't mean you have to douse your yard with chemicals. Instead, try earth-safe solutions— such as feeding your lawn less— and you'll have terrific turf.

Rx for a Weed-Free Lawn

Here are three easy, organic approaches that can help you win the fight against weeds.

FEED YOUR GRASS WHEN IT STARTS TO GROW. Apply a slow-release organic fertilizer to your lawn just as robust new growth begins—early spring for bluegrass, early summer for warm-season grasses, and fall for turf-type fescues.

MOW YOUR GRASS HIGH. Set the blade of your mower at its highest, and leave it there. Tall blades of grass have more surface area exposed to the sun, which will help them produce greater root growth. And that will leave you with healthier grass that's better able to outcompete weeds.

USE HAND-TO-HAND COMBAT. Just get out there with a fishtail weeder and dig those weeds out, roots and all.

Bargain-Basement Lawn Food

If your lawn has champagne taste and a beer budget, here are some inexpensive and natural fertilizers that may satisfy it. Look for them in 50- to 100-pound bags at local farm supply stores.

Fertilizer Type	NPK Ratio	Usage Guidelines
Alfalfa meal	5-1-2	35 lb. per 1,000 sq. ft.
Cottonseed meal	6-2-1	25 lb. per 1,000 sq. ft.
Fish meal	5-3-3	20 lb. per 1,000 sq. ft.
Soybean meal	7-0.5-2.3	25 lb. per 1,000 sq. ft.

Managing Moles

Moles can take out an otherwise-healthy lawn by cutting off grass roots while they tunnel around in search of earthworms, grubs, and other protein-rich tidbits. Here are some tips on keeping your yard looking mole-free.

At the first sign of mole activity, go out and flatten their tunnels by walking over them. This might give them the message to build their trails in someone else's yard.

When you identify a tunnel route that's used over and over again, open a hole in the tunnel with a stick and pour in a castor oil–based mole repellent. You can buy MoleMed (made from castor oil, soap, and water) and mix according to label directions to either pour down the tunnels or spray on the grass. Or, you can make your own brew by mixing together 1 cup of water, 3 ounces of castor oil, and 4 tablespoons of dishwashing liquid. Mix 2 tablespoons of this concentrate with 1 gallon of water before sloshing it into your mole holes.

Minimize the evidence of mole damage by repairing damaged spots with fresh seed or patches of sod taken from the edges of your lawn.

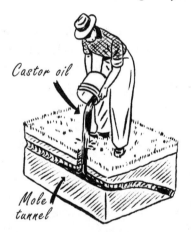

LET MOLES KNOW THEY'RE NOT WELCOME BY POURING A CASTOR OIL–BASED REPELLENT INTO THEIR TUNNELS.

SNUBBING GRUBS

Probably the worst (and certainly the ugliest) lawn pests that you'll encounter are insect larvae that dig a diet heavy on grass roots. The worst of

Solutions at a Glance

PROBLEM: Your grass is growing faster than normal, meaning you have to mow a lot.

CULPRIT: Chemical fertilizers

SOLUTION: A no-brainer—switch to organic fertilizers. Organic fertilizers release their nutrients slowly, giving your lawn a long, luscious feast, meaning it won't grow so fast that it's impossible to keep up with the mowing.

these are beetle larvae—the white grubs usually found 1 to 2 inches below the surface of your lawn. And though you don't need to launch a full-scale war on just a few grubs, you may find that you have so many that they're eating the feet right off your grass. If that's the case, you can get them under control by using milky spore disease or beneficial nematodes. See page 95 for more information on these solutions.

NO SPOTS FROM SPOT

If you have a dog, you already know that his urine can easily burn yellow spots into a lawn—especially if he uses the same place over and over again. But try this resourceful tip and you'll regain your lush lawn in about 3 weeks.

"Before I trained my golden retriever to go in his small patch of gravel, I used this simple solution," reports Mike Holman of Brantford, Ontario. "I mixed a small (8-ounce, or 227-gram) box of baking soda into a full watering can of water (about 1 gallon) and walked around the yard saturating the dog spots every few days. The solution looks like watery milk, and you have to pour it shortly after it's mixed or the baking soda will settle in the bottom. The baking soda takes the acidity out of the soil where the urine is and helps the turf green up again. It does take a little time, but at least it's nontoxic to you and Rover, and it's cheap."

A MIXTURE OF BAKING SODA AND WATER IS A NONTOXIC WAY OF GETTING RID OF THE SPOTS FROM Spot.

Hair Plugs for Lawns

To make postweeding repairs to her large lawn in Moreno Valley, California, Tamara Utens keeps up to five flats of homemade fescue sod growing at any given time.

"I take the plastic flats that many plants come packed in, and I line them with foil, leaving one side of the flat with a low lip of foil so excess water can drain away. I fill them with ordinary soil from the garden and then sprinkle grass seed on top." Utens says she started out using potting soil, then switched to garden soil after she ran out one day. "With regular soil, there's less transition stress when the sod gets planted," she

says. "I keep the flats near my patio door so I can wet them down twice a day. A thick turf grows in a few weeks, which I can peel out and place whole or in pieces into bare spots."

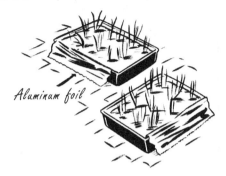

GROWING YOUR OWN TURF IN PLASTIC FLATS MEANS YOU'LL ALWAYS HAVE SOME SOD TO REPLACE BARE PATCHES IN YOUR LAWN.

Repairing Rips and Ruts

Accidents happen everywhere, and lawns are no exception. Maybe a shrub or tree had to go, or perhaps you missed your driveway on a dark and muddy night and left a nice tire rut in your turf. Never fear, though—here are the secrets to seamless patching.

Repairs are easy if your lawn is bluegrass, improved tall fescue, or a cool-season blend that includes these two species along with a little perennial ryegrass. Simply fill in the spot with soil and rake it level, and plant seed that matches the rest of your yard. To allow for natural compaction, the freshly prepared soil should sit about $\frac{1}{2}$ inch higher than the surrounding soil before planting.

The fix isn't quite as easy with vegetatively propagated zoysiagrass or bermudagrass. Instead of patching with purchased sod that may be slightly different in terms of color, size, and vigor, take plugs from the edges of your

Pest Detective

Notice some less-than-desirable patches or spots turning up on your lawn? You might have a lawn disease that you can resolve by fine-tuning your fertilizer habits.

Symptom	Cause	What to Do
Large, circular sections of the lawn look scorched	The fungus *Rhizoctonia solani*, which thrives during hot, humid weather	Stop overwatering and overfertilizing, and rake out dead growth.
Brown circular patches just a few inches across	The fungi *Lanzia* and *Moellerodiscus* spp. (formerly *Sclerotinia homeocarpa*)	Dollar spot, as this disease is known, is most serious in lawns that need food. So give your lawn a moderate fertilizer followed by deep watering, done early in the day so the grass is dry by nightfall. Rake up infected grass clippings to reduce the spread of disease.
Lots of purple spots on grass blades that make patches look like they have melted	Melting out or leaf blotch (formerly *Helminthosporium* fungus, now thought to be several fungi, including *Drechslera*, *Bipolaris*, and *Exserohilum*)	Adding fertilizer that provides both nitrogen and potassium can help as can *not* watering your lawn after dark. (Just don't get carried away feeding your lawn because too much fertilizer can encourage the fungus that causes this disease in the first place. When using any type of lawn fertilizer, always use a drop spreader, and don't exceed the application rates given on the fertilizer label.)

lawn and plant them close together where you need new grass. Cut out plugs with a sharp knife, making sure the roots are still attached. After transplanting, fill the crevices between the plugs with a mixture of sand and soil to help the plugs grow together quickly.

COME OVER TO CLOVER

Beef up your lawn with Dutch white clover. It has a lot going for it—it fixes enough nitrogen from the air to share with grass, it produces loads of bee-pleasing flowers, and it even puts up with a fair amount of foot traffic.

ADD DUTCH WHITE CLOVER TO YOUR LAWN BY SOWING SEEDS IN FALL OR SCATTERING THEM IN VERY EARLY SPRING.

Lettuce Problems

Although lettuce is one of the most reliable spring garden crops, this leafy green loves the cool temperatures of fall, too. Growing the goods for great salads is trickier in summer (you have to fool the greens into thinking it's still spring), but it's doable. Lettuce is pretty easy to grow, but you do need to watch out for slugs so they don't make dinner of your lettuce before you do. Here are some "slug beaters" as well as other tips for growing great lettuce.

PACE YOURSELF

To get the most lettuce from your plantings, don't plant it all at once. Mature lettuce only holds a week or two in the garden before bolting to seed or getting bitter, so plant small quantities every couple of weeks.

HEAT-BEATING HELPERS

A cooling shower in the middle of a hot summer day is just the ticket for people—and for lettuce, too. Market gardener Hui Newcomb uses micro-sprinklers to put out a fine mist on the summer lettuce growing on her Vienna, Virginia, farm. You can create the same effect with a sprinkler attached to a timer. Shower the lettuce from 12 noon until 2 P.M. when the sun is at its most intense.

A bit of shade helps, too. Greenhouse operators put shade cloth over their houses to cool them in the summer. You can apply the same principle to your lettuce patch with nylon netting or cast-off lace curtains stretched over wire hoops and fastened with clothespins. Or plant the summer crop under an overhang or next to a building or shrub that blocks the hot afternoon sun. Lettuce grows well with half-day sunshine.

SUMMERTIME, BUT THE LETTUCE LIVING IS EASY—WITH A LITTLE SHADE.

PROBLEM: Something's eating your lettuce.

CULPRIT: Slugs

SOLVE IT! Make the slugs uncomfortable (and do a little recycling at the same time) by mulching with excelsior strips or the shredded computer paper commonly used as packing material. The slugs will detour to avoid dying of a thousand paper cuts. Got a sweet gum tree or know someone who does? Sweet gum seedpods look like prickly balls. Surround your lettuce with a layer of those and send the slugs elsewhere.

PROBLEM: Your lettuce has yellows, a disease that makes lettuce leaves deformed and sickly looking.

CULPRIT: Leafhoppers

SOLVE IT! Gum up their plans by coating disposable plastic picnic cups (preferably yellow ones) with Tangle-Trap or Vaseline and tacking them upside down to short stakes in the lettuce patch.

PROBLEM: The lettuce looks great from the top, but the leaves are turning brown and slimy at the base.

CULPRIT: Bottom rot

SOLVE IT! Bottom rot is caused by fungus, and it's most common in warm, humid conditions. If your summers are hot and humid, give lettuce extra space (at least 8 inches between plants), and grow romaine from late spring through summer. Lettuce that grows upright is less susceptible to bottom rot.

PROBLEM: Less than half of the seed you planted germinated.

CULPRIT: Warm storage temperatures

SOLUTION: Store leftover lettuce seed in the refrigerator during June, July, and August. Keeping the seed cool during these hot months will help improve its germination rate.

Lettuce Varieties to Match the Season

How do you keep the lettuce coming from the balmy days of spring until well past fall's first frosts? "Careful variety selection allows for a crop from spring through fall," says Melanie DeVault of Pheasant Hill Farm in Emmaus, Pennsylvania. Tender leaf and Bibb lettuces are the first to bolt when the weather gets hot, and romaines and summer Batavians, like 'Sierra' and 'Nevada', hang in there longer. Lettuce doesn't need long days of sunshine, so if you live where the winters aren't too severe—or are willing to provide some protection—some lettuces produce even while the snow flies.

Spring	Summer	Fall	Winter
'Black-Seeded Simpson', 'Tango', and 'Royal Oak' (green leaf); 'SuperPrize', 'Red Oak Leaf', 'Red Sails', and 'Lolla Rossa' (red leaf); 'Pirat' (red Bibb)	'Summertime' and 'Ithaca' (iceberg); 'Nevada', 'Sierra', and 'Santa Fe' (Batavian); 'Buttercrunch', 'Bronze Arrow', and 'Red Deer Tongue' (Bibb); 'Cimmaron' and 'Green Towers' (romaine); 'Red Fire' (red leaf); 'Slobolt' (green leaf)	'Freckles' (romaine); 'Bronze', 'Green Mignonette', and 'Tom Thumb' (baby Bibb); 'Salad Bowl' and 'Waldemann's Dark Green' (green leaf); 'Brunia' (red leaf); 'Merville de Quatre Saisons' (Bibb)	'Rouge d'Hiver' (red romaine); 'Winter Density' and 'Selma Wisa' (Bibb)

LEFTOVER SALAD MIX

It's easy to overbuy lettuce seed when you need only a pinch for each planting. But then what do you do with all the extra seed? Hui Newcomb, a market gardener from Fairfax County, Virginia, mixes the seed together and sows it in late summer as a cut-and-come-again salad mix. Or, you could save the seed and use it for next year's summer sowings. Fresh lettuce seed is usually reluctant to germinate in warm soil; older seed germinates more readily when the thermometer soars.

Mexican Bean Beetles

The black sheep of the lady beetle family, Mexican bean beetles can turn a bean patch into a scene of devastation worthy of a science fiction movie. Preventive strategies include keeping a clean garden in winter and growing fast-maturing bush beans, which usually produce before the beetles cause serious damage. But pole beans seldom escape damage from this pest. So cover your plants with floating row covers to help keep the beetles out. And make a habit of checking under a few leaves in search of eggs and larvae. Pinch off egg-bearing leaves, and squash the larvae with your fingers. You might also want to try some of the following remedies, such as horticultural oil.

TRY AN OILY TREATMENT

For small outbreaks, try spraying the leaf undersides with light horticultural oil, which smothers the larvae. Be sure to mix the oil at the rate recommended on the label for summer use. (That's because bean leaves are especially susceptible to damage from oil sprays during hot weather.)

WIN WITH WASPS

If you have problems with Mexican bean beetles year after year, enlist the help of beneficial *Pediobius foveolatus* wasps in your garden. Called *pedios* by gardeners, these tiny parasitic wasps are a plague on pesky bean beetles. Wait until you see Mexican beetle larvae actively feeding on your beans to release the wasps. In recent experiments in gardens in Wisconsin and Washington, the wasps wiped out nearly every last larvae. And don't worry that the pedios will turn into a pest. Native to India, this tiny wasp seldom survives winter north of Zone 8.

CLEAN UP AFTER YOUR BEANS

To reduce future problems with Mexican bean beetles, be sure to clean up promptly after your beans finish producing. Remove the remains of your bean crop from the garden, or dig it into the soil along with any remaining beetles, eggs, and larvae.

PLANT A DECOY

Mexican bean beetles and their hungry yellow larvae are almost guaranteed to show up when you plant beans in your garden. So try planting a trap crop of soybeans away from your other beans to lure these pests into an early exit. When the beetles flock to the preferred soybeans, pull up the plants and remove them—pests and all–from your garden.

FOIL MEXICAN BEAN BEETLES BY PLANTING A TRAP CROP OF SOYBEANS AWAY FROM YOUR OTHER BEANS.

KNOW THY ENEMY

Knowing what Mexican bean beetles look like—as well as knowing their habits—can help you take the upper hand in keeping them under control.

The brownish beetles with eight black spots hide out in weeds and woods during the winter and flit about in spring until they find some beans. After feeding a bit, they lay clusters of orange-yellow eggs on the undersides of bean leaves. The eggs hatch in 1 to 2 weeks, and the slow-moving yellow larvae, shaped like blobs with soft points over their backs, quickly begin rasping away at the undersides of bean leaves. If left uncontrolled, the larvae will feed on the bean pods and stems after chewing away all but the veins from every bean leaf.

GO FOR THE PURPLE

Yellow wax beans seem to have been voted the bean of choice by this pest. If you have a bean beetle problem in your garden, you might want to try growing 'Royal Burgundy' or other purple-podded snap beans instead, which suffer less beetle damage than yellow wax beans.

Mosquitoes

By the time you feel the bite and slap your arm, it's too late—you've been bitten by summer's perennial pest, the mosquito. The silent-but-deadly females need a bit of your blood so they can lay their eggs, but all you'll get out of the deal is an itchy red welt that could last for days. Take heart, though: We have some great tips to keep these thirsty flyers from bugging you all summer long!

GET 'EM WHILE THEY'RE YOUNG

If you want to control mosquitoes, you've got to start at the beginning—their beginning, that is. Mosquito larvae need standing, undisturbed water to survive the first 2 weeks of their lives, so your mission is to make sure that the water in your yard isn't someplace that would make a great mosquito nursery.

You can keep your waters mosquito-unfriendly by doing something as simple as changing the water in your birdbaths often. Or, if you have a pond in your yard, you can add native fish or goldfish to its waters—the fish will enjoy snacking on the mosquitoes.

You might also try placing donut-shaped rings made out of BTI (*Bacillus thuringiensis* var. *israelensis*), which are available through garden-supply catalogs (see "Resources" on page 196), in your pond. These rings are also safe for use in water barrels, birdbaths, and water gardens.

And while you're eliminating potential mosquito-breeding grounds, don't forget any unintentional water sources that surround your home and garden. Fill in or drain off depressions where water pools, and you'll be less likely to end up sharing your yard with swarms of biting insects.

BTI ring

LET MOSQUITOES KNOW THEY'RE NOT WELCOME BY PLACING BTI RINGS IN YOUR WATER GARDENS AND PONDS.

LATHER AWAY LARVAE

Banish mosquitoes from your rain barrels and buckets with a simple squirt of liquid dish soap. Use just enough soap to kill any larvae that hatch in your rain-collecting containers, but too little to do any harm to the plants that'll be soaking up that water. About 1 teaspoon of soap per gallon of water should be perfect for washing away your mosquito problems. (You might also want to consider keeping lids over your barrels and buckets to help prevent mosquitoes from laying larvae in the water in the first place.)

USE GOOD "SCENTS" WHEN REPELLING MOSQUITOES

Some scents will draw mosquitoes to you the same way fresh-baked cookies may draw you into a neighbor's home. So when you're outside in mosquito country, avoid smelling like perfumes, shampoos, soaps, and hair spray—to mosquitoes, they all have that "come hither" appeal. Instead, use aromatic herbs like lavender, geranium, lemon balm, and lemon thyme to repel these biting pests. Simply grow these herbs in containers or beds around your patio, and when you need a little mosquito protection, crush a few of their leaves to release their oils. Or you can apply the herbs directly to your skin, but be sure to patch test a small area first to make sure you aren't allergic. If your skin shows no signs of irritation 15 minutes after the test, go ahead and use that herb to chase away these bloodsuckers.

Solutions at a Glance

PROBLEM: Something is snacking on you.

CULPRIT: Mosquitoes

SOLVE IT! Mosquitoes are attracted to the heat retained by dark colors, so stick with white, yellow, or beige clothing, and chances are good you'll fly in under the mosquito radar.

You can also try diffusing a scent mosquitoes hate—such as rosemary, spearmint, or geranium—into the air. Surround yourself in a mist of these mosquito repellents and the pests will give your yard a wide berth. To make these scents airborne, combine 10 to 20 drops of rosemary, spearmint, or geranium oil with 2 ounces of water in an atomizer, says Mindy Green, director of education at the Herb Research Foundation in Boulder, Colorado, and co-author of *Aromatherapy: A Complete Guide to the Healing Art*. Lightly spray the mixture on your skin or clothes no more than five times a day. You can also use these oils undiluted in an electric diffusor, she notes. Or, if you have a potpourri burner, simply add water to the receptacle, and 5 to 10 drops of oil to the water, and light the candle below. Then sit back, relax, and enjoy a mosquito-free evening by candlelight!

Mulch Problems

Savvy gardeners have been using mulch for generations. The ideal mulch keeps weeds down, prevents water from evaporating, moderates soil temperature, provides nutrients to plants, adds organic matter to the soil, and improves soil texture. But despite all its positives, mulch does have some downsides. Depending on your mulch of choice, it may blow away, rob the soil of moisture or nitrogen, or form a hard crust that water can't penetrate. These problems are easily solved, however, with just a little effort on your part. Here's how.

TERRIFIC TWOSOME

Two mulches earn the distinction of not having any problems at all—compost and leaf mold—which makes them wise choices for your mulching needs.

Compost is a wonder mulch for several reasons. First of all, you can make it yourself without having to buy any special ingredients—it's free, and it's the ultimate in recycling. Compost does everything a mulch should, plus it contains disease-fighting microorganisms. It looks fine in the garden as is and doesn't blow around. Compost also really holds moisture without waterlogging the soil. Since Nancy Engel, a gardener from Cold Spring, New York, started adding compost to her window-box planting mix, she cut her watering down from three to four times a week to once a week—even for her boxes that get full sun.

LEAVES ARE A PRICELESS SOURCE OF MULCH—AND FREE FOR THE TAKING. ALL YOU HAVE TO DO IS RAKE THEM UP, SHRED THEM, AND LET THEM DECOMPOSE.

Solutions at a Glance

PROBLEM: A hard crust has formed on top of your soil.
CULPRIT: Sawdust
SOLVE IT! Occasionally break it up with a cultivating fork.

PROBLEM: Your plants aren't getting the nitrogen they need.
CULPRIT: Fresh bark chips
SOLVE IT! Use shredded bark instead.

PROBLEM: Corn cob mulch and newspaper mulch are blowing around.
CULPRIT: Wind
SOLVE IT! Water the mulch as you lay it down, then anchor it with a covering of something more attractive, such as wood chips.

PROBLEM: Nitrogen is being robbed from the soil.
CULPRIT: Wood chips, sawdust, and leaves
SOLVE IT! Add bloodmeal or alfalfa meal to your soil.

PROBLEM: Something's hanging out under your mulch.
CULPRIT: Slugs and voles
SOLVE IT! Remove the mulch.

Leaf mold is wonderful, too, and if you have deciduous trees, then you have an inexhaustible source of leaf mold. All you need is a lawn mower to shred the leaves and a place to pile them while they decompose. Like compost, leaf mold puts valuable nutrients back into the soil, improves the texture of the soil, and is a great mulch for all types of plants.

FREE CHIPS

If buying bags of wood chips for mulch is putting a good dent in your budget, don't throw in the towel. Instead of paying for wood chips, check with a tree trimming company. They may be more than happy to supply you with free wood chips.

TOO MUCH OF A GOOD THING

Don't go overboard on the mulch. Too much mulch around a tree can smother its roots and cause bark rot on its trunk. So how much should you use? A good rule of thumb is to not put more than a 2- to 3-inch layer of mulch around a tree and keep mulch 4 inches away from the trunk.

Poison Ivy

As gardeners, we all do our best to avoid the plant with three shiny green leaves. But occasionally we still manage to find ourselves covered in the red, itchy rash that tells the world we've tangled with a patch of poison ivy. If your yard is crawling with it, you may be at your wit's end trying to avoid the stuff. But don't give up—here are some great suggestions for a rashless year outdoors, plus some home remedies to help relieve the itch if poison ivy has already gotten to you this season.

THIS OIL REALLY GETS AROUND

You may not know it, but the leaves of the poison ivy plant aren't the bad guys.

According to Susan Carol Hauser, author of *Nature's Revenge: The Secrets of Poison Ivy, Poison Oak, Poison Sumac, and Their Remedies*, it's the oil urushiol (you-ROO-she-ol),

which is found in the plant's sap, that gives you the rash. And that oil can be carried around on animal fur, garden tools, or any other object that it touches. But that's not even the worst of it: The oil retains its rash-spreading, itch-starting properties for up to a year while it sits on those objects. That means that if your gardening gloves, tools, or boots come in contact with poison ivy at the end of this season and you put them away until next spring—surprise! You can get poison ivy again just by touching them.

THE ITCH-CAUSING OIL IN POISON IVY CAN HANG AROUND FOR A LONG TIME, SO MAKE SURE TO THOROUGHLY WASH ANY GLOVES, TOOLS, OR BOOTS THAT COME IN CONTACT WITH IT.

So what's your best strategy for avoiding this perennial irritation? Whether you already have the telltale rash or you just know you've had a brush with poison ivy, "make sure you clean everything you've been in contact with," Hauser says. "The rubber boots you were wearing, your clothing, tools, gloves." A thorough cleaning with water should do the trick, but your defensive strategy doesn't end there. Even after you've stripped and washed yourself, you could still expose yourself to the oil simply by coming in contact with your soiled clothing. So take care when handling your clothes, and wipe down the outside of the washing machine after tossing them in, Hauser says. And also hose down your garden tools.

TREAT THE SKIN YOU'RE IN!

Prevention is your best bet when it comes to poison ivy, but even the most cautious gardener will find herself elbow deep in the stuff at least once in her life. If you do get ivy-oiled, here are a few things you can do to stop the itch before it starts.

REMOVE YOUR CLOTHING AND TAKE A LONG SHOWER RIGHT AWAY AFTER YOU FINISH OUTDOOR ACTIVITIES. Immediately flooding the skin with water is the best way to get rid of the urushiol oil, according to Susan Carol Hauser, author of *Nature's Revenge: The Secrets of Poison Ivy, Poison Oak, Poison Sumac, and Their Remedies.*

HAVE A POISON IVY KIT HANDY. Hauser uses a mason jar filled with rubbing alcohol and a washcloth. If you think you've come in contact with poison ivy, simply slosh the wet cloth over the area of skin you're worried about. Then wipe down your hands and the outside of

Solutions at a Glance

PROBLEM: Your yard is overrun with a weed, and you're sure removing the plants is the only way to keep from getting a rash again and again.

CULPRIT: Poison ivy

SOLVE IT! Dig the plants out—carefully!—by the roots. Make sure you wear protective clothing, and wash with plenty of water afterward. Or, suffocate the plants by covering them with black plastic or cardboard. It takes some time, but eventually the plants will die. Be sure to seal down the edges of the cover, and keep a sharp lookout for runners that can sneak out and start new plants. (You can also keep mowing poison ivy off; the plant will weaken and eventually die.)

the jar, and return the cloth to the jar for the next ivy emergency.

TRY THE HERBAL RELIEF OFFERED BY JEWELWEED OR TOUCH-ME-NOT, HAUSER SAYS. If you think you've brushed against some poison ivy, simply break off a stem of jewelweed and apply the juice as you would aloe. This pale green plant can grow to 5 feet tall, is a succulent, and prefers moist and partial shade locations. It has slipper-shaped seedpods, and the healing juice is a watery orange that flows freely from broken stems or torn leaves.

BUT MA, IT ITCHES!

We've all heard it: "Don't scratch—you'll only make it worse." But is it true?

"People tend to think scratching spreads the rash," explains Susan Carol Hauser, author of *Nature's Revenge: The Secrets of Poison Ivy, Poison Oak, Poison Sumac, and Their Remedies.* "Itching may feel good, and it won't spread the rash," Hauser assures us. But scratching can cause infection or nerve damage, so you should still listen to your mother—she really does know best.

Try these ideas for some quick relief while you're busy *not* scratching your rash.

- One garden remedy you can try is a peppermint tea compress. Add 1 cup of hot water to 1 tablespoon of fresh peppermint leaves. Steep for 10 to 15 minutes. "Keep the tea covered as it steeps," says Betzy Bancroft, an herbalist from Port Murray, New Jersey, because evaporation will make your tea less effective. Soak a cloth in the liquid, and apply it to the skin.
- You can use hot tap water to release the histamines (which cause the awful itching in the first place) in the skin and gain some relief, says Hauser. Use tap water that's as hot as you can stand, but not so hot that it will burn you. Immerse the part of your body that has the rash in a basin of hot water, or hold it under running water (where you can gradually increase the temperature). After several minutes, you'll feel the histamine release from your skin in little bursts. Keep the water hot until the bursts stop (change the basin water if needed)—usually in 10 minutes or so. Relief from itching lasts up to 8 hours, so using this treatment before going to bed should help you get a good night's sleep.
- Try applying a paste made with water, cornstarch, baking soda, oatmeal, or Epsom salts to relieve the itch. Use 1 teaspoon of water to 3 teaspoons of the dry ingredient, and apply to the skin as needed.

GET MUCH-NEEDED ITCH RELIEF BY APPLYING A PASTE MADE FROM CORNSTARCH AND WATER TO YOUR IRRITATED SKIN.

Potato Problems

There's nothing like digging your hands into the earth and coming out with a bounty of delicious, homegrown potatoes. These subterranean veggies are universally loved (have you ever met someone who *didn't* like potatoes?) and are super easy to grow—especially if you know a few expert tips. Read on to discover the secrets to planting, growing, and harvesting picture-perfect potatoes year after year.

Rx for Healthy Potatoes

There's a lot that can be said about how to grow healthy potatoes, but all potato experts agree on one thing: You should only plant seed potatoes that are certified to be disease-free. Follow these tips to have the healthiest taters in town.

TRY TO AVOID SAVING YOUR OWN POTATOES TO PLANT FROM YEAR TO YEAR. That's because various viruses can affect potatoes, and if you save your own seed potatoes, over time you'll probably see a decline in the size and quality of your spuds.

DON'T TRY TO USE SUPERMARKET SPUDS. Odds are good that they won't grow because they've been sprayed with chemicals to keep them from sprouting.

BE TWICE AS SURE OF YOUR SEED POTATOES. Use double-certified seed potatoes, if you can. They're becoming more readily available, and they're both free from disease and produced without any chemicals whatsoever.

Spring Ahead with Green Sprouting

To help ensure a successful crop and to get a head start on the growing season, potato experts recommend a practice called "green sprouting." Here's how it works.

"About 30 days before you plant, put the potatoes in a dark, 70° to 75°F area," says Megan Gerritsen, co-owner of Wood Prairie Farm, an organic potato seed supplier in Bridgewater, Maine. "Then, as soon as you see sprouts, move the potatoes to cooler temperatures (50° to 55°F) in the light. You want the tubers and sprouts to turn green." Exceptionally vigorous seed potatoes (the sprouts get too long too fast) should be held at 42° to 45°F.

Keep the sprouted potatoes in the cool and light conditions for about 3 weeks. By then, sprouts will be about ½ inch long and the tubers will be ready to plant.

Jim Gerritsen, the other co-owner of Wood Prairie Farm, gives green sprouting the credit for their successful crops in an area where the season is very short and the crops have a lot of late-season challenges. "If we can give those potatoes a good head start indoors, where there are no bugs and no blight, we gain 2 weeks on our season," Gerritsen says, adding that green sprouting is great for areas where cold or wet weather might rot seed potatoes. "If the potatoes are green sprouted, they're already in gear before they have a chance to rot." Even holding potatoes for 24 to 48 hours at 70°F is a huge benefit."

IF YOU'RE PRACTICING "GREEN SPROUTING," YOU'LL NEED TO MOVE YOUR POTATOES OUT OF THE DARK AND INTO THE LIGHT AS SOON AS YOU SEE SPROUTS.

SAVE TIME SPENT SLICING

Don't bother cutting up small seed potatoes (those about half the size of a golf ball or hen's egg)—you can plant them whole. Cut larger seed potatoes so that each piece has at least two or three eyes and weighs an ounce or two. And be sure to allow cut seed spuds to dry in the sunshine for 24 hours before you plant them.

WHEN YOU CUT LARGER POTATOES FOR SEED, MAKE SURE EACH PIECE HAS AT LEAST TWO EYES.

STICK IT IN THE FRIDGE

Don't toss that old refrigerator that still works—it's a great place to store your potatoes after the harvest (as long as it's not self-defrosting—which would cause your potatoes to shrivel). The tubers should be stored in a completely dark place, at about 40°F, so if you were planning on just sticking them in the basement, you might want to rethink that strategy. (Make sure your fridge doesn't get too cool, though; potatoes convert their sugars to starch at temps below 36°F.)

Powdery Mildew

If your plants look like someone just dusted them with baby powder, you know you have powdery mildew. Actually a fungus, powdery mildew thrives in summer when evenings are cool and days are warm and humid. But don't despair. Powdery mildew seldom kills or causes serious damage—it just looks ugly. And clever gardeners can avoid even that.

PESTERED BY POWDERY MILDEW

Half the battle against powdery mildew is knowing which plants are most likely to be affected. If you know, then you can be more careful about taking steps to prevent powdery mildew in the first place. Here's a list of common victims.

Trees and Shrubs
Hackberries (*Celtis* spp.)
Euonymus (*Euonymus* spp.)
Crape myrtle (*Lagerstroemia indica*)
Privets (*Ligustrum* spp.)
Honeysuckles (*Lonicera* spp.)
Crabapples (*Malus* spp.)
English oak (*Quercus robur*)
Roses (*Rosa* spp.)
Lilacs (*Syringa* spp.)

Flowers
Dahlias (*Dahlia* hybrids)
Hybrid delphinium (*Delphinium × elatum*)
Bee balm (*Monarda didyma*)
Garden phlox (*Phlox paniculata*)
Common zinnias (*Zinnia elegans*)

Fruits and Vegetables
Apples
Cucumbers
Grapes
Melons
Peas
Pumpkins
Squash
Strawberries

5 WAYS TO PREVENT POWDERY MILDEW

PLANT DISEASE-RESISTANT VARIETIES. As a rule of thumb, newer varieties tend to have more powdery mildew resistance. As much as possible, read the label or check the seed catalog description.

GIVE 'EM ROOM. Good air circulation keeps leaves drier and prevents fungi from getting a foothold. Plant at the recommended spacing to prevent crowding.

GIVE 'EM LIGHT. If a plant is prone to powdery mildew, plant it in (or move it to) to full sun. There, the leaves will dry faster and better.

DESTROY DISEASED PLANT PARTS. Even if the plant can't be saved, fast action may prevent the spread of the disease to another completely different plant. As much as is practical, trim or pick off diseased leaves or stems and destroy them. Rake or pick up diseased leaves that fall to the ground.

WATER WITH CARE. Don't water overhead, spraying leaves. Instead, water the soil directly. Not only does this prevent the leaves from staying wet, creating ideal fungi-spreading conditions, it also prevents powdery mildew spores that may be in the soil from splashing up onto leaves.

PREVENTIVE POTION

You can help keep powdery mildew at bay with this home brew of baking soda, water, and Murphy Oil Soap. The baking soda alters the pH of the leaf, making it harder for fungi to get started. The oil soap serves as a sticker-spreader to help the spray spread and stay. Simply mix together 1 gallon water, 3 tablespoons baking soda, and 1 tablespoon Murphy Oil Soap.

Spray before powdery mildew strikes, in early spring—as soon as plants have leafed out. Start spraying those that have been plagued by powdery mildew in the past. Spray every 7 to 10 days, getting in at least four applications before temperatures hit the 70s.

You can also apply the spray at the very first sign of powdery mildew, repeating every 7 to 10 days until temperatures hit the 70s. (Spray it on when it's any warmer and you might burn the leaves.)

SPRAY PLANTS WITH A NONTOXIC "HOME BREW" THAT PREVENTS POWDERY MILDEW.

Propagation Problems

Propagating plants is kind of like raising animals, only better, because you don't need one of each sex to get new ones—you can propagate your own offspring from cuttings. Propagation is a great way to increase your plantings or to share a favorite plant with friends. And it's easy, as long as you avoid a few pitfalls.

Rx for Healthy Propagating

As we said before, propagating is easy, if you avoid a few pitfalls. Because we want to help you do just that, we've put together a few tips for avoiding common mistakes.

USE GENTLE BOTTOM HEAT. Gentle bottom heat can hasten rooting, "but be careful not to fry them," says Tony Ricci of Three Springs, Pennsylvania. If you do a lot of propagating, it might be worthwhile to invest in an electric propagation mat because you'll be able to regulate the heat easily.

WATCH THE MOISTURE LEVEL CAREFULLY because heat also dries out the rooting medium. Regular misting helps keep cuttings from drying out, or you can cover the pots holding your cuttings with a clear plastic bag to create a miniature mist tent. It's fine for the plastic to fog up, but if it starts dripping moisture, the medium is too wet. Take the plastic off temporarily to prevent the cuttings from molding in the excess moisture.

AVOID DIRECT SUNLIGHT. Don't put your propagation flats in direct sunlight, either, because direct sun can cause leaves to scorch and wilt. In fact, cuttings need no sun at all until they have rooted and are starting to produce new leaves.

A Nick Saves Time

If you want to get hardwood and softwood cuttings to root faster, try wounding the lower stem by nicking it with a sharp knife or the blade of your pruning shears. This is especially helpful if the cutting is from older wood, which roots more slowly than new wood.

Smaller Equals More Success

Smaller cuttings tend to root better and faster—you'll root close to 100 percent of 1½-inch-long rosemary cuttings, for example, while only

PROBLEM: Your cuttings are infected.

CULPRIT: Fungal spores

SOLVE IT! Add a few drops of hydrogen peroxide to the water when you water or mist the cutting flat to reduce the chance of infection.

about 10 percent of 4-inch cuttings will root. (The only drawback is that smaller cuttings are also more prone to wilt, so they need more immediate attention.)

FLAG THAT PLANT

Few perennials should be divided when they're in bloom, but that's when you're likely to notice that one plant is superior to its neighbors. And, of course, that's the plant you want to propagate. Use a bamboo stake with a colorful strip of plastic stapled to the top to mark the special plant so you won't forget which one it is when the time is right to propagate.

Timely Cuts

One tricky aspect to propagation is knowing the right time to take cuttings. Soft-stemmed plants—like impatiens, geraniums, and many perennials—will root from cuttings anytime. Perennials are usually best divided in the early spring when they first show growth or propagated from cuttings in midsummer. Some woody plants—like berry bushes, shrubs, and trees—will root successfully only if the cuttings are taken at certain times of the year. Trial and error usually works best, but here are some guidelines to get you started.

Plant	When to Take Cuttings
Hydrangeas (*Hydrangea* spp.)	Softwood cuttings, spring and summer
Privets (*Ligustrum* spp.)	Anytime
Ornamental cherries (*Prunus* spp.)	Softwood cuttings in spring
Currants and gooseberries (*Ribes* spp.)	When dormant (late fall to early spring)
Azaleas (*Rhododendron* spp.)	During active growth in spring
Lilacs (*Syringa* spp.)	During active growth in spring
Deciduous trees and shrubs (hardwood)	When dormant (late fall to early spring)
Deciduous trees and shrubs (softwood)	Spring (when budded) to early summer
Evergreens	During a growth flush (there are several annually)

Solutions at a Glance

PROBLEM: The impatiens (or coleus or geraniums), which were started from cuttings, are growing straight up and won't branch out.

CULPRIT: Cuttings from the wrong shoot

SOLVE IT! The temptation is to root the leading shoot from annual bedding plants when you pinch them to encourage bushiness. That shoot is already programmed to grow upright. Take cuttings from side branches instead, and your plants will be bushier.

PROBLEM: Your divisions of oriental poppy (*Papaver orientale*) die.

CULPRIT: Wrong form of propagation

SOLVE IT! Oriental poppy is one perennial that's hard to divide successfully. Take root cuttings instead in July or August when the plant is dormant. Dig it up and cut the fleshy roots into 4- to 5-inch pieces. Be sure to insert them in your rooting medium the same way they were growing in the garden. Cutting the bottom at an angle and the top straight will help you remember which end was up.

PROBLEM: Your cuttings wilt and die before they develop roots.

CULPRIT: Loss of moisture

SOLVE IT! The cuttings are losing moisture too fast. Strip all but the topmost leaves from cuttings to prevent excess moisture loss, and never let the rooting medium dry out.

PROBLEM: Your cuttings mold before they develop roots.

CULPRIT: Excess moisture

SOLVE IT! If you're covering the propagation flat to increase humidity, remove it occasionally to vent excess moisture. Sprinkle milled sphagnum moss over the surface of the flat to wick moisture away from the cutting stems.

Lots of Herbs

Cuttings are an easy way to grow lots of herb plants for yourself and for your friends. Basil, scented geraniums, lavender, rosemary, and sage are just a few of the herbs that grow well from cuttings. To take cuttings, use a sharp knife, then remove the leaves on the bottom half of the cutting and push it into the soil mix in your container. Cuttings need high humidity—put the pot with your cuttings inside a plastic produce bag that has slits for ventilation. Keep your new cuttings out of direct sunlight for a few days. Then be patient—your cuttings will need at least a month before they form new roots.

Putting Down Roots

Although many plants root in nothing more than plain water, some harder-to-root species need a little help. Here are a couple of tricks of the trade.

USE WILLOW BRANCHES. "Willow trees (*Salix* spp.) have a natural rooting hormone (salicylic acid) in them," says Tony Ricci, an organic grower from Three Springs, Pennsylvania. "Take some twigs, soak them in water for a few days, and then either dip the cuttings in the water or water the flats with it."

USE BORIC ACID. Trying to root hollies (*Ilex* spp.)? Do the above, and add a pinch of boric acid to the willow water. Researchers have found that boron enhances holly rooting when used with rooting hormones.

ADDING A PINCH OF BORIC ACID TO WILLOW WATER IS ONE TRICK TO HELP GET HOLLIES TO ROOT.

Humidity Helper

Give cuttings the humidity they need by placing your containers of cuttings on a tray of pebbles. Put just a small amount of water in the tray—enough to create humid conditions, but not enough to touch the bottom of the pots. (Also use fingernail-size pebbles.)

Pruning Problems

Many plants and trees in your landscape can benefit from pruning now and then. But how often have you taken a little too much off? Or not enough? What about the hydrangea you pruned that subsequently failed to flower? Results like these can be enough to make you want to turn in your loppers. Pruning doesn't have to be an ordeal, however. Take the following tips for healthy pruning, including how to do it safely, to heart and we're sure you'll have better luck the next time that tree or bush needs a trim.

REMOVING LARGE LIMBS SAFELY

You've probably been there. In one fell swoop you hack a large branch off of a tree—and the wood splinters, tears away and leaves you with an injured tree. You can avoid such damage in the future, however, simply by knowing how to remove large limbs correctly. Here's what to do:

1. Make an undercut about one-third to one-half of the way through the branch.
2. Make a second cut into the top of the limb just outside of the first cut. (The weight of the limb should make most of the branch snap off at that spot.)
3. Make your third—and final—cut just outside of the branch collar.

REMOVING LARGE LIMBS WITH THREE CUTS INSTEAD OF ONE CAN HELP PROTECT YOUR TREE—AND YOUR HEAD.

DISEASE PREVENTION AND CONTROL

Bill Adams, extension horticulturist for the Texas Agricultural Extension Service in Houston, recommends dipping pruning tools in a 10 percent bleach solution in between fruit trees with disease symptoms to prevent spreading the disease. "Dipping is particularly important when pruning peaches and nectarines, to avoid spreading bacterial canker," Adams says. Prune the diseased trees last and try to prune well below any disease cankers.

Patrick Curran, owner of Curran's Orchard in Rockford, Illinois, uses a simple rule to prevent disease in his apple orchard. "If two limbs are close together, or if they cross, or if they touch, one of them should come out," he says. "Two limbs rubbing together will eventually result in disease." Not only does this help to ensure a healthy orchard, it encourages superior fruit production. "Open trees allow more sunlight and air to enter the tree canopy—this helps fruit stay dry and reduces growth of fungus and bacteria."

"Cut it out!" says Tom Galazen, owner of North Wind Organic Farm in Bayfield, Wisconsin. "Airborne fungal diseases can easily spread from one perennial fruit, such as blueberries, to another." One way to prevent disease from spreading is to remove diseased leaves or branches from the plant.

RX FOR HEALTHY PRUNING

Here are a some points to keep in mind before you begin pruning so that you end up helping your plant rather than hurting it.

When pruning shrubs, use loppers to cut off a few large stems right at ground level, instead of using hedge shears. Plants will then need fewer cuts and will maintain a better form, says Lee Reich, Ph.D., garden writer and author of *The Pruning Book*.

The best time to prune to promote quick healing and help prevent disease is just before growth begins in the spring, advises Reich. But hold off on pruning early bloomers such as forsythia until after they've finished blooming, or else you'll be removing some flower buds whose blossoms you could have otherwise enjoyed!

"Orange flagging tape is a great thing to use if you aren't an experienced pruner," says Carol Bradford, a Master Gardener and garden columnist from Syracuse, New York. "Use the tape to tie good-sized bows around the branches you want to cut off—then visualize the way the tree will look without the branches."

Make sure your loppers are sharp because sharp blades will make cleaner cuts and won't bruise the back sides of branches. Clean cuts and a lack of tree damage will also help to prevent disease.

Flagging tape

AVERT A PRUNING DISASTER BY USING ORANGE FLAGGING TAPE TO HELP YOU VISUALIZE HOW YOUR FINISHED MASTERPIECE WILL LOOK.

KEEP ON BLOOMIN'

Hate to say good-bye to those delphinium blooms? You can extend the plants' bloom time by pruning out all but three growing stems when the delphiniums reach 18 inches tall, says Jeff Cox, noted garden author from Kenwood, California. After pruning the plant, stake the three remaining stems. The plant's roots will compensate by sending up new stems that will produce a second bloom much later in the season, giving you more time with these gorgeous flowers.

PRUNING PATIENCE

You can help your peach trees fend off the deadly cytospora canker by making sure not to prune them too early, says Frank Pollack, who runs an organic fruit and vegetable farm in Pennsylvania's Pocono Mountains. "Research has shown that cytospora will do more damage to peach trees if you prune them before the sap is moving again," he explains. "So wait to prune the trees until things have warmed up—that way, any pruning-related wounds will have a chance to heal quickly because the sap is moving," says Pollack.

WHACK THOSE BLUEBERRIES BACK

David Martinson, an organic fruit farmer from northern Wisconsin, errs on the side of over-pruning his blueberries in early spring. "You may think you're pruning too much," he explains. "But blueberries are resilient shrubs that thrive on pruning." In fact, when pruning individual canes, Martinson recommends pruning them back to ground level. "In the growing season following pruning, my blueberries increase in size." What better way to encourage vigorous shrub growth?

Solutions at a Glance

PROBLEM: Something's getting the better of your stone fruits (peaches, plums, and cherries).

CULPRIT: Frost

SOLVE IT! Wait to prune until the flower buds are just beginning to swell. Pruning tends to spur the trees into growth and bloom, so waiting to prune delays the bloom and helps avoid frost damage.

LILAC TIME-SAVER

Pruning, as you well know, can take a lot of time. When it comes to lilacs, save yourself some work later on by cutting lots of lilacs for your house when they're in bloom. Don't think of it as robbing the bush, but rather as saving work later, because you should also cut off all the old flower heads when pruning the bush.

INCREASING APPLE PRODUCTION

You can help your apple trees produce more fruit simply by fashioning them after a Christmas tree.

"Apple trees should resemble evergreen trees," says to Patrick Curran, who gardens in Rockford, Illinois. An apple tree should be wider at the bottom than it is at the top, so prune your trees so the upper limbs are shorter than the lower ones. This will allow enough sunlight to penetrate through the tree canopy to the lower limbs, will increase photosynthesis, and will increase the overall fruit production of your tree.

LET THE SUN SHINE IN ON YOUR APPLE TREE BY PRUNING IT SO THAT IT'S WIDER AT THE BOTTOM THAN THE TOP.

BUSHIER BLOOMS

Want to have bushier fall-blooming asters? Simply cut them back to half their height when they're 12 to 15 inches tall. By cutting them back they'll bear more flowers on shorter stems that require less staking.

FLUSH CUTS ARE OUT

Create a healthy cut when you prune by leaving $\frac{1}{16}$ inch of branch on the tree, says Frank Pollack, an organic fruit and vegetable farmer from the Pocono Mountains in Pennsylvania. "You'd think an absolute flush cut with the tree is the way to do it," says Pollack, "but leaving just the barest piece of the branch permits the outer ring of the pruned cut to grow back and heal faster than a flush cut."

REIGNING IN STRAWBERRY RUNNERS

You can control vigorous runner growth in strawberries by gently clipping them back so they aren't as long and are less dense, says Tom Galazen of North Wind Organic Farm in Bayfield, Wisconsin. "Ideal spacing for the new plantlets formed on the runners is 4 to 6 inches," says Galazen. "Keeping rows narrower—around 18 to 24 inches across—should result in greater production than wider rows."

Rabbit Problems

Remember back before you were a gardener, back when you thought that rabbits were just so cute? Now that you have a garden, though, you're aware of the fact that Thumper could be the one taking out your bean, lettuce, or carrot seedlings or nibbling off your bulb foliage. Cutting it right down to the ground, in fact! And though you haven't caught the rabbits red-handed, you're pretty sure they're the culprits. So what can you do to save your crops and your sanity in the face of marauding bunnies? Plenty—including fencing them out or repelling them with the scent of rotten eggs.

Positive I.D.

Before you initiate a full-scale war on Peter Cottontail, make sure that's actually who you're dealing with. There are a few surefire ways you can determine that rabbits are the ones destroying your garden.

First, rabbit tracks are unique. With two back thumper legs propelling them, the indentations of their prints are easy to spot. Second, you can tell rabbits have been around if you find small, hard, pea-size dark brown pellets, generally left in neat little piles. Third, rabbits use their sharp teeth to cleanly clip small branches from a stem or trunk, as opposed to deer, who bite twigs bluntly off and chew leaves, or plow through a vegetable patch willy-nilly, leaving a mess.

PETER RABBIT'S TRACKS ARE UNIQUE IN THAT THE INDENTATIONS OF THEIR PRINTS—ESPECIALLY THEIR TWO BACK THUMPER LEGS—ARE EASY TO SPOT.

Solutions at a Glance

PROBLEM: Your tender young seedlings are being eaten.

CULPRIT: Rabbits

SOLVE IT! Sprinkle wood ash on and around vulnerable crops. (If you have a wood stove or fireplace, you can save the ash in a bucket all winter.) And remember to reapply wood ash after it rains.

PLAY CHICKEN WITH RABBITS

If rabbits are the major pest in a small yard, a simple, sturdy chicken-wire fence (1-inch mesh or smaller) works like a charm. The important thing to remember when designing the rabbit-proof garden with rabbit-impenetrable fencing is to bury at least 6 inches of the wire fencing in your trench so that these furry fellows can't burrow underneath the fence.

BARRIER PROTECTION

Maybe you don't mind sharing parts of your yard or garden with rabbits, but you have a few plants whose safety you want to ensure. In that case, you can make simple protective barriers from ¼-inch hardware cloth for specific plants and young trees (because rabbits also enjoy snacking on tree bark). Make hardware cloth cylinders that cover the bottom 2 feet of the tree, plus a few inches of trunk below the surface of the soil. Keep the cylinder loose enough to accommodate several years' growth of the tree or plant. (Overlap the hardware cloth and

secure it by inserting a piece of wire through the mesh and twisting it like a twist-tie.)

You can also cut strips of chicken wire into cylinders to wrap around young trees. (Commercially made tree guards are also available.)

Early in the season, protect small plants from rabbits with plastic milk jugs. Cut the bottom out of a jug, place it over a plant, and pile dirt around its base to keep it from blowing away. Remember to remove the jugs once the weather gets warmer, or the plants will get too hot and shrivel up.

Milk jug
Bottom cut out

RECYCLE PLASTIC MILK JUGS AND USE THEM TO PROTECT YOUNG PLANTS FROM HUNGRY BUNNIES.

SMELLY RESOLUTION

Some gardeners swear by homemade rotten egg sprays, bloodmeal, and hot pepper sauce as rabbit repellents. But if you don't feel like whipping up a batch of something homemade and smelly, commercial sprays are also available from mail-order sources (see "Resources" on page 196). One such spray, N.I.M.B.Y., is an emulsion of natural oils, available in a 32-ounce trigger spray bottle, that's an environmentally safe way to help repel rabbits.

Rose Problems

Who can imagine a world without roses? For song writers, poets, and lovers—not to mention those of us who find sheer delight in their fanciful names—it would be a pretty bleak place without them. Yet multitudes of gardeners are convinced roses are more trouble than they're worth. Sure, roses can hand you a challenge or two. (What living thing can't?) But once you've learned a few tricks of the trade for beating fungus and pests and for putting into practice some general growing guidelines, roses are as easy to live with as any other shrub.

RX FOR HEALTHY ROSES

Your surest road to rose-garden bliss is preventing problems before they happen. That includes making sure you choose varieties that are hardy and are resistant to the diseases that occur in your growing area (if you're not sure which roses will do best where you live, call your local Cooperative Extension office for information). Also use the following techniques.

PRACTICE GOOD HYGIENE. Like you, roses want their bodies and their homes clean and tidy. It makes them better able to fend off pests and disease. Keeping them shipshape is easy, says Akron, Ohio, gardener Mary Frances Jarrold. "Pick up debris when you see it," she advises, especially from the bases of the plants, where fungal spores can thrive. Cut off anything that doesn't look right—spent flowers, odd-looking leaves or canes. Then burn the pickings and prunings or dispose of them in sealed containers with your household trash—never compost them, or else you'll end up with fungal woes throughout the rest of your garden.

DON'T BE AFRAID TO PRUNE. New, vigorous wood is far less susceptible to pests and disease. Every year in late winter or early spring, cut out all diseased or damaged canes and some of the older canes of hybrid tea roses and grandifloras so that new canes can develop. Prune once-blooming roses like old garden roses and ramblers right after they finish blooming because they bloom on 1-year-old wood. (If you prune during the dormant season, you'll cut off your blooms.)

PROVIDE AIR CIRCULATION. You tend to pick up germs when you're in a hot, stuffy, crowded space. So do roses. When you plant, make sure to give them elbow room. And prune them so air can circulate freely to all parts of the plant. Your aim is "a bowl shape of branches," says Jane Anders, a Master Gardener from Portland, Oregon. "Open up the structure so the air and sunlight can get to the bud union where new canes develop."

HELP AVOID DISEASE BY PRUNING YOUR ROSES TO AN OPEN, BOWL-LIKE FORM THAT LETS IN AIR AND LIGHT TO ALL PARTS OF THE PLANT.

SUPPLY GOOD NUTRITION. We all feel, look, and perform our best with a healthy diet. Roses are no different. Furthermore, where nutrition is concerned roses are bottomless pits. The food of choice for roses, of course, is manure. "Roses love manure and lots of it," says Anders. It scarcely matters what kind— cow, horse, llama—as long as it comes from an herbivore and it has had at least 6 months to cool down so it doesn't burn delicate roots.

The exception to the waiting period: rabbit droppings. "They work like time-release capsules," Anders says. Sprinkle the rabbit pellets around the drip line, cover them lightly, and each time water hits them the nutrients will soak into the soil and to the hungry rose roots.

Feed roses heavily in spring, when the soil temperature reaches 50°F or so, and again in summer, just after the first big flowering. Then in late fall (around Thanksgiving in Portland) cover the whole root zone with compost, and mound it up over the bud union if you have a grafted rose plant.

In mid-March and mid-July, Anders gives her roses a dose of Epsom salts to stimulate new growth. "Sprinkle about a third of a cup around the drip line, where the feeder roots are, and water it in," she says.

RECIPE FOR SUCCESS

Do your roses traditionally get off to a slow start each year? Here's a way to give them a boost from Master Gardener Marilyn Dube of Portland, Oregon. (This recipe makes enough for one plant.)

Fill a large bucket with about 5 gallons of water. Then add

2 dried banana peels
1 cup Epsom salts
2 cups alfalfa meal or pellets
½ to 1 cup dolomitic lime

Stir the ingredients together and pour the mixture around the base of the plant. Then work the solids into the soil along with any remaining winter mulch such as compost. "Your roses will be off and running," Dube guarantees.

FEND OFF FUNGI

Most of the diseases that plague roses are caused by fungi. A few of the worst are black spot, powdery mildew, rust, and canker. Black spot, the best-known ill in all of rosedom, occurs mostly in rainy or humid climates. Small black spots show on leaves; later, yellow haloes appear. In advanced stages, leaves drop off. Powdery mildew appears as a white or gray powder on leaves and flowers—never on canes. It thrives where cool nights follow hot days. Rust first appears as orange pimples on the undersides of leaves; later leaves turn orange or yellow. Spores can lie dormant in leaves, stems, or plant debris until rain, overhead watering, or high humidity spur them to action. Canker shows as brown areas on canes and usually attacks plants that have been under stress.

To prevent these fungi, follow these practices.

- Choose resistant plant varieties.
- Water early in the day so foliage dries out before nightfall.
- Diligently practice the preventive techniques described in "Rx for Healthy Roses" (on page 127).
- If your favorite roses are susceptible to disease and you have humid, damp growing conditions, spray once a week with the following organic fungicide developed at Cornell University. In 1 gallon of water, mix 3 teaspoons of baking soda and 1 teaspoon of canola oil *or* 1 teaspoon of nondetergent dishwashing liquid like Ivory (not both).
- If your roses do succumb to a fungus, the best thing to do is remove and destroy infected leaves or canes. To avoid spreading the disease, dip your pruners in alcohol or other disinfectant after each cut.

BLACK SPOT

IN THE LATER STAGES OF BLACK SPOT, YELLOW HALOES APPEAR IN ROSE LEAVES.

POWDERY MILDEW

YOU'LL FIND THE GRAY OR WHITE POWDER OF THIS FUNGUS ON ROSE LEAVES AND FLOWERS.

RUST

THE FIRST SIGN THAT YOUR ROSES HAVE RUST IS ORANGE PIMPLES ON THE UNDERSIDES OF LEAVES.

CANKER

KEEP YOUR ROSES STRESS-FREE TO HELP THEM AVOID FALLING VICTIM TO CANKER.

Note: The pests and diseases most likely to bully your roses—and the critters most likely to charge to your rescue—vary from one part of the country to another. See page 196 for some comprehensive rose books and regional problem solvers.

Pest Detective

The bugs that chow down on roses aren't the arch-villains they're cracked up to be, Master Gardener Jane Anders from Portland, Oregon, says, and most of them have natural predators. Even if the bad guys seem to get the upper hand now and then, they rarely do permanent damage. Here are some to watch for, including leaf-cutting bees and borers.

Symptom	Cause	What to Do
Curled, distorted, and sticky foliage	Aphids	Knock aphids off with a strong spray of water, and use insecticidal soap. Also, keep in mind that lady beetles and other predators will eat them.
Clean circular, oval, or scalloped holes in leaves	Leaf-cutting bees	Nothing—these bees are important pollinators of many garden plants, and they don't do serious harm to roses. If the damaged leaves bother you, cut them off.
Skeletonized leaves and holes in buds and flowers in midsummer	Japanese beetle and other beetles	Apply milky spore disease to the lawn to control the grub stage of the beetles and hand-pick the adults.
Spirals at the ends of cut canes in the pithy part of the cane	Borers. There are many types, and none fatal to rose plants. The most common, and the least damaging, is the pith borer.	Prune off canes below the infested part, destroy the prunings, and put a dab of petroleum jelly or white glue on all pruning cuts.
Small holes in foliage and eventually skeletonized leaves	Bristly rose slug	Spray the underside of the leaves (where the slug is) with insecticidal soap.
Flower buds and shoots that turn black and die	Rose midges. Unchecked, a heavy midge infestation can eliminate all bloom from late spring through early fall.	As soon as you spot midge damage, remove and destroy infected growth.

GOING TO TOWERING HEIGHTS TO BEAT THE COLD

When you run a nursery on Alaska's Glacier Highway, you develop some pretty inventive ways to coddle plants. Says Mike Barrett, co-owner of Auke Bay Gardens north of Juneau, "Many of the best roses in these cold parts are untidy in habit—meaning they need support—and bloom best when they aren't cut back much. We like to train them on towers rather than trellises, not only because we like the way they look but also because a tower makes a nice cage to wrap the canes in when drying winter winds come up." Here's how to wrap roses that are trained on towers. (*Note:* You *don't* want to take such extreme measures unless you live an area with severe winters.)

1. Bury the rose's crown with a mound of soil (about 6 inches or so).
2. Wrap the rose-covered tower in floating row cover, such as Reemay.
3. Drop enough wood chips in through the opening at the top of the tower to cover the soil at the bottom (the chips should be about 1 foot deep).
4. Fill the rest of the structure with straw.
5. Fit a heavy plastic bag over the top to keep the straw from rotting and matting.

6. Pile a 1-foot layer of wood chips around the outside base to further protect the plant's crown and help brace the whole setup against the wind.

If you're in a very windy spot, Barrett says, "you could anchor it even with guy lines and stakes, but so far we haven't had to do that." Don't be surprised if your garden draws startled looks from passers-by. Says Barrett, "The finished structure looks just like a mummy."

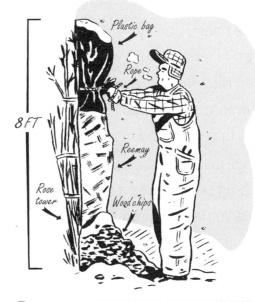

TURN YOUR ROSES INTO MUMMIES AND HELP THEM BEAT WINTER WINDS AND FREEZING TEMPS.

Seed Problems

How hopeful we start out! A packet of seed, a flat of soil, and a leap of faith. Then the things don't germinate, or they do and then promptly die, or they lag behind their fancy greenhouse-bought counterparts. Are seeds really worth all that work and disappointment?

Yes! Just like riding a bike, starting plants from seeds takes a certain knack. But once you've acquired that knack, it's as easy (and fun) as coasting that bike down a gentle hill on a sunny day. And, of course, seeds save you money big time. A flat of established seedlings can cost you $25 or more at a greenhouse—but the cost would be just a dollar or two if you started them yourself. Also, variety selection is so much better from the seed racks and mail-order catalogs. A whole new world of plants are suddenly open to you for less than a cup of fancy coffee.

MIX YOUR OWN

Disappointed with the results of sowing a packet of mixed annual seed? Why not make your own and have a wonderful cottage garden effect? You'll save money and you'll get to include only the flowers you love in the colors you adore. To get you started, mix and match your choices of the following easy-to-grow annuals. (Many of these will even reseed next season if you let some of the flowers go to seed, providing a free garden!)

Calendula (*Calendula officinalis*)
Cleome (*Cleome hasslerana*)
Larkspur (*Consolida ajacis*)
Cosmos (*Cosmos bipinnatus*)
Snow-on-the-montain (*Euphorbia marginata*)
Sweet alyssum (*Lobularia maritima*)
Nicotiana (*Nicotiana alata*)
Nigella (*Nigella damascena*)
Four o'clock (*Mirabilis jalapa*)
Marigold (*Tagetes* spp.)
Johnny-jump-up (*Viola tricolor*)

EGGSHELL TONIC

If you have a history of ending up with spindly, leggy seedlings, you might want to try feeding the next batch eggshell water. You'll need

1 gallon container with a tight-fitting lid (a milk jug works fine)

1 scant gallon water

1 dozen or more eggshells

Simply fill the container nearly full with water. Then, as you use the eggshells over a week or two, crush them lightly and pitch them in the container (no need to rinse the shells). Keep the container on the porch or in the garage; you'll know the water is ready to use once it starts to smell like, well, rotten eggs. Before you pour it on your plants, dilute with an equal part water.

MAKE A COMFORTING BREW OUT OF EGGSHELLS AND WATER TO HELP SEEDLINGS GET OFF TO A GOOD START.

READ THE LABEL

Not sure when those seeds are supposed to go into the ground? Confused over the planting depth? Next time you go to buy seeds, take a good look at the packets and make sure they have explicit planting directions on them. The best packets give detailed instructions, right down to optimum planting temperatures and ideal seed-starting mediums—and should provide guidance when you aren't sure what to do.

LET THERE BE ABSOLUTELY NO LIGHT

When you're planting seeds indoors and the package says to cover the seeds with soil, use vermiculite instead. Its light color lets you see exactly where you've covered and where you haven't. And its special moisture-holding properties prevent damping-off.

BLOW YOUR DAMPING-OFF TROUBLES AWAY

Dave and Delores Johnson of Golden Valley, Minnesota, seldom have problems with damping-off, even though they start thousands of plants from seed. They create good air circulation in their basement by turning on a fan or two. Don't put the fan right on the seeds—just a gentle breeze in the general vicinity will do fine.

SAY GOOD-BYE TO DAMPING-OFF WITH THE GENTLE BREEZE FROM A FAN.

SWEET SEEDS

Here's an easy way to see just where you're planting those fine seeds, such as carrots or poppies. Mix them with sugar before planting.

Sugar's light color and sparkle helps you better see where seeds are scattered and the sugar feeds helpful soil organisms.

MIX FINE SEEDS WITH SUGAR TO PLANT MORE PRECISELY.

EASY GERMINATORS

If starting seeds gives you gray hair, you might want to take a look at the seeds you're using before throwing in the towel. After all, some seeds are easier to germinate than others. As a rule, annuals are usually less tricky than perennials. And nearly all annual vegetables are easy to start from seed. So before you call it quits, try starting seed from some of the easy germinators listed on this page.

Very Easy
Hollyhock (*Alcea rosea*)
Snapdragons (*Antirrhinum* spp.)
Centaureas (*Centaurea* spp.)
Cosmos (*Cosmos* spp.)
Common sunflower (*Helianthus annuus*)
Sweet basil (*Ocimum basilicum*)
Marjorams (*Origanum* spp.)

Annual poppies (*Papaver* spp.)
Marigolds (*Tagetes* spp.)
Garden nasturtium (*Tropaeolum majus*)
Pansy (*Viola* × *wittrockiana*)
Zinnias (*Zinnia* spp.)
Most vegetables

Moderately Easy
Swan River daisy (*Brachycome iberidifolia*)
Sweet woodruff (*Galium odoratum*)
Globe amaranth (*Gomphrena globosa*)
Impatiens (*Impatiens walleriana*)
Parsley (*Petroselinum crispum*)
Petunias (*Petunia* cultivars)
Salvias (*Salvia* spp.)

More Difficult
Wax begonias (*Begonia Semperflorens-Cultorum* hybrids)
Heliotrope (*Heliotropium arborescens*)
Lantanas (*Lantana* spp.)
Geraniums (*Pelargonium* spp.)

BABY FOOD FOR PLANTS

Regular potting soil and garden loam won't do any more for starting seedlings than raw steak would do for a baby. So give this special seed-pampering soil mix for seedlings a try:

    1 part compost, purchased or sifted
    1 part perlite
    1 part vermiculite

SOME LIKE IT HOT

Ever threw out a flat of ungerminated seeds and decided you must have a black thumb after all? The problem may not be your black thumb, but rather, that you aren't providing the proper soil temperature required for germination, says Roy Ann Moulton, a horticulturist at Thompson & Morgan in Jackson, New Jersey.

Different species require different temperatures to germinate. To ensure success, you need to provide a soil temperature that's at least in the same ball park as the one required for the seeds you're growing. "If the seed packet says to germinate the seeds at 75°F, that means the *soil* must be 75°F, not the air," says Moulton.

The most accurate way to measure soil temperature is to use a soil thermometer. However, keep in mind that warm air rises. If the room temperature is 70°F and you're aiming for a soil temperature of 75°F, place the seed container on top of the refrigerator or a high shelf to help raise the soil temperature.

MONEY-SAVING MESCLUN

Want to grow your own mesclun but don't want to pay the extra money for a seed packet of prepared mesclun mix? Then create your own. Here's a recipe for budget gourmet mesclun to get you started.

> 1 seed packet 'Très Fine' curly endive
> 2 seed packets 'Salad Bowl' lettuce
> 1 seed packet 'Red Oak Leaf' lettuce
> 1 seed packet 'Rouge d'Hiver' lettuce
> 1 seed packet arugula

If you decide to deviate from the above recipe and come up with your own, keep these points in mind.

- Use annual greens that have about the same maturation date (check the seed packet).
- Go for a combination of colors—a little red lettuce helps.
- Try to include at least one bitter green and one mild green for a contrast of flavors.

Solutions at a Glance

PROBLEM: Something's eating your newly planted seedlings.

CULPRIT: Birds, particularly crows

SOLVE IT! After planting the seeds and covering them with a little soil, cover the planting area with about 1 inch of dried grass clippings before watering, says Al Bridgers of Maryville, Tennessee. Besides discouraging birds, the clippings also prevent the seeds from washing away and keep them moist.

- For the most interesting mesclun, also go for a variety of shapes, such as a feathery endive with an aptly named oak leaf lettuce.

DON'T FORGET TO REMEMBER

If you're a seed saver, keeping track of when you bought those old packages of seed can be a problem. A simple trick is to jot down the year purchased on the outside of the seed packet in permanent marker. No more guessing how old those seeds might be!

DESIGNER SEED PACKETS

Baby food jars and camera film canisters make fine containers for seeds you've saved from a package or collected in your own garden. But these seed storers tend to take up space.

You can make your own space-saving seed packet with wax paper and tape. Simply fold the paper over, tape both sides, and create a flap. Then tape the flap down, and lift and reseal it as needed. Label the packet with a marker or cut out and tape the seed catalog or seed packet photo and description on your new waxed paper packet.

USE TAPE AND WAX PAPER TO CREATE A CONVENIENT SEED PACKET.

MOIST MIX

Before filling your seed-starting containers, you always need to wet the soil mix. But commercial soil mixes can be difficult to wet thoroughly. To make sure your mix is moist throughout, put it in a plastic bucket or basin, add a bit of warm water, and stir. Keep adding water until the mix is evenly moist. You'll know the mix is evenly moist if you squeeze a handful tightly and only a few drops of water ooze out. (If the mix is too wet, add more dry mix.)

THE BIG CHILL

Make your spring plantings a success by following these tips when direct seeding in cold weather.

- Choose cold-resistant varieties whenever you can.
- Pre-sprout seeds. Layer the seeds in a damp paper towel until tiny sprouts emerge, then plant them.
- Plant on a south slope or in an area that collects warmth from a nearby brick or stone wall or light-colored building.
- Plant in well-drained humus-rich soil, which warms more quickly than heavier soils.
- Use tunnels and row covers to protect your plantings and to collect heat.
- Cover the seeds with compost. Research shows that having fertilizer immediately available during cold spring plantings boosts yields in the long run.

Shade

Do most of your garden beds happen to fall where the sun doesn't shine? Or is your once sunny garden getting shadier and shadier with each passing day? If so, you aren't alone. Marilyn Dube, owner of Natural Design Plants in Portland, Oregon, says that in terms of her sales, "Shade plants represent a larger piece of the pie every year." Whether your sunlight is disappearing behind your own growing trees or new houses are rising around you, don't throw in the towel. You *can* have luscious beds—you just need to work with the shade. Here's the lowdown on analyzing shade, fighting shade pests, and brightening those shady spots.

THE MANY SHADES OF SHADE

Shade isn't an absolute like a pH number or a mark on the thermometer that you can measure quickly and easily. Before you set out to replace sun-loving plants that are languishing in shade, find out how much shade you have, when you have it, and where it's coming from. Knowing those shade factors is important because different plants thrive in different types of shade.

Vicki Webster, who has gardened for many years behind high brick walls in Boston, recommends making a drawing of your garden and its immediate surroundings. It needn't be a work of art—a rough sketch will do fine—but be sure to include the following items:

- All sources of shade (such as your neighbor's giant spruce tree, a lattice-topped fence, the walls of your house, and the roof of your garage).
- Circumstances that could alter the light level in the near future (for instance, young trees that will block more light as time goes on, a diseased street tree you know is destined for removal, a house under construction next door).
- Conditions you can change if you want to (such as trees or shrubs you could remove or prune, or a solid fence you could replace with lattice panels).
- For a full day (about every 30 minutes), track the sun's light as it travels across your garden from dawn until dark. It is important to note on your sketch the times the sun's

light enters and leaves each planting area and established bed.

- Repeat the above tip at each of the next three seasons.

Capture your shade on paper to find out how much, when, and where you have it. Knowing these things will help you decide which types of shade-loving plants will do best in your shady spots.

Analyzing Your Shade

Armed with your raw data from your four seasonal sketches, you'll be able to tell which kind of shade you have in which places and at what times—you're bound to have at least a couple of types (unless your garden is entirely in the shadow of a neighboring building). Here are the basic types.

DENSE SHADE is cast by north-facing walls or fences, or by the low, dense branches of evergreen trees. Your plant choices here will be limited. Says Marilyn Dube, owner of Natural Design Plants in Portland, Oregon, "Depending on how much reflected light you get, you're probably better off with hardscaping—attractive pavers or bricks, with a shade-tolerant vine, such as climbing hydrangea, dutchman's pipe, or trumpet honeysuckle on a fence."

DAPPLED SHADE comes from large-leaved trees like maples (*Acer* spp.) or oaks (*Quercus* spp.). They block the sun but still allow light to enter the site. Your plant palate is a little broader here. Many ferns and hostas will grow well in dappled shade, as will early-blooming wildflowers and spring bulbs.

BRIGHT LIGHT in a garden sense means that no direct sun reaches the site, but nothing blocks the sky. It's a situation common in city gardens, or on the north sides of houses. Many plants, including rhododendrons, camellias, and other broad-leaved evergreens, thrive in bright light, as do ferns, lungwort (*Pulmonaria saccharata*), and violets.

FILTERED LIGHT drifts through the small leaves of trees such as birches (*Betula* spp.) or laburnums (*Laburnum* spp.) or through openings in a lath-covered arbor. This is what many plant catalogs *really* mean by shade. Plants such as hostas, bleeding hearts (*Dicentra spectabilis*), and goat's beards (*Aruncus dioicus*) do well in filtered light.

PARTIAL SHADE, also referred to as part shade or part sun, means a site gets direct sun for part of the day—as few as 2 hours or as many as 5. (Usually a site that gets direct sun for 6 or more hours a day is described as being in "full sun.") Partial shade is the trickiest kind to work with but it's also the most fun to experiment with because the effect of sunlight on plants depends not only on how long it lasts but also how intense it is—and that varies depending on the season, the time of day it arrives, and the part of the country you live in. Some plants that do well in partial shade include columbines (*Aquilegia spp.*), foxgloves (*Digitalis spp.*), and coral bells (*Heuchera sanguinea*).

FOR PLANTS THAT NEED FILTERED LIGHT, SUCH AS BLEEDING HEARTS, AN ARBOR OR PERGOLA PROVIDES THE RIGHT CONDITIONS.

FEATHERY SEEDLING PROTECTION

Even up north, a freshly sown bed can benefit from some shade, and a few fern fronds snipped from your garden can be the perfect thing for creating instant shade. That's how Sunia Yang protects delicate seedlings in her Menlo Park, California, garden: "Cut a fresh fern frond and stick it in the ground so it shades the area you've just sown. As the seeds germinate, grow, and need more sun, the frond dies back and lets in more light." This method works best, she says, with something light and feathery, like brackens (*Pteridium* spp.) or wood ferns (*Dryopteris* spp.), rather than heavier sword ferns (*Nephrolepis* spp.).

GETTING THE SHADY STORY

Just moved to a different part of the country and not sure what shade is really like on your new landscape? Take a tip from Rosalia Kung, who currently hails from Skillman, New Jersey, but who has planned gardens from scratch and has given new life to old ones in many a state: Start a newcomers' garden group, as she did when she first moved to Shaker Heights, Ohio. "The group was very informal," she says. "We'd gather every week or so in one of our gardens—bag lunches in hand—and talk about our problems and what we wanted to accomplish. We'd exchange plants. We'd walk through our neighborhoods, look at the gardens, study the light levels, and see what plants were doing best." Since then she's made a habit of rallying newly transplanted gardeners. "The group is a wonderful extension of friendship," she says, "and it's a great problem solver."

FABULOUS FOLIAGE

If you can't adjust the light conditions in your garden (that is, you have to live with shade), the one thing you can do is adjust your vision for your garden. Instead of pining for ornamentals with lots of blooms, turn your thoughts to foliage.

A well-planned foliage garden can have a dramatic impact without the need for flowers. Make the best of leaves—they come in all colors, sizes, shapes, and textures. Use bold leaves as focal points, brightly colored leaves for dramatic effect, silver and variegated leaves to brighten a dull spot, and fine-textured leaves such as ferns for the background.

FIGHTING THE SLUG WARS

Without a doubt the most dreaded denizen of moist shade is the slug, and its close cousin the snail. In the Pacific Northwest—which, to hear the locals tell it, ranks as the moist shade capital of the world—keeping the slimy pests at bay takes on all the attributes of trench warfare. Here's how some otherwise peaceful gardeners do battle with the arch villains.

- "I mulch with seaweed. Something about it—probably the salt content—keeps them away, though it isn't high enough to damage the plants," says Jack Talerico, from Vashon Island, Washington.
- "I went to a salvage yard and bought enough copper radiator strips to make a border around my whole shade garden. They don't climb over it," says Penny Grist, also from Vashon Island.
- Connie Kiener of Portland, Oregon, comments that slugs and snails "make me so mad I go out at night and chop them in half with a sharp scissors."
- Jane Anders of Portland, Oregon, picks slugs up and drops them into a bag of salt, and Susan LeMaster of Portland notes, "I feed them to my turtle, Mister Big. He considers them a great delicacy."
- "The slugs I whack with my Japanese knife," says Judy Davison of Seattle. "The snails—I have so many snails I could raise escargot—I pick up and throw over the back fence.

They make a satisfying plunk when they hit the pavement in the alley, and I've developed a terrific hook shot."

PUBLIC ENEMY NUMBER 2

Aside from slugs and snails, the critter that most plagues shade plants is the black vine weevil, also known as the taxus weevil because the choicest items on its menu are plants of the genus *Taxus* (known commonly as yews). The adult weevils chew the edges of leaves, which causes merely cosmetic damage, but their eggs hatch into grubs which in turn tunnel into the soil and eat the roots of whatever plants they encounter—in many cases with fatal results. Your treatment options are as follows:

- Trap adult weevils by wrapping double-faced tape around the base of the trunks of your yews or—if you aren't squeamish about scurrying bugs—wrap a piece of cloth loosely around the trunk. The weevils will duck under it for shelter during the day. At dusk, remove the cloth and shake it over a bucket of soapy water.
- Wipe out weevils by encouraging their natural predators: birds, beneficial nematodes, ground beetles, and spiders. (The best way to encourage natural predators is to avoid using pesticides. You can also attract birds by erecting bird houses for them; beneficial nematodes will automatically appear if you keep your soil well laced with compost.)
- Dig up any plants that are too far gone to save and destroy them.

Prevention is simple. Weevils and their grubby offspring thrive in dead plant debris, so *Taxus* devotee Rosalia Kung of Skillman, New Jersey, says, "Just keep everything clean." She has an easy, tidy-as-you-go approach: "I carry a plastic bin with me all the time, lined with a trash bag. That way I can set the bin on the ground and use both hands to toss in litter. It's faster than using a wheelbarrow," Kung says, "because you have to handle the stuff only once."

KEEP BLACK VINE WEEVILS FROM HELPING THEMSELVES TO YOUR SHADE PLANTS BY ENCOURAGING PREDATORS SUCH AS GROUND BEETLES.

DRY SHADE

One of the most problematic conditions for gardeners is a dry, shady spot. But some plants will grow even in this difficult site. Here's a list of perennial plants that will at least tolerate dry shade:

Fairy bells (*Disporum* spp.)
Lenten rose (*Helleborus orientalis*)
Hostas (*Hosta* spp.)
Solomon's seal (*Polygonatum odoratum*)
Christmas fern (*Polystichum acrostichoides*)
Candy tuft (*Iberis saxatilis* (candytuft)
Crested iris (*Iris cristata*)
Canada columbine (*Aquilegia canadensis*)

LETTING LIGHT IN

If the source of your problem shade is the tall building across the street or your neighbor's treasured fir trees, you have little choice but to plant shade-loving plants. Oftentimes, though, you *can* shed more light on the scene simply. Topping trees is tree abuse, says Marilyn Dube, owner of Natural Plant Designs in Portland, Oregon, so here are some other ways to lighten up.

- Increase reflected light by painting walls white or installing mirrors in strategic spots.
- Insert lattice panels into solid fences.
- Replace solid overhangs or porch roofs with lattice or panels of clear fiberglass.

A PATIO WITH A LATTICE ROOF CAN HELP YOU LET IN MORE LIGHT TO A SHADY AREA THAN A PATIO WITH A SOLID ROOF CAN.

Slugs and Snails

Ugh—a slug. Or a snail. Slimy with a penchant for popping up every time you lift a stone or pot, slugs and snails also do real damage to many a broad-leaved plant. Telltale signs are small holes and tears throughout the leaf where these little critters have dined in style.

You *can* outsmart slugs and snails, though, without resorting to beds filled with plastic plants. All it takes is a little resourcefulness—such as changing the time of day you water your plants.

SLUG MOTEL

Here's how to create a "slug motel" where slugs and snails can check in but they can't check out, courtesy of Marianne Binetti, a garden columnist and writer in Enumclaw, Washington. Cut the top off an empty, clean, small (not 2-liter) plastic soda bottle right where it begins to taper inward. Put slug and snail bait (such as beer, or a solution of 1 teaspoon dry yeast dissolved in ¼ cup of water) in the bottle and firmly insert the cut-off portion upside down. Place the bottle on its side in your garden among your hostas and other slug-prone plantings. Change the bait every few days or as needed when you empty out the slugs and snails.

For a more elegant, Stone Age version of the slug motel—and one that naturally attracts snails and slugs—arrange four small rocks in a square and top with a larger, flat stone. Put the bait underneath in an empty, small cat food can; the moisture that collects under the stone will make the motel even more inviting for slugs and snails. (Again, remove the bait every few days and replace it with fresh bait.)

SLUGS CAN CHECK IN BUT THEY CAN'T CHECK OUT OF THIS SODA BOTTLE SLUG MOTEL.

DON'T HAVE A SODA BOTTLE? ALL YOU NEED IS FIVE STONES TO CREATE A STONE AGE VERSION OF THE SLUG MOTEL.

Avoiding Slugs and Snails

Need some easy solutions for minimizing the slug problem in your garden? Here are six to get you started.

DON'T OVERWATER. Slugs love moisture. The wetter the soil, the happier they'll be.

MULCH SPARSELY. Particularly in problem areas, use compost as your mulch or no mulch at all. Slugs and snails love to hide under thick layers of wood chips and such.

MOVE SLUG-RIDDLED PLANTS INTO THE SUN WHEN PRACTICAL. The more sun and less moisture, the less slugs are likely to bother a plant.

PINCH OFF LOWER LEAVES WHEN PRACTICAL. Leaves dragging on the soil are an invitation for slugs and snails to climb on. If the growth habit of your plant makes it feasible, allow as few leaves as possible to touch the ground.

INSTALL COPPER STRIPS. Available at most garden centers, you can put these strips around prized plants. Slugs dislike the copper and the strips' sharp edges. Follow installation instructions exactly.

GET RID OF PLANTS THAT SLUGS DECIMATE EVERY YEAR. Or seek out cultivars of those plants that are less prone to slug damage. Some hosta cultivars, for example, are less tempting to slugs and snails than others.

Outsmart Slimy Slugs

"If you water in the morning instead of the evening, you can reduce your slug damage by up to 80 percent," says Cheryl Long, senior editor at *Organic Gardening* magazine. "One study found that with lettuce, morning watering reduced slug damage just as well as using slug baits. Morning watering lets the soil dry out during the day, so the moisture-loving slugs can't feed as much when they come out at night," she says.

Handle with Care

Avoid touching those icky slugs and snails when you're picking them off plants by using a pair of long, scissor-handled tweezers—technically called hemostats. They give a firm grip without the gross-out. (You can buy hemostats at a drugstore or medical supply store.)

USE LONG-HANDLED TWEEZERS TO GET A GRIP ON SLIMY SLUGS.

Copper Cut-Off

You've built raised beds, hoping the height factor will deter slugs, but yet they still find their way in to dine. Don't worry, all isn't lost. Deter them by rimming your beds with copper. Simply cut a sheet of copper into strips (or purchase strips at your local garden center) about 3 inches wide. Nail the strips to the inside of the raised bed, then make notches using metal (tin) snips about every $3/4$ inch or so along the top of the strips. Fold the notches outward with pliers, and you'll have a slug-proof barrier.

FOIL SLUGS BY REINFORCING RAISED BEDS WITH COPPER STRIPS.

THEY LIKE SLUGS

Encouraging natural slug predators to your garden is one way to keep these slimers in check. Downy woodpeckers, robins, and other garden birds are happy to bite into a nice juicy slug. Other slug enemies include garter snakes, grass snakes, salamanders, shrews, toads, and turtles. To encourage predators to work in your favor, provide plenty of water sources and places for predators to hide in your garden. (And keep Kitty and Fido inside.)

AN OUNCE OF PREVENTION

Slugs and snails will arrive in your garden in early spring. Monitoring for the first arrivals is time well spent—eliminating the first slugs and snails of the season will prevent future generations. So set out your beer traps early and check them often whether or not you've actually seen any problems.

When falls arrives, take action to prevent slugs and snails from spending the cold months in your garden. Removing boards, rocks, clippings, and other debris will deny slugs and snails a ready shelter for the winter. And keep a sharp eye out for egg clusters.

Soil Problems

Just as no one is ever happy with their weight, no one, it seems, is ever happy with their soil. It's either too full of clay or of sand, too acid or too sweet, too rocky or too riddled with hardpan. But, just like those extra pounds, bad soil can become a thing of the past. With some ingenuity and a few labor-saving tricks, you can have the black, loamy stuff all gardeners dream about.

CREATE A TRUDI PIT

Chicago-area gardener Trudi Temple has come up with an innovative method of getting rid of garden waste and enriching the soil without ever spending time turning a heap. Instead of building a compost pile, Temple digs a hole in an inconspicuous spot in her garden. The hole might be as small as 1 × 1 foot or as large as 5 × 5 feet. "It depends if I just do a little bit of weeding and how much space I have," Temple says. "Sometimes I do dig the hole right be-tween two perennials and even take a little of their roots off. It doesn't hurt the plants at all."

Temple puts weeds, trimmed plant parts, cardboard boxes, and whatever organic matter she finds during her gardening chores into the hole. Then she puts 5 to 6 inches of soil on top of the hole to speed decomposition, and puts a stepping stone on top of the soil to mark the spot. After 6 months to a year, the site is ready to be planted.

CREATE A NO-TURN COMPOST PILE BY USING A PIT THAT DOES ALL THE WORK FOR YOU.

Solutions at a Glance

PROBLEM: Lavender, rosemary, thyme, oregano, and other Mediterranean-type plants don't do well in your climate.

CULPRIT: Your soil is too rich. These are plants that like lean, rocky, soil and hot, dry conditions. Too much moisture and nutrients in the soil lead to fungal problems and poor flavor or fragrance.

SOLVE IT! Create a "bad soil" bed. First, dig a pit, preferably next to a driveway or sidewalk that gets baked by the sun much of the day. Excellent drainage is a must, so a slight slope is ideal. Then fill the bottom of the pit with crushed rock or broken bricks. Next, fill the top foot or so with soil that is 4 parts garden loam, 1 part sand, 1 part perlite, and 1 part vermiculite. For good measure, arrange various stones or rocks on the soil surface to further re-create the warmth-drenched Mediterranean climate.

PLOW IT UNDER

Building a new bed? Don't worry too much about getting rid of that sod, says Gloria Seborg of Seattle, Washington. She just tills

hers under, figuring it adds important organic matter to the soil.

First, Seborg tills the area she wants to plant. Then she spreads any soil amendments and tills again, which chops the sod more finely. As she rakes the bed smooth with a ground rake, she tosses out any remaining chunks of sod she might find.

The first year after tilling the sod under she has to be diligent in weeding any grass that crops up. But weeding is much less work, Seborg says, than the traditional method of first cutting or digging off all that sod.

TOPSOIL TRIBULATIONS

If you're thinking about buying some topsoil, take care not to get dumped on, warns Alvin Cruise, an avid gardener in Tulsa, Oklahoma. Too often, what is billed as topsoil might be of poor quality, laden with sand or clay, and filled with debris. Cruise recommends that you be present when the topsoil is delivered to your home so you can inspect it before a ton or two is dumped on the driveway. Another alternative is to inspect the soil beforehand. "You really need to check out the source because what would be one person's good soil isn't necessarily a gardener's good soil," Cruise says.

RAIN DRAIN

Living on Bainbridge Island near Seattle, Shelly Johansson knows that flowerbeds need good drainage. But as a garden designer, she often encounters the worst soil, laying on top of hardpan a foot or so down, which obviously isn't conducive to good drainage.

When she's presented a problem site like that, Johansson creates drainage from the flowerbed by digging a trench along the bed's lowest part, where water would naturally collect. She then lays a length of perforated drainage pipe into the trench, making sure the pipe taps off onto a driveway or other good drainage area. She covers the pipe with gravel or rock, and it provides excellent drainage even in the wettest weather.

ENSURE GOOD DRAINAGE IN PROBLEM SITES BY INSTALLING A DRAINAGE PIPE.

A Forkful of Air

Try this fast, easy way to aerate small areas of soil—those places where you step down from a deck, the area along a driveway, or the place where kids cut across a lawn.

After a good rain, when the ground is moist but not wet, plunge a spading fork 3 to 6 inches into the soil. Rock the fork back and forth a couple of times to widen the holes and then repeat in other areas as needed.

Leafy Soil Amendment

You don't have to spend time bagging all those fall leaves—or even raking them up and hauling them to your compost heap. Instead, just throw them right on top of your beds, where they'll add valuable humus and leaf mold to the soil, absolute candy for beneficial earthworms.

Rae Haws of Ames, Iowa, has incorporated fall leaves into her abundant vegetable garden for several years and says the most efficient way to do it is to first mow over the leaves with the lawn mower or chop them with a chipper/shredder. Then spread them over the vegetable garden and till them in. If you don't have a tiller, you could simply toss spadesful of soil on top of the leaves to keep them from blowing and to speed decomposition.

Easy-on-the-Back Beds

Digging new beds takes time—and can take a toll on your back. So instead of digging, create new beds by simply layering materials in three easy steps. You can build a huge bed in less than an hour—and your back will feel great when you're done! Here's how.

1. As long as the soil is reasonably good and the area isn't badly infested with tall, highly invasive weeds, simply spread three or four layers of newspaper on top of the area where the new bed will be. Wet the newspapers down to prevent blowing and speed decomposition.

2. Spread on any soil amendments you wish to use, such as sand or sphagnum peat moss. Then add good-quality topsoil, compost, or better yet a mixture of the two. (It doesn't even matter if the compost is only half-rotted. Just be sure you mix it in thoroughly.) In all, the new bed should be 2 to 8 inches high (it will settle over time).

3. Plant! Waiting 4 to 6 weeks or over the winter is ideal, but you can also plant immediately if you need to.

SAVE TIME AND BACK PAIN WITH THIS BED THAT TAKES JUST LESS THAN AN HOUR TO CREATE.

SEASONAL SOIL IMPROVER

Improving bad soil isn't as difficult as you might think. You just need to have patience. Here's a season-by-season approach to turning your soil into stuff beds are made of.

PROBLEM: You're missing out on valuable planting space.

CULPRIT: A stump right in the middle of your flowerbed or garden. You've tried to dig it up but can't.

SOLVE IT! Plunk a bird bath basin on the stump and suddenly you have a rustic focal point to plant around.

FALL. Dig the bed. Plant a cover crop, such as annual rye (*Lolium multiflorum*). The roots help break up the soil, as does the freezing and thawing of winter and early spring.

SPRING. Till in the rye, which adds important organic matter. Then plant annuals only. Go for plants with well-developed root systems, such as tall marigolds and sunflowers; their roots further break up the soil.

SUMMER. Mulch the annuals with compost about 3 inches thick. By the end of the season, you'll have vastly improved soil in which you can plant just about anything you want.

Squash and Melon Problems

Squash and melons, being members of the same family, have similar growing habits. And if you've ever grown zucchini, you know they can be really easy to grow and grow and grow. . . .

But a surprising number of home gardeners don't grow beyond zukes. Too many problems, they say. Too many squash bugs on the summer squash. Too many wilted vines! Too hard to grow melons, and even harder to know when they're ripe. But these great tips and problem solvers will squash your fears in no time!

Rx for Healthy Squash

Squash expert Dr. Richard Robinson, vegetable breeder at the New York State Agricultural Experiment Station, Cornell University, in Geneva, New York, recommends the following tips. Remember: An ounce of prevention and preparation may, indeed, bring you a pound of great little patty pan squash.

USE PLENTY OF ORGANIC MATTER. Squash don't like a starvation diet, so make sure there's plenty of humus in your garden bed.

HEAT THINGS UP. Use black plastic to warm the soil. Remember to prepare your ground with the organic matter and lay the plastic before you plant out seeds or transplants.

GIVE 'EM SHELTER. Plastic tunnels with wire hoops covered with row cover can get squash off to a bit of an earlier start, plus the cover keeps pest bugs at bay.

CHOOSE DISEASE-RESISTANT VARIETIES. These are some of your best defenses against perennial squash pests. (See "Holy Disease Resistance!" on page 150.)

MAKE 'EM FEEL AT HOME. Start seeds indoors, 2 to 3 weeks before the last predicted frost. (Squash seeds are so large that they'll quickly grow out of their pots, so bear that in mind when you sprout seeds.) Or direct seed them outdoors when the ground is warm (at least 70°F).

KEEP THEIR FEET DRY. Whether you use a row system or a "hill" system (a grouping of five or six seeds together in a raised section of garden soil), make sure you have good drainage. "Drip irrigation is a help," Robinson says, adding that with raised beds or hill systems it's especially important to watch moisture during dry days because the hills dry out quickly. "I personally like to have the seeds evenly spaced, rather than grouping several in one spot," he adds. (And if crows are a problem in your garden, hills are usually too convenient a stop, so make marauding harder on the black birds and plant seeds individually.)

PICK 'EM SMALL. It'll send the plant a signal to keep producing fruit. And that means more squash for you!

IF YOU DECIDE TO GROW YOUR SQUASH USING THE HILL SYSTEM, MAKE SURE TO WATER REGULARLY BECAUSE THE HILLS DRY OUT QUICKLY.

STARVE OUT THE ENEMY. If squash bugs seem to be everywhere at the end of the growing season, your best strategy may be to deny them their favorite food the following year. Substitute another crop for squash — potatoes, for example. In the third year, skip the potatoes, but plant the squash. You should find that the squash bug population has decreased.

HOLY DISEASE RESISTANCE!

If you're looking for a disease-resistant squash, 'Whitaker' is a godsend for the organic gardener. It's the only squash variety resistant to four of the most devastating diseases faced by the home gardener, especially in the Northeast: powdery mildew, zucchini yellow mosaic virus, cucumber mosaic virus, and papaya ring spot virus.

"This disease resistance, especially to powdery mildew, makes 'Whitaker' very useful to the organic grower," says Dr. Richard Robinson, vegetable breeder at the New York State Agricultural Experiment Station, Cornell University, in Geneva, New York, who developed the squash variety with research support specialist Joseph Shail and virologist Rosario Provvidenti. Robinson notes that the variety is open-pollinated and will set fruit even if it isn't pollinated. That makes it a natural for growing in low plastic row tunnels or hoop houses.

'Whitaker' resembles an Italian Cocozelle-type squash in character and taste. It has medium green fruit that's straight, with blocky ends and dark green stripes. The white flesh is firm, and the compact bush plants are erect and tend to hold the fruit up off the ground.

WHEN IT COMES TO SQUASH, 'WHITAKER' WINS THE PRIZE FOR DISEASE RESISTANCE—ESPECIALLY AGAINST POWDERY MILDEW.

Rx for Healthy Melons

Dave Wolverton grows killer melons, even though he lives in Arlee, Montana—a beautiful valley surrounded by high mountains that cause tremendous variation in temperatures, even in August, the crucial month for melon maturity. Wolverton also has to work around a short growing season. So how *does* he do it? Here are his tips for raising incredible melons, against all odds.

DON'T RUSH TO START YOUR SEEDS. Wolverton starts his indoors May 1 because melons don't need a lot of lead time. But, especially for a short season, starting seeds indoors is an absolute must, he says.

HEAT IS CRITICAL FOR A HEALTHY START. "I place seeds on the surface of moist vermiculite inside a covered plastic tray, then place the tray where the temperature stays in the 80s," Wolverton says. The living room of his parents'

home next door works great for him. Heat mats will also work.

LET SEEDLINGS LIE. As the seeds sprout, Wolverton transfers them to Paperpots (30-pot size for melons, available through mail-order suppliers) with two or three sprouted seeds to a pot. (The paper stretches out to form a honeycomb design, which he fills with planting mix.) At planting time, the paper separates into individual pots that can be carefully removed, which is important because melons don't like their roots to be disturbed.

PREPARE THE PLANTING AREA. Wolverton incorporates compost and fish meal (about 3 pounds per 100 square feet) into the area that will become home to his melons. He spaces rows 9 feet apart, mounds rows about 6 inches higher than the surface of the bed, and positions drip irrigation. Then he lays black plastic over the mounded rows.

GET 'EM IN THE GROUND. Wolverton plants one Paperpot of two or three seedlings every 5 feet. Smaller varieties can be spaced $2\frac{1}{2}$ feet apart in rows 6 feet apart. He covers his seedlings with row covers to create a warmer microclimate. (In other parts of the country, he notes, the covers may be more important for helping fight insect pests.) He pulls the covers back around July 1, but leaves them near the melon plants in case quick cover is needed on a cold night.

SPRAY, SPRAY, SPRAY—NATURALLY. Of course we aren't talking harmful chemicals here! Wolverton says the plants respond very well to fish fertilizer sprays, seaweed sprays, and a twice-a-season baking soda and water spray, which keeps mildew at bay. "Spray the leaves with 1 tablespoon of baking soda mixed with a

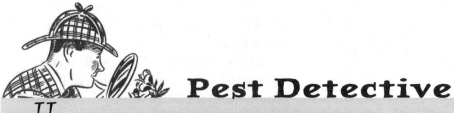

Pest Detective

Having a problem with your squash or melons? Here are some of the most common pests and ailments—and the best organic solutions for dealing with them.

Symptom	Cause	What to Do
Holes chewed in leaves	Cucumber beetles	Use row covers until flowers open. Try planting later in the season to avoid this spring pest, and set out yellow pans with soapy water to trap beetles once they arrive.
Leaves and fruit with mottled spots, and stunted growth	Mosaic viruses	Use resistant cultivars and don't touch wet plants, to avoid spreading the disease. Control sucking insects such as aphids by knocking them off plants with a strong spray of water. Use floating row covers to protect the plants, and remove and destroy virus-infected plants immediately.
Wilted leaves with pale blotches, blackened shoots	Squash bugs	Hand-pick these gray-brown, oval bugs. You can lay boards on the soil near the plant at night, lift the boards up in the morning, and pick and destroy bugs off the board daily. Religiously clearing plant waste at the end of the season can prevent recurrence.
Vines that suddenly wilt and die, and orange sawdustlike droppings at base of the plant	Vine borers	Plant resistant cultivars, such as 'Butternut' winter squash. Use floating row covers until blossom. Then use preventive methods, such as wrapping the base of the vine in aluminum foil, spraying with garlic or hot pepper solution, or wiping the vine base often. If you spot a borer in a vine, slit the vine, remove the borer, and mound soil over the cut portion of the vine. Or you can inject BT (*Bacillus thuringiensis*) into the vine with a syringe if you notice borer symptoms.
White powdery coating on leaves, and plant dies	Powdery mildew	Choose resistant cultivars such as the melons 'Sweet' and 'Edisto 47', allow good air circulation, and remove and destroy affected vines. To control the disease and prevent recurrence, spray weekly with 1 tablespoon of baking soda and $2\frac{1}{2}$ teaspoons of summer oil mixed with 1 gallon of water. Plant squash and melon varieties (such as 'Redlands Trailblazer' winter squash) that are resistant to cucumber mosaic virus and other viral diseases that cucumber beetles transmit.

gallon of water around July 25 and again around August 15. This is all the more important in my marginal climate, where leaf disorders are likely to occur," he says. One caution, though: "The fish fertilizer spray needs to be timed so as not to offend visitors; it smells horrible," he says.

VARIETY SELECTION IS IMPORTANT. His favorite watermelon is 'Lucky Sweet'; 'Earlidew', his favorite melon. He's also experimenting with long-keepers, with hopes of extending the growing season.

FOLLOW THE WASP RULE. "For the muskmelon types that slip easily from the stem when they're ripe, the 'wasp rule' is useful: One wasp sipping nectar where the stem meets the fruit means leave it another day or two. Two wasps sipping nectar means you may pick it now. Three wasps on the stem means pick it immediately—but watch out for the wasps!" he explains.

FOLLOW THE WATERMELON RULE. Wolverton's watermelon rule is that when the underside touching the ground turns a rich, golden yellow, it's ready. Also, the tendril closest to the melon dries up fully. (Wolverton prefers these tests to the traditional thumping test—where you thunk a melon with your finger and listen for a hollow "ripe" sound—because that takes a lot of skill and different varieties thump differently.)

WHEN THE UNDERSIDE OF YOUR WATERMELON TURNS A RICH YELLOW, THE MELON IS READY TO MEET YOUR TASTE BUDS.

PROP 'EM UP. Melon fruits can rot in the field even before they ripen. To prevent this from happening, raise them up on overturned cans or plastic containers to keep them dry and intact.

Squirrel
Problems

Squirrels are fun to watch when they're harmlessly gathering acorns in fall. But as anyone with a bird feeder and garden can attest, squirrels can be stubborn and downright gluttonous. They've also been known to dig up bulbs, corms, and newly sown seed—as well as dine on tomatoes and other soft fruit. And 9 times out of 10, they'll find a way to your birdfeeder—in spite of any high-tech squirrel-thwarting contraption you've installed! But you can keep peace in the garden. Read on for some tips to help you outsmart these persistent pests.

FENCE TACTICS FOR SQUIRRELS

Squirrels are good climbers, and that means that nice, sturdy wire fences that deter rabbits or groundhogs may not faze the them. They may just skip the fence entirely, climb a post, and hop right over. But one way to deter climbing squirrels is to use chicken wire

fencing, leaving a floppy roll of wire (about a foot) at the top, to act as a baffle. That way, as a squirrel climbs the fence, the fence flops backward and Mr. Squirrel won't be able to make the hop over: humans, 1; squirrels, 0!

SQUIRREL-BE-GONE

If it seems like nothing in your yard can be kept safe from squirrels, you might want to try one of the chemical-free commercial products available to help keep squirrels away. In fact, Squirrel Away can be found at most major discount stores and garden centers. It's an all-natural formula that uses powdered capsicum pepper, which is distasteful and harmlessly irritating to squirrels, and which provides birds with a good source of Vitamin A—talk about a win-win situation! You can sprinkle Squirrel Away in bird food, over rows of bulbs, or around tender seedlings.

Also available is N.I.M.B.Y., an emulsion of natural oils designed to help keep squirrels, chipmunks, rabbits, and deer away from precious plants and other areas (see "Resources" on page 196). You can also find organic pepper spray deterrents at garden-supply companies and nursery centers, or you can even try whipping up a batch at home (see "Cabbage Problems" on page 21).

HAVE A DRINK ON ME

A Springfield, Virginia, gardener had a problem with squirrels chewing her tomatoes. But this observant gardener also noticed that this usually happened when there wasn't much water around. So she positioned several birdbaths around the garden and yard, and lo and behold, the squirrels left her tomatoes alone. (But alas, they still ate the bird feed.)

PROVIDE PLENTY OF WATER SOURCES AROUND YOUR GARDEN SO THAT SQUIRRELS WILL BE ABLE TO QUENCH THEIR THIRST WITHOUT HAVING TO NIBBLE ON YOUR TOMATOES.

Solutions at a Glance

PROBLEM: Something's eating your just-planted bulbs and seeds.

CULPRIT: Squirrels

SOLVE IT! Put wire screening or hardware cloth over the soil where you've planted bulbs and seeds to deter squirrels from digging.

THE FELINE FACTOR

It doesn't take a rocket scientist to figure out that squirrels and cats don't get along. To trick squirrels into thinking a hungry cat is lurking near your flowerbeds, apply a light sprinkling of used cat litter around the base of your tulip bulbs (don't use the litter in your vegetable or herb gardens, though).

Ticks

After a day of working in your yard or garden, you might come in to find one of these unwelcome guests—ticks—attached to your skin or clothes. Besides being nasty (they're blood suckers) and just plain ugly, some ticks can carry blood-borne diseases (such as Lyme disease and Rocky Mountain spotted fever, both serious threats to your health). But before you start thinking about hiding indoors all summer, read on for ways to prevent ticks from getting the better of you.

TICKS ARE SUCH A DRAG

According to Stan G. Green, Ph.D., an urban entomologist with the Pennsylvania State Extension Service, based in Philadelphia, dragging tall vegetation growing on the edge of your property is a great way to check on tick populations. It won't help you wipe out ticks if your property is teeming with them, but it will give you a good idea of whether you're dealing with a small army of ticks or just a handful.

You can create a drag from a piece of smooth cotton cloth or an old sheet—use a piece as large as you can comfortably handle. Staple the edge of the cloth or sheet to a piece of wood that's about 1 inch wide (and the length of the sheet). Then tie a piece of string to the wood. Hold on to the string, and pull the drag around the edge of your property. As you pull the drag over your turf, any ticks hanging out in the tall grass or weeds will attach themselves to the sheet. (Just make sure you wear long sleeves and pants while dragging, or you may end up with a few ticks on yourself.)

When you're finished, dispose of any ticks on the drag, or put them in glass jars with tight-fitting lids so they can be analyzed, especially if you live in an area with a high incidence of Lyme disease. (If you find a lot of ticks covering the drag, you should drag daily until you end up with fewer ticks. To keep tick numbers low, drag every 2 weeks throughout spring and summer.)

CHECK ON THE TICK POPULATION ON YOUR PROPERTY BY TURNING AN OLD SHEET INTO A TICK DRAG.

DON'T HOLD AN OPEN HOUSE FOR TICKS

Has your yard become a haven for ticks? Here are a couple of easy tricks that take in the welcome mat on these blood-thirsty critters.

Start by keeping your yard neat. By eliminating brush and leaf piles, you'll eliminate some prime hiding spots for ticks. Woodpiles should be kept off the ground, too, so that mice—another favorite tick host—don't set up housing there.

You could also consider giving your lawn a crew cut, advises Stan G. Green, Ph.D., an urban entomologist with the Pennsylvania State Extension Service, based in Philadelphia. Tick larvae, which usually aren't carriers of the disease, need moisture to survive. By cropping your lawn shorter than 6 inches, the sun can dry out the larvae and kill them off. And while this won't cure a tick problem, it will definitely cut down on tick populations, Green says.

Keep one thing in mind, though: Short lawns aren't happy, healthy lawns, so if you're going to try this tactic, target spring and early summer to best get at the larval cycle, and then let your lawn grow longer for the rest of the season. (There's no point trying this later in the season, anyway; once tick youngsters grow up, they're able to take the heat.)

Solutions at a Glance

PROBLEM: Something's infesting your backyard.

CULPRIT: Ticks

SOLVE IT! Keep a flock of guinea hens. These hungry gobblers of deer ticks are the perfect solution if you have the space and ability to keep them.

Fortunately, lawns aren't the favored habitat of most tick species. You're more likely to pick up ticks from hiking through brushy, wooded areas and meadows of tall grass. If you're out in natural areas, wear a light-colored, long-sleeve shirt and tuck your pants into your socks. When you get back, be sure to check yourself carefully for ticks. (Ticks need to feed for several hours before transmitting any diseases.) If you do find an attached tick, use a narrow tweezer to slowly and carefully remove the tick, then drop it into a jar of alcohol. Observe the bite area for the next several weeks to make sure you don't exhibit any symptoms of disease, such as a rash that looks like a bull's eye.

Tomato Problems

Chances are, tomatoes are your favorite vegetable. After all, who doesn't enjoy sinking their teeth into a freshly picked love apple? Even small space gardeners grow tomatoes in tubs or patio containers. But for all their goodness, tomatoes aren't problem-free. Diseases are the most common headache, but sometimes critters or insects go after them. Too much fertilizer can reduce yield; too much or too little water can spoil the fruit. To err is human, and tomatoes are forgiving. But heeding a few rules will make for happier plants and lots of luscious fruit.

HARVEST HINTS

Pick fruit when it's still firm and a bit underripe and let it finish ripening indoors in a dark, cool place (but not the refrigerator). By picking fruit while it's a bit underripe, you'll lose far fewer tomatoes to ravenous critters and molds, and you won't lose much flavor, either. When picking, be sure to remove the stem to keep the tomatoes from piercing each other in the harvest basket. Ripen them by laying them out stem end down, on their shoulders, and don't let them touch each other. Fully ripe tomatoes will stay in good condition for a week with care, but even gentle pressure on the flesh will cause a ripe tomato to soften and rot.

RIPEN TOMATOES STEM END DOWN TO PREVENT BRUISING AND ROT.

TO PINCH OR NOT TO PINCH?

Should you allow a tomato seedling to blossom before you plant it? Most market gardeners say it depends on the size of the plant. If the seedling is small, maybe in a six-pack with its siblings, it's better to pinch off any blossoms before setting the plant into the garden. If it's in a quart-sized or even larger pot, it's likely to have a large enough root ball to set that early fruit and ripen it. The moral? Move your seedlings into the largest pot you can manage if you want robust plants and early fruit.

PRUNING: ONCE AND DONE

You want early fruit but don't want to decrease overall yield? Do what market gardener Sylvia Ehrhardt does. "We want fruit as early as we can have it, so we prune to two stems early in the season," says Ehrhardt. "But then we don't prune them anymore." In Ehrhardt's Knoxville, Maryland, garden, early tomato varieties start ripening their fruit in May.

A STAKE IN TIME

Staking tomatoes is a must to help prevent fruit from being attacked by insects or rotting on the ground. Cone-shaped or collapsible wire cages are convenient if you only have a few tomato plants in your garden, but off-season storage of these monstrosities is a problem if your tomato plants number in the dozens. A solution? Stake-and-weave trellises. Here's how to create one.

1. Drive a metal T-stake into the end of the tomato bed, and another after every third tomato plant. Heavy-duty stakes are best if you grow indeterminate tomatoes; lighter-weight stakes are fine for more compact determinates.

2. When the tomatoes are about 1 foot tall, attach a strand of plastic baling twine to the first stake. Draw the twine to the second stake, loop it around the stake, and pull it tight. Continue to the next stake, and the next, until you reach the end of the tomato row.

3. Do the same on the other side of the tomato row. This creates a twine "cage" on either side of the tomato plants.

4. Once a week or so, as the tomatoes grow, add another level of twine. Four or five levels should be enough to corral the tomatoes.

STAKE-AND-WEAVE TRELLISES ARE QUICK TO PUT UP AND EASY TO PULL DOWN IF YOU GROW LOTS OF TOMATOES.

Solutions at a Glance

PROBLEM: It's the end of the season, and you have lots of green tomatoes out there.

CULPRIT: Frost

SOLVE IT! About 6 weeks before the first expected frost, give your tomato plants a haircut. Doing this prevents new fruit from forming and hastens the ripening of the fruit already set. You can still have vine-ripened fruit if you pull the entire plant before frost, lay it on top of some straw in a frost-free area (such as a barn), and put another layer of straw on top of the plant.

Pest Detective

Gardeners aren't the only ones who love tomatoes—so do all kinds of pests and diseases. But that doesn't have to mean you'll end up with a measly couple of love apples at harvest time. Solutions to tomato problems are at hand; in fact, here are five common bugaboos and what to do about them.

Symptom	Problem	What to Do
Holes in leaves and stems of plants—maybe even severe defoliation	Colorado potato beetles	Use beetle-busting straw mulch. Young potato beetles come up from the ground and can't fly for a week. So if you mulch early, they end up dying while crawling through the mulch.
Little sunken black spots on the tomatoes, which sometimes don't show up until the fruit is fully ripe	Anthracnose	As soon as you see the first evidence of anthracnose, spray the tomatoes with a solution of 1 cup of hydrogen peroxide to 1 gallon of water, and repeat every 7 to 10 days.
The tomatoes bloom like gangbusters but set no fruit	Blossom drop	Tomatoes won't set fruit at very low (below 40°F) or very high (above 85°F) temperatures. Cover early tomatoes to help keep them warm. When it's sweltering outside, throw a shade cloth over the plants (an old lace curtain or tablecloth works well) or give them a cold shower with a sprinkler in midday to keep the blossoms cool.
Black, sunken spots on the bottoms of tomatoes	Blossom end rot	Blossom end rot means the tomato isn't getting enough calcium. Even if the soil has plenty of calcium, too much or too little moisture will prevent the tomato plant from taking it up. Keep the tomatoes steadily watered by poking pinholes in the bottoms of plastic milk jugs and half-burying them next to the plants. Fill the jugs once a week or so from the garden hose.
Leaves curl up, turn yellow, and drop off	Verticillium and fusarium wilt	Pull up and destroy infected plants. Choose tomato varieties that are resistant to these diseases.

Transplant Problems

You have to plant some crops as seedlings, not seeds, or they won't have time to do their thing before the season ends. But young plants are tender, making them easy victims of weather and pests. So no matter whether you grow your own or buy seedlings from a garden center, you'll want to be sure they get off to a good start.

plastic and to the top outside edge of the plywood to hold the plastic in place at night and on windy days.

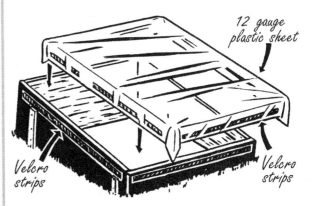

12 gauge plastic sheet

Velcro strips

Velcro strips

THIS EASY-TO-BUILD COLDFRAME SERVES AS A HALFWAY HOUSE FOR GARDEN-BOUND SEEDLINGS.

HALFWAY HOUSE FOR HARDENING OFF

You know that you have to harden-off those transplants before setting them in the garden, by gradually introducing them to outdoor conditions. Instead of having to constantly be moving garden-bound seedlings from indoors to out and back again, you can make a simple coldframe as a halfway house for them. Just nail together a plywood frame, then staple Velcro strips to heavy

RX FOR HEALTHY TRANSPLANTS

If your green thumb turns to black when trying to start transplants, don't despair. You might just need to tweak your technique a bit. Here are four tips to help you back on the road toward starting seedlings successfully.

SOW DRY, SET WET. This old-time advice still holds true. Transplanting works best when the soil is damp. And if it isn't? "I carry buckets of water into the garden and fill the holes with water before I put in the transplants," says Jerry Worrell of Ferry Landing Farm in Dunkirk, Maryland. "I do that with tomatoes, peppers, eggplants, and all my perennials." The water settles soil around the roots of the plant, preventing potential air pockets that could dry out the roots.

PLANT TOMATOES DEEP. Bury tomato seedlings all the way up to their top leaves and they'll sprout roots along the buried stem. (A long-handled bulb planter makes it easy to dig a deep hole).

BE GENTLE WITH SQUASH, FOR PEAT'S SAKE. Squash, cucumbers, and melons have tender roots that are easily broken, which can send the plant into transplant shock. Start these seedlings in individual peat pots and plant them pot and all before the roots start to penetrate the sides of the pot. Too many plants in a peat pot? Pinch off, don't pull, the excess plants, to avoid disturbing the roots of the ones that remain.

FOIL CUTWORMS. Cutworms can mean death to transplants. To protect seedlings, wrap plant stems loosely with small strips of aluminum foil. (The shiny foil helps repel aphids, too!) You can also keep cutworms at bay by placing tuna or cat food cans with the tops and bottoms cut out over your seedlings.

A Little TLC

Transplants need extra care when you put them out into your garden. To avoid shocking them with bright sunlight, try to transplant on a cloudy or drizzly day or in the evening to spare transplants. You'll also need to protect them from extremes of drought, heat, cold, and wind for the first week after transplanting. Overturned baskets, milk jugs, or fabric row covers work well to keep them from the elements.

Tough or Tender?

You'll have better luck hardening-off seedlings outdoors if you know whether or not the plants can take a visit from Jack Frost. That's because seedlings of hardy vegetables can withstand some frost; half-hardy vegetables benefit from some frost protection; and tender vegetables can't take any frost at all. (If frost is predicted while you're hardening-off seedlings, protect half-hardy transplants by covering them at night. To protect tender seedlings, bring them indoors overnight.)

Here's a list of how tough or tender your crops are.

Hardy: broccoli, brussels sprouts, cabbage, collard, kale, kohlrabi, leek, onion, spinach

Half-hardy: cauliflower, celery, chard, chicory, Chinese cabbage, endive, lettuce

Tender: cucumber, eggplant, muskmelon, okra, pepper, pumpkin, squash, tomato, watermelon

Tree and Shrub Problems

Trees and shrubs truly are the backbone of any landscape. We count on them to bring a sense of grandeur and timelessness to our plantings and to provide form in our yards when the last annuals or perennials have said good-bye for the season. But even trees and shrubs aren't immune to problems such as poor drainage, nitrogen deficiency, or scale. That's why this section covers ways to head off problems before they start, along with troubleshooting tips.

AVOIDING TROUBLE

Avoiding trouble is always easier than coping with it after it strikes—especially when you're dealing with something as big as a tree. Says Matt Vehr, manager of horticulture at Cincinnati's Spring Grove Cemetery and Arboretum, "Most problems with trees and shrubs occur because you have the wrong plant for your site." It's fairly easy to alter growing conditions enough to please a few perennials; it's often impossible when you're dealing with trees and big shrubs. If your woody plants are constantly plagued by pests and diseases, if their growth is sickly and stunted, or if those cute little saplings have grown into monsters you hadn't bargained for, says Vehr, "You're probably better off getting rid of them and starting over again."

Before you even start perusing catalogs, spend some time analyzing your site, advises Vehr, along with Ray McNeilan, retired extension agent for Multnomah County, Oregon. Here's how to do that in four easy steps.

1. Analyze your site for prevailing winds, temperature ranges, humidity levels, and the amount of sunlight your tree or shrub will get. Look at nearby trees and shrubs. Are branches missing on one side that would indicate damage from strong winds on that side? You can gauge temperature ranges by finding out which USDA Hardiness Zone you're in (see the map on page 216). To determine humidity levels, look at the weeds that are growing at the site. Are they weeds like common purslane (*Portulaca oleracea*), which can survive under dry conditions, or are they weeds like pigweeds (*Amaranthus*

Cultural Culprits

If your formerly happy trees and shrubs are looking haggard, the source of the trouble may not be pests or disease; it could be cultural problems. Here are some common things to look for and what to do if you find them.

Symptom	Possible Cause	What to Do
Dropping, scorched or wilted leaves	Not enough water is reaching the roots	Soak the ground slowly and thoroughly from the trunk to the drip line, then mulch with compost or well-rotted manure.
General decline in appearance and vigor	Compaction of the soil from foot or vehicle traffic	Re-route traffic (erect a barrier around the root zone if you have to). Dig organic matter such as compost into the soil as far as you can without disturbing the roots, and then add mulch.
Leaves mottled, speckled tan or white, or turning silvery in color; branches dying	Air or ground pollution, or damage from road salt	Avoid using salt to melt snow. Instead, use cinders, sand, or clay cat litter to provide traction on ice and snow, or check in your local hardware store for an environmentally friendly ice melter. Feed and water the tree thoroughly or remove it and plant a more resistant variety.
Older, lower leaves turn yellow and may drop; plant growth is slow and spindly	Nitrogen deficiency	Dig in compost, supplemented with a high-nitrogen additive such as bloodmeal or fish meal. Avoid low-nitrogen mulches such as wood bark.
Leaves wilted or turning brown; top branches dying; general decline in appearance and vigor	Poor drainage	If the plant is small enough, move it to a better site. Otherwise, improve the drainage (you may need help from a professional landscaper).

spp.) and common lamb's-quarters (*Chenopodium album*), which grow best in areas where humidity is higher? To determine how much sunlight your tree or shrub will get, see "Shade" on page 137.

2. Test your soil for pH, fertility, and drainage.

3. Think about what you want the trees or shrubs to accomplish. Do you want a background for your perennial border? A leafy canopy to shade your hammock on hot summer days? A soldier in the war against winter gales and high heating bills? Also, consider how big the tree needs to be to do its job and how long it will take to grow to maturity.

4. Get help. Trees and shrubs can be big investments in terms of money. If you aren't sure what will feel most at home on your range, ask the advice of a knowledgeable friend or a professional arborist.

Rx for Healthy Trees and Shrubs

For healthy, problem-free trees and shrubs, follow this three-part formula, says Akron, Ohio, gardener Mary Frances Jarrold.

RELY ON NATIVE PLANTS. "They look better, and they're much less susceptible to pests and diseases," she says.

ENCOURAGE PREDATORS THAT PREY ON PEST INSECTS. Jarrold's favorites: toads and bats. "I used to spray," she admits. "Almost immediately after I quit, a family of toads showed up. Soon after that my husband put bat houses in all the trees, and that was the end of the pest problems."

KEEP IT CLEAN. "Never go into the garden without a bag and a pair of pruners," she advises. "Pick up debris as soon as you see it, and clip off any leaves or twigs that don't look right. Diseases thrive in litter and weakened tissue."

Get a Good Start

If you've inherited a tree or shrub that has never performed up to snuff, the trouble might well stem from improper planting. Trees and large shrubs need to be treated differently from perennials if they're going to grow up strong, healthy, and able to fend off pests and disease. If you're fond of the plant and it's small enough for you to manage, move it to a new site and give it a fresh start. Here's how to transplant a tree or shrub, from Ray McNeilan, retired extension agent for Multnomah County, Oregon.

1. Dig a planting hole wide enough to accommodate the roots without circling or kinking, but only deep enough to set the plant at the same depth as it was planted before. (Don't add soil amendments. If you do, the roots will confine themselves to the beefed-up area, rather than spreading out as they need to do. The plant's growth will be stunted, maybe severely.)

2. If a tree can't stand on its own, you'll need to stake it. (Young trees develop stronger root systems and sturdier, more resilient trunks when they're allowed to move with the wind.) When the rootball is in its planting hole and before you replace the soil, drive in two posts, one on each side of the hole and well clear of the roots.

3. Fasten the tree to the posts with soft, broad straps; never use wire or wire-filled hose, which can girdle the bark.

4. Allow enough slack so the trunk can move 2 inches in every direction.

5. Remove the stakes and ties within 6 months to 1 year after planting.

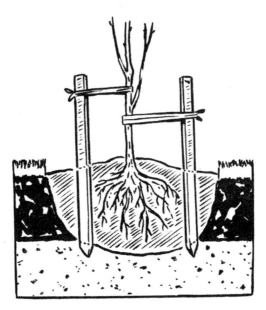

STAKE YOUR TREE PROPERLY TO AVOID INJURING — OR EVEN KILLING — IT.

Solutions at a Glance

PROBLEM: Your trees are losing their bark.

CULPRIT: Deer (They're using your trees as scratching posts to get the velvet off their new antlers.)

SOLVE IT! Loosely wrap green plastic construction fence around the trees to a height of about 4 feet. The bucks will get their head rubs elsewhere.

BALDING FROM THE BOTTOM

Got a hedge that's looking sparse and scraggly toward the bottom? That's probably because it's suffering from the shade brought on by the leaves above it. Advises Skillman, New Jersey, gardener Rosalia Kung, "When you prune, make sure you keep the top of a hedge narrower than the bottom, so the light reaches all parts of it equally." Another advantage to a thin-topped hedge: Snow won't pile up on it and break the branches.

YOUR HEDGE WILL STAY HEALTHIER IF THE SUN CAN REACH THE BOTTOM FOLIAGE AS WELL AS THE TOP.

HOME SWEET POT

Itching to plant a certain tree or shrub but know it will be a struggle to make it survive on your home ground? Give up the fight before you begin—the results are sure to be marginal at best. Instead, advises Linda Waller, container-plant specialist and owner of Doolittle Gardens in Seattle, pot it up. Here's how.

- For best results, plant dwarf varieties with limited growth potential. For example, a sugar maple (*Acer saccharum*) won't find happiness in a pot, but plenty of its little cousins will, such as Japanese maples (*A. palmatum*).

- Choose a container that's big and sturdy enough to handle the rootball and that has good drainage. High-fired terra cotta (not the thin, mass-produced kind), fiberglass, or wood will all work fine—but if you opt for wood, use a plastic liner or the roots will grow into the container.

- Raise the pot an inch or two above the ground to allow air circulation. A wheeled plant caddie the size of the container will do the job nicely, and will allow you to move the plant easily for maintenance, winter protection, or simply to change the scene in the garden.

- Whatever you do, Waller warns, don't line the bottom of the pot with clay shards, stones or foam peanuts. "Roots confined to a pot need all the room they can get. If you use well-amended soil your drainage will be plenty good enough without adding material that deprives roots of soil in an already limited space."

After that, says Waller, "The two crucial factors are water—never let the container dry out completely—and placement." In particular, she says, be aware of reflected sun from glass doors or light-colored walls. It can work for you or against you. On the plus side, the added warmth can extend the season and let you grow more tender plants than you could otherwise. On the flip side, intense light will give them a thirst that won't quit—and if it's too brutal, it could cook them. If your sunbathing tree starts looking stressed, move it to a cooler spot.

SMALL AND DWARF VARIETIES OF TREES AND SHRUBS CAN LIVE HAPPILY EVER AFTER IN POTS. JUST GIVE THEM ROOT ROOM, GOOD AIR CIRCULATION, AND SOIL AMENDED TO SUIT THEIR TASTE.

Solutions at a Glance

PROBLEM: Crust white or brown patches are all over your shrub's branches.

CULPRIT: Scale

SOLVE IT! Put rings of double-faced tape around several branches, says Judy Wong, a Master Gardener from Menlo Park, California. As the tiny scale hatchlings scamper about, some of them will be trapped on the sticky stuff (they'll look like grayish dust). Be sure to leave a little tab at the end of the tape so you can get it off the plant easily.

DOING THE ROOTBALL ROCK

When planting a tree, getting the top of the rootball even with the soil surface can be tricky. So what do you do if you slide the tree into the hole you just dug, only to find the tree is at the wrong height?

Simply pull on the trunk a little to rock the still-intact rootball onto an angle. If the tree is set too low, add some soil under the rootball. If it's too high, remove some soil. Then rock the tree back in the other direction, and add or remove soil under the other side of the rootball.

Tree and Shrub Problems   **167**

Vegetable Garden Problems

Working in a vegetable garden on a beautiful summer day can be terrifically relaxing, and it can also bring tremendous rewards to the dinner table. But as you know, to reap a garden's rewards you have to battle weeds, weather, and pest bugs. The following hints will give you some insight on the best bug beaters, how to use compost for a healthy garden, and more, so you'll be well on your way to vegetable riches.

RX FOR A HEALTHY GARDEN

Veteran gardener Paul Doscher follows six basic tenets to ensure a healthy vegetable garden. Here are this Weare, New Hampshire, expert's resourceful tips to help you plan a picture-perfect vegetable garden and stop problems before they start.

SITE IT RIGHT. It's important to site your garden rows or plants so that they get optimum sun during the day, says Doscher. "Running rows or beds from north to south ensures that as the sun tracks across the sky in summer (in an arc from northeast to southwest) every plant that needs full sun will get some," he explains. And remember to plant taller plants at the north end of a bed so they won't shade smaller plants early and late in the season, when the sun is lower in the sky.

If, however, your land is on a slope, the sun orientation rule doesn't apply—stopping erosion is more vital. In that case, Doscher notes, you should run your rows parallel with the slope so that heavy rains won't create erosion gullies.

IF YOU HAVE TO PLANT YOUR GARDEN ON A HILL, RUN THE ROWS PARALLEL WITH THE SLOPE SO YOU DON'T END UP WITH HEAVY EROSION.

RAISE YOUR GARDEN'S POTENTIAL. "I've used raised intensive beds for more than 20 years now. They're the most efficient way to produce high yields with less work," Doscher says. In the North, the beds don't take a lot of work to make. You don't need to double-dig, because the freezing and thawing of soil in winter breaks it up, aerates it, and lets plant roots grow down deep.

Doscher uses his rotary tiller to build beds easily. First, he tills an area, then he uses the furrower device on the rear of his tiller to push up soil from the paths into the beds. This ensures deeper soil in the beds (where you *don't* walk) and less soil in the paths (where you do).

MAKE COMPOST. One of the most important keys to a successful organic garden is compost, and making it doesn't have to be a chore, says Doscher. "We make lots of compost, but not with fanaticism. You'll find no compost starters or special biological injections here," he says. "Compost makes itself," along with the natural organisms that are found in soil, he says. And by having several compost piles in various stages of development, you'll always have some ready to nourish your garden with. See "Whip Up a Batch of Homemade Compost" on page 170 for Doscher's compost-making tactics.

REMEMBER TO MULCH. Keeping moisture in the garden is another key to success. Doscher accomplishes this by mulching the entire garden, especially the paths between the beds, early in the season. (He uses spoiled hay, but grass clippings or other organic covers will work, too.) But don't put the mulch down too early, he warns, or slugs and cold soil will stop your plants before they get started. Put the mulch down after the soil has warmed (the exact timing will depend on your location and a particular year's weather). Doscher then waters

Solutions at a Glance

PROBLEM: You tilled your veggie garden midseason, and now it has more weeds than veggies in it.

CULPRIT: Weeds

SOLVE IT! Tilling in summer brings weed seeds to the surface, where they can germinate, causing a weed-farm effect. Till only twice a year: once in spring, to turn over the soil and mix in organic matter, and once again in fall, to turn in waste organic matter, such as spent plants and spoiled veggies.

with soaker hoses, giving each bed a good soak about twice a week.

CONTROL GARDEN PESTS. There's more than one way to fool a bug, but the best way to keep them guessing, says Doscher, is to faithfully rotate your crops from year to year. Don't plant tomatoes or cabbage or beans in the same spot 2 years in a row. And a 3-year or longer rotation is most effective.

Another antipest tactic is to choose resistant varieties that are less susceptible to pests. "We have a standard collection of varieties we use because, in our experience, they suffer from fewer pests in our location," he says. Check with your neighbors or the Cooperative Extension Service for variety recommendations in your area.

Finally, when these tactics don't control a pest problem, Doscher's weapon of choice is Sunspray oil for dormant perennials and occasional use on the garden in summer. Floating row covers also will help keep bugs off the small plants, he says.

KEEP FEATHERED PESTS AT BAY. Doscher uses bird scare or flash tape (available from a number of seed catalogs and nursery centers) to keep birds out of his strawberries and crows away from his young corn seedlings. He attaches the shiny red-and-silver tape to stakes and runs it the length of the garden rows, about 12 inches off the ground. The wind makes the tape flash in the sun, scaring birds away. "It really works," Doscher says.

Keep 'Em from Bolting

Having your lettuce or other leafy greens bolt before you get the chance to even enjoy a couple of salads can be a frustrating experience. But you can't blame the plants—when their biological clock tells them it's time to make a flower stalk, they just can't refuse. But there are some tips that can ensure a few salads before the inevitable occurs.

Your first option is to move your timetable. Many plants that bolt when grown in spring show great staying power if grown in the fall, when days are getting shorter. Your second option is to choose varieties that are less likely to bolt (such as 'Green Ice', 'Red Sails', 'Sierra', and 'Matchless'). Bolt resistance also has been bred into many vegetables, so start looking for it when you shop for seeds.

Whip Up a Batch of Homemade Compost

Veteran gardener Paul Doscher of Weare, New Hampshire, makes a quick-and-easy compost to supply his garden with all the nutrients it needs. Here's his surefire method:

1. Shred or chop all the waste to put in the pile for the fastest results. (You'll still get compost if you don't shred—it will just take longer.)
2. Add a layer of fresh manure (chicken works well, but any animal manure will do), soil, or finished compost every 6 inches or so as you build the pile.
3. Keep your pile moist, but not soggy, and open up air holes in the pile with your pitch fork.
4. Use garden waste that's fresh or green so you capture the nitrogen in it for feeding the organisms that are so important to making compost.
5. Once you've finished the compost—brown, crumbly material with a lot of the waste so decomposed you don't recognize it—cover the pile with a sheet of black plastic. This will protect it from rain and keep it from losing important nutrients through leaching.

SHREDDING FALL LEAVES BEFORE ADDING THEM TO YOUR COMPOST PILE WILL HELP THEM DECOMPOSE FASTER.

Beat Back Bugs

There's no reason to let the bugs take over your garden. With the great expert tips on page 172, you can keep everything from aphids to Mex-

Pest Detective

Not all garden pests have four (or six) legs and a healthy appetite. Some of your foes are microscopic organisms that sneak in and leave your plants diseased and ailing. But don't fret if your garden gets sick—resourceful organic cures exist for most garden diseases. The main thing is to act fast, so keep a close eye on your vegetable garden and identify diseases before they take a firm hold. Then try these solutions when you spot a problem.

Symptom	Cause	What to Do
Flesh-tone spore masses that ooze out of lesions; dark brown spots on bean plants, melon leaves, and cucumbers; or tomatoes with dark, sunken lesions	Anthracnose caused by fungus	Remove infected plants, and don't work in the garden when leaves are wet. Rotate crops and keep plant leaves off the soil surface to help prevent the disease.
Young, just-emerging seedlings rot at soil level and die, or fail to emerge at all	Damping-off caused by parasitic fungi	Indoors: Remove dying seedlings if the problem isn't too severe; for a severe problem, discard the whole flat. Provide good air circulation (a fan works well), and be careful not to overwater. Also, use a commercial soilless growing mix and bottom heat at 70° to 75°F. Outdoors: Wait until temps warm up to plant, or put black plastic over the soil to warm it up. Thin seedlings for good air circulation.
Nightshade crops, especially tomatoes, potatoes, and eggplant, develop circular leaf spots; their leaves yellow and the plants die	Early blight caused by fungus	Pick bottom leaves as they brown, and remove and destroy badly infected plants. To prevent early blight, avoid subjecting plants to stress and overhead irrigation, use mulch, plant crops in full sun, space them for good air circulation, clean up garden debris in the fall, and rotate crops.
Small, pale green spots develop on tomato, potato, and eggplant leaves; spots grow into large brown areas, leaves shrivel, and plant dies; fruit is infected with brown spots that look greasy	Late blight caused by fungus	Promptly remove infected leaves or, if necessary, destroy infected plants. To reduce late blight in your garden, plant certified disease-free potato varieties with late blight resistance (such as 'Elba'), avoid overhead irrigation, space plants for good air circulation, and rotate crops.
Whitish gray powder coating on leaves and buds	Powdery mildew caused by spores of fungi spread by wind	Plant resistant varieties and water them with a strong stream of water during dry conditions, when powdery mildew thrives. Spray affected plants once a week with 1 tablespoon each of vegetable oil and baking soda, plus a drop of dishwashing soap in a gallon of water. Prune and destroy infected parts that don't improve after spraying.

ican bean beetles under control and away from your tender eggplant seedlings or thriving filet beans. (See individual entries for tips on controlling pests specific to certain veggies.)

USE FLOATING ROW COVERS AS BARRIERS to keep insects (and those pesty moths that start many problems) off crops. Row covers work well on cabbage, Asian greens, eggplant, squash, melons, and more. Just remember to remove the covers when your plants blossom (for pollination purposes). Row covers are available from most seed companies and nurseries in various widths and weights.

HAND-PICK THOSE BAD BUGS. If your garden is small, it's easy to find pests with the help of a good insect guide. Check leaves often for egg masses and young and adult pests (or the damage they leave in their wake), and you'll soon become an expert at identifying them. Just watch out that you don't remove beneficial insects. Early removal of pests goes a long way toward improving the health—and the production—of your crops.

HAND-PICKING PESTS IS A GREAT WAY TO KEEP GARDEN BAD GUYS UNDER CONTROL.

EXPERIMENT WITH HOMEMADE, NATURAL SPRAYS. Auburn University entomologist Geoff Zehnder says that sprays made with ground red pepper and garlic work well on cabbage. (See "Cabbage Problems" on page 21 for de-

tails.) Commercial hot pepper and garlic pest repellents are also widely available. Animal pests can be chased off with these sprays, too.

ENCOURAGE BENEFICIAL INSECTS. This can be done by planting a border of companion plants, such as dill and yarrow, which are rich in nectar and pollen, to attract many beneficials. Add stones to containers of water or birdbaths around the garden so little beneficials can drink without drowning. Beneficial insects include the aphid midge, braconid wasp, lady beetles, lacewings, dragonflies, minute pirate bugs, scale predator beetles, and spined soldier bugs.

USE BIOLOGICAL INSECTICIDES WHEN NECESSARY. Products with BT (*Bacillus thuringiensis*) can control both moth and butterfly larvae, cabbageworms, loopers, hornworms, and crop-damaging caterpillars.

DO SOME CLEAN UP IN FALL. Remove diseased plants and any crops where you've had pest problems—or where you know the pest overwinters in the debris. (Leave flower borders for spring to provide overwintering sites for beneficial insects.)

MAKE VEGGIES WAIT ON YOU

Nothing feels worse than watching your veggies spoil before you have a chance to harvest or enjoy them. So seek out veggies that keep, and you'll be able to feast on them over a long period. Some of those "keepers" will wait in the ground until you have a chance to gather them. Others will store well into winter with the right conditions. Here are a few friends to the harried gardener who just doesn't have the time to deal with her veggies right now:

● Cabbage can be a real trooper, but there are two tricks to keeping it—pick it young and store it cold (but not so cold it freezes). Ideal conditions are between 32° and 40°F and 90 percent humidity.

- Carrots, beets, and parsnips all store well in the ground through fall. In fact, carrots and parsnips sweeten as the temperature turns colder. Before the ground freezes, mulch the plants with 8 to 12 inches of straw. Or, harvest them, brush off the soil, cut off the tops of the leaves (leaving an inch of greens), and store the veggies in sand in a cool place.

- Long-keeper tomatoes will last you well into winter. Just pick them when they turn a pale white-green, wrap them in newspaper, and store them in a cool (around 60°F), dark place to ripen slowly.

- Onions, leeks, shallots, and garlic are all good long keepers.

- Potatoes, especially 'Yukon Gold' and 'Butte', are also good keepers. Just remember to store them where it's cool (about 40°F) and dark because light produces green potatoes with poisonous alkaloids that will make for bitter potatoes and sick potato eaters.

- Winter, butternut, and spaghetti squash are all great keepers. Store at 45° to 50°F and 65 to 70 percent humidity.

STORE LONG-KEEPER TOMATOES IN NEWSPAPER AND YOU CAN ENJOY BLT SANDWICHES IN JANUARY.

BABY VEGGIES ARE IN!

You can get vegetables to do double-duty by harvesting some when they're "babies" rather than waiting until they're mature. Lettuce is a great example of a natural baby veggie, taking only about 5 weeks to be ready for harvest (from transplant). Some romaines and Batavian varieties are fine for baby lettuce, but the best varieties are those bred to be compact, such as Bibbs. Other great baby veggies include:

- Beans, particularly haricot vert or filet beans
- Beets, which are flavorful when young
- Broccoli, which can be spaced closely (8 inches apart) so heads will stay small
- Carrots, such as 'Kinko' and 'Thumbelina', which can be planted closely and are ready about 55 days after seeding

YOU CAN ENJOY SOME VEGETABLES EARLY IN THE SEASON, SUCH AS CARROTS AND BEETS, BY HARVESTING THEM WHEN THEY'RE YOUNG.

- Corn (an early-maturing variety), which can be planted 6 inches apart and picked when there is a bulge inside the husk
- Eggplant, which is delicious when young
- Squash, including patty pan, zucchini, and all summer squash

Vole Problems

Voles (also called meadow mice or field mice) are so small that you might be tempted to look at them and think "How much damage can that little thing do?" But these 1- to 2½-ounce critters eat almost their own weight in vegetable matter every day. And because they can have 5 to 10 litters of four to seven young at a time, an awful lot of your garden can get eaten up by voles in just one season. Read on for great ways to spare your plants from these voracious vegetarians.

BUILD A BETTER VOLE BARRIER

Master Gardener Joan Reese-Gorecki decided that enough was enough after watching—and hearing—a gladiolus keel over one morning in her suburban Memphis garden. That's when she came up with a plan to take care of her vole problem once and for all.

"My husband built a wooden frame the size of a raised bed. Before I put the frame in place, I turned the frame on its side and stapled a piece of hardware cloth across the bottom," she explains. (Hardware cloth is wire welded into mesh that comes in rolls from the hardware store. To protect against voles, use mesh that's ¼ inch or smaller in size.)

"I set the frame into my bed, filled it with a mixture of soil and compost, and then planted my vegetables and flowers right into the frame, where they remained all season," says Reese-Gorecki.

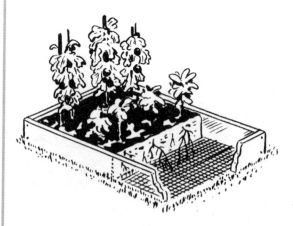

HARDWARE CLOTH STAPLED TO THE BOTTOM OF A FRAME KEEPS VOLES OUT BUT LETS ROOTS REACH THE SOIL.

"It worked out spectacularly well!" she says. Plant roots easily grow down into the soil through the 1/4-inch openings in the hardware cloth, but voles can't reach the bulbs and tender plant shoots.

"I plant asparagus the same way. The asparagus beds need to be 8 inches high, though, so we use a double width of lumber," Reese-Gorecki says. (And remember: Avoid using pressure-treated lumber to build raised beds.)

WINTER WARFARE

The worst vole damage comes during winter, when they feast on the trunks and root systems of your trees and shrubs. You can put an end to their snacking, though, by removing any wood chips or mulch from the base of young trees and shrubs in fall. (Without the wood chips or mulch, voles won't have any protective cover.) You can also wrap hardware cloth around the tree trunks (keep the cloth about 6 inches away from the trunks so the trees will have room to grow), then push the cloth about 6 inches into the ground.

FIGHT FOR YOUR TULIPS

Voles can be the guilty party if your prize tulip bulbs fail to appear in the spring. Try planting tulips in plastic pots with drainage holes, and

Solutions at a Glance

PROBLEM: Critters are eating their way through most of your precious plants.

CULPRIT: Voles

SOLVE IT! Reduce their presence in your yard and garden by making them feel unwelcome. Remove weeds and brush piles and keep tunneled areas mowed regularly. Pull mulch away from trees and shrubs in the fall so voles won't move in and eat roots and bark through the winter.

---

then sinking the containers into the ground, keeping the pot rim at the soil surface. You can also put a handful of sharp crushed gravel around bulbs when you plant them to deter voles from digging down to your bulbs. For the most fool-proof technique—plant daffodils. They're poisonous to voles, so the voles won't bother them.

Water Garden Problems

Who doesn't love a water garden? They're beautiful, restful, cooling, and calming, no matter if they're big or small. But they can also be green, algae-ridden messes, fraught with a host of problems: predators that eat fish, plants that become invasive, and slippery surfaces that pose a hazard for children.

Forethought and resourcefulness, however, can put the fun back into water gardening. Plan and manage your water garden (instead of just building one willy-nilly and letting it care for itself), and you'll have the delight of water for years to come.

KEEPING FISH SAFE

No matter if you have $200 koi or $2 goldfish in your water pond, you'll want to help protect them from predators. Shelly Johansson, a gardener and garden designer from Bainbridge Island, Washington, recommends creating a pond 4 to 5 feet deep. A deep pond lets fish dive away from predators. If you can't build a deep pond, put a pot turned on its side on the bottom of the pond, so the fish can dive in and hide there.

DON'T LET YOUR FISH BECOME A TASTY SNACK; PROTECT THEM FROM CRITTERS BY GIVING THEM A POT TO HIDE IN.

HOW LOW WILL IT GO?

That low-lying spot on your property may look like the perfect place to build a water garden, but it isn't, says Jamie Beyer, a water garden writer and consultant in Ames, Iowa. In fact, a low-lying area is among the *worst* places to locate a water garden because runoff from the surrounding landscape may contain contaminants such as pet feces and lawn chemicals, which will collect in the spot. So what to do? You can either burm up the edges of the pond to divert runoff or convert the area into a bog garden, which can take excess runoff, says Beyer.

SAVVY SUBSTITUTES

Don't panic if you can't afford to shell out top dollar for special water-gardening supplies. Here are some ways to keep your hard-earned money in your pocket and still have what you need to create a great water garden, from Jamie Beyer, a water garden writer and consultant in Ames, Iowa.

RECYCLE BLACK PLASTIC POTS. Avoid buying those expensive water garden planting containers. Instead, use ordinary black plastic pots left over from other plant purchases. Just rinse them off and cover the holes in the bottom with plastic window screen or landscape fabric to prevent the soil from washing out.

USE ROOF LINER. Roof liner is an economical substitute for regular pond liner. Although some pond experts recommend pond liner because it's guaranteed fish safe, Beyer says he has never known a fish to have gotten lost because of roof liner. One of the best pond liners is 45 mil EPDM, and Beyer says you can buy roof liner made out of the same material. (If you still aren't sure the roof liner is fish safe, ask the supplier about using their product in a pond.) The savings, especially for large gardens, are substantial because roofing liner costs about one-third less than pond liner.

LOOK AROUND THE HOUSE FOR CUSHIONING MATERIAL. Although you can buy special cushioning liners to lay between the soil and liner to prevent rips and tears, you can save big by cushioning with either old carpet scraps or several layers of newspaper.

SAVE MONEY BY USING LEFTOVER PLASTIC POTS FOR WATER GARDEN PLANTS.

SQUARE FOOT FISH

You're all ready to add some fish to your water garden. But will they have enough room? Fish require a surprising amount of space—and your water garden isn't any goldfish bowl. As a rule of thumb, each inch of fish should have about 6 square inches to 1 square foot of water surface. Koi are the exception, needing about 25 square feet for each fish. But for other fish, here's the space you need—at a minimum.

- One 2-inch fish: 1 square foot of water surface
- Two 8-inch fish: 8 square feet
- Six 6-inch fish: 18 square feet
- Twelve 4-inch fish: 24 square feet

Pest Detective

Hmmm. Something suspicious is happening in your water garden, and it isn't pretty. Here are some symptoms, causes, and cures.

Symptom	Cause	What to Do
Chewed holes in foliage, often skeletonized	Aphids	Keep aging, yellowing, and dying foliage trimmed from plants; apply an oil spray of two parts vegetable oil to eight parts water and a teaspoon dishwashing detergent; then remove oil film from water surface by skimming or carefully absorbing it with paper towels.
Foliage is yellowing and dying; traces of tiny webs	Red spider mites	Spray plants with garden hose. If that doesn't work, apply an insecticidal soap, removing the plant from the pond for spraying if possible.
Holes chewed around the edges and throughout floating vegetation; tiny brown stippling as well	Water lily beetles	Prune damaged vegetation; wipe any eggs from bottom of plants, especially water lilies (*Nymphaea* spp.). If problem is severe, remove plants and isolate them in a special tub.
Large oval chunks eaten out of water lily leaf margins	China moth larvae	Remove caterpillar cases from the underside of leaves, spray with *Bacillus thuringiensis* (BT).

RX FOR AN ALGAE-FREE POND

Algae—yucky, thick, mucky algae—is the bane of many a water garden. You can control algae, however, by doing the following:

GET SNAILS. Black Japanese snails are voracious algae eaters, and they won't feed on your water plants.

PLANT FLOATERS. These plants, such as water lilies (*Nymphaea* spp.), grow in colonies on the surface of the water and shade it, thereby keeping it cool (algae loves warm water). Floaters also block out light algae need to thrive.

HAVE A FEW FISH. They also eat algae.

CONSIDER A BIOLOGICAL FILTER OR UV CLARIFIER. Both of these defend your pond or pool from algae, as well as destroy many types of bacteria, viruses, and fungi that can harm fish. (You can purchase filters or clarifiers from water-gardening supply stores.)

RAKE IT UP. You can remove smaller amounts of filamentous algae, which looks like floating seaweed, by hand or with a leaf rake.

SCRUB IT. If algae forms on rocks, waterfall, or other hard surfaces, turn off the pump and let the algae dry. Then scrape or brush it off with a stiff brush. If that doesn't work, rewet the algae and sprinkle it with noniodized table salt. Leave it for several hours and then scrub again.

USE A LEAF RAKE TO KEEP YOUR WATER GARDEN CLEAR OF SEAWEEDLIKE FILAMENTOUS ALGAE.

ROCK SOLID ADVICE

If you want your water garden to have a natural look—as if it just happened to crop up in your backyard—then using stone is the way to go. For the most natural effect, follow these tips for using stone in a water feature.

USE WHAT'S LOCAL. Not only is local stone usually less expensive than stone that has been hauled in, it also tends to fit in better with your region's trees and landscape.

PLACE STONE RANDOMLY. Study naturally occurring creeks and ponds and follow their lead. Nature plunks stones down right along the edges and in the middle of streams

FIND A PLACE FOR STONE ELSEWHERE IN YOUR LANDSCAPE. If you have a flagstone path and a low flagstone retaining wall, the flagstone edging around your pond is going to look more at home.

VARY STONE SIZES. Again, nature includes very large, some medium, and very small stones (in the form of gravel) in her landscape. Mix it up in your landscape, too.

Water Problems

Garden plants are pretty resilient, and they'll put up with a lot of neglect and laziness on our parts. But there's one thing they can't survive over the long haul: a lack of water. Unless, of course, you set them up to be camels from the get-go. Prepare their beds the right way and employ a few expert tricks, and they'll pull through any dry spell without so much as a wilted leaf, and without inviting in any moisture-loving pests and diseases. Read on for the hows, whens, and whys of watering so every drop counts.

HAVE AN ORGANIC DEFENSE

Protect your garden by making sure your soil is high in organic matter, and your plants will come through a drought like champs. Even if dry times don't come, your plants will still thank you for the nice meal!

Your best bet is to enrich your soil with plenty of compost, animal manure, or leguminous green manures, such as clover or alfalfa. For a drought-hardy green manure, try a perennial clover, or cowpeas (*Vigna unguiculata* subsp. *Unguiculata*). (See "Resources" on page 196.) This enrichment helps the soil act like a sponge, hanging on to moisture long after less-rich soils have completely dried out and turned to cement. This cooling moisture can mean the difference between life and death for your plants, especially if your area imposes watering restrictions during a drought.

ENRICHING YOUR SOIL WITH A GREEN MANURE HELPS ENSURE YOUR PLANTS WILL MAKE IT THROUGH A DROUGHT.

Solutions at a Glance

PROBLEM: Your plants are left high and dry during drought.

CULPRIT: Sandy soil

SOLVE IT! Sandy soil is no day at the beach for your garden plants, so you'll need to add plenty of organic materials and a heavy organic mulch to it if you want your plants to come through looking green and happy.

PROBLEM: Blossoms are dropping, tomatoes are cracking while ripening, and blossom end rot is taking over your tomato plants.

CULPRIT: You haven't watered enough, or you've watered unevenly.

SOLVE IT! Run soaker hoses through the beds a few inches below the mulch, and you'll be able to provide even watering when and where your plants need it most.

CHOOSE WISELY

If year after year you find yourself wishing for rain during the summer months, try following these words of wisdom from gardeners around the country; they'll help you deal easily with a lack of the wet stuff.

MAKE IT QUICK. Grow short-season varieties that are ready for harvest more quickly and therefore require less water than long-season varieties, recommends D. Keith Crotz, an avid organic gardener and college biology instructor in Chillicothe, Illinois.

IMPORT SOME REINFORCEMENTS. Plant southern varieties in the North, and you'll generally get better results during extended hot, dry spells, says Jim Gerritsen, co-owner of Wood Prairie Farm in Bridgewater, Maine. (This also works in the reverse: Northern varieties of many vegetables will show increased vigor and yield in longer, more hospitable southern climes.)

MAKE SOAKER HOSES DO DOUBLE-DUTY

Paul Doscher of Weare, New Hampshire, has an ingenious way to get the most use out of the fewest number of soaker hoses.

"We don't have enough soaker hoses to put them out in each and every bed, so I've made most of our beds the same length and cut hoses to that length," explains Doscher. "I move them around the garden so each bed gets a soaking about twice a week." To make moving the hoses easier, Doscher uses quick-connect, snap-type couplings, available at garden or home centers.

PROBLEM: Plants in some parts of your yard are being wiped out, while others are spared.

CULPRIT: Drought

SOLVE IT! Take a good look at the places where plants seem to be persisting—is the soil there wetter, of a slightly different type, or slightly more shaded from the sun? Design your garden to take greatest advantage of these microclimates, and you'll bolster your defenses against drought.

For extra insurance, Doscher uses soaker hoses and mulches the entire garden (especially the paths between the beds) with spoiled hay early in the season.

SET IT AND FORGET IT

Sometimes we see our plants wilting and know Mother Nature isn't doing her part, but we just can't find the time to get out there and give our gardens a nice, long drink. When this is the case, Cheryl Long, senior editor at *Organic Gardening* magazine, recommends that you get an automatic shut-off attachment, like an oven timer, for your watering system (see "Resources" on page 196). Then, before you head to work in the morning, "you can set it to run for whatever length of time

you want, and it will turn off automatically," says Long. (When you water in the morning, you ensure that your plants will be dry by the end of the day, making them less susceptible to diseases that prey on wet foliage and waterlogged roots.)

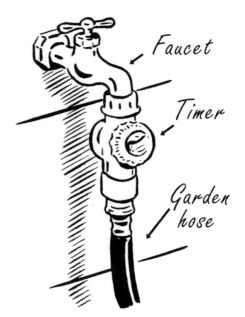

A TIMER ATTACHED TO YOUR WATERING SYSTEM IS A CONVENIENT WAY OF WATERING YOUR PLANTS IN ABSENTIA.

HARVEST THE LITTLE ONES

If it starts to get dry and you can see your crops becoming parched, don't try waiting it out to let vegetables grow to full maturity. Instead, harvest your crops early as so-called baby vegetables. Besides saving water that you'd otherwise spend nursing these veggies to maturity, you'll also enjoy better-tasting, more tender vegetables with shorter preparation and cooking times, says Pennsylvania market gardener Cass Peterson.

Weeds

Gardeners who truly love to weed are rare. But it's a fact of life that soil made rich and hospitable by loving care is bound to sprout some uninvited guests. Not all weeds are a scourge, and the wise gardener learns to appreciate—or at least tolerate—the helpful ones. The rest can be kept under control with some savvy, timely action, and the right tools. Worry about weeds? Nah. Take a few tips from market gardeners, who have *acres* of vegetables to keep clean. What works for them will work for you, too.

Rx for Healthy Mulching

Most gardeners have a single-word answer for weed problems: mulch. Straw, hay, newspaper, chopped-up leaves—almost any kind of mulch will do. The "best" mulch is whatever you happen to have on hand. But there are ways to mulch and "whens" to mulch, which make the practice easier and more effective. Here are a few tips.

GROW THE MULCH IN PLACE. "Broadcast oats over the strawberry beds in the fall and let it winter-kill," says Tony Ricci of Three Springs, Pennsylvania. "Your mulch will already be in place in the spring." Other gardeners grow living mulches such as perennial rye (*Lolium perenne*) between their garden beds and mow the mulch periodically, using the side-delivery chute of their lawn mower to blow the clippings onto the beds.

WAIT UNTIL THE WEATHER WARMS UP TO MULCH HEAT-LOVING PLANTS. Mulch cools the soil, which is good when summer heat sets in but is an early-season disadvantage to tomatoes, peppers, and eggplant. Conversely, cool-weather plants like broccoli and kale will produce longer if you mulch them while the soil is still cool.

PUT DOWN A FEW LAYERS OF NEWSPAPER BEFORE MULCHING. Newspaper is an added barrier to weeds, and it will keep some mulches, like sawdust or wood chips, from robbing nitrogen from your soil as they break down. "You can even use fresh sawdust if you want," says Sylvia Ehrhardt of Knoxville, Maryland. "By season's end, you can till it into the ground because it will be rotted enough by then."

RECYCLE YOUR NEIGHBOR'S MULCH. Ask your neighbors if you can have their unwanted bags of leaves and grass clippings (just make sure their leftovers haven't been sprayed with herbicides or pesticides).

GROW MULCH RIGHT WHERE YOU WANT IT INSTEAD OF HAVING TO LUG IT AROUND.

PERENNIAL MULCH FOR ASPARAGUS

Some crops are just plain hard to keep weed-free. Asparagus is one of them. It's difficult to hoe because spears pop up all over the place. It's tedious to hand-weed. Here's a labor-saving alternative that's *good* for the asparagus: Grow it in a bed of clover, which will feed the asparagus while it crowds out weeds. Just follow these steps.

1. In the fall before you plant the asparagus, seed the patch with white Dutch clover (*Trifolium repens*), a low-growing variety.
2. Early the following spring, till or spade a narrow, 8-inch-deep trench for the asparagus crowns (get year-old crowns, which will be fairly small). Plant them as usual, filling the trench halfway with soil.
3. When the asparagus sprouts appear above the soil level in the trench, finish filling it in, and then seed more white Dutch clover over the top.
4. Once or twice in the first season, pull any weeds that come through the clover (if the clover was planted thickly enough, there won't be many).
5. Each fall, reseed any spots where the clover looks thin.

The technique works well with rhubarb, fruit trees, perennial berries, shrubs, and many perennial flowers such as bleeding heart (*Dicentra* spp.) and peonies. But don't use it with strawberries—the spring growth of the clover traps too much moisture, setting the strawberries up for fungal disease.

LAZY WAY TO WEED

One of the easiest ways to prevent weeds is to grow plants that have allelopathic properties, meaning the plants secrete substances that prevent other plants from growing around them. Both common sunflower (*Helianthus annuus*) and annual rye (*Lolium multiflorum*) are allelopathic. If you decide to plant annual rye, plant it as a winter cover crop. It will inhibit weed growth for several weeks after you till it in the spring.

A FRESH IDEA: "STALE BEDS"

You know the drill: Every time you stir the soil, another batch of weed seeds sees the sun and sprouts. But you can use a technique called "stale beds" to avoid tilling up new weed seeds before planting crops. Here's how to do it.

1. Prepare the seed bed by tilling or spading and raking.
2. Water the bed well to encourage weeds to sprout.
3. When the weeds have sprouted but are still very small (½ inch or so tall), rake or hoe very shallowly (don't spade or till again, or you'll bring up even more weed seeds!).
4. Water once more and let the weeds sprout in the beds again.
5. Rake or hoe again, and then plant your crops. You'll have done in most of the weeds in the top inch or so of soil—enough to give you a great head start on a season's worth of weeds!

No, No, No. Don't Hoe, Hoe, Hoe

Some plants have fragile, shallow root systems and can actually be damaged by overzealous hoeing. What to do? Cultivate shallowly or mulch around squash, cucumbers, and melons. If the weeds get away from you in a planted row, it's better to cut them off than to pull them out—especially when they're in peas and beans.

Read Your Weeds

Before you yank them all out, take a look at what weeds are growing where in your garden because they can tell you useful things about your soil. Where docks (*Rumex* spp.) and lady's thumb (*Polygonum persicaria*) grow, the soil is strongly acid. A good place for blueberries, perhaps, but not for lavender. Hawkweeds (*Hieracium* spp.) and knapweeds (*Centaureas* spp.) grow in slightly acid soil.

Where the soil is compacted, plantains (*Plantago* spp.), dandelion (*Taxacum officinale*), and smartweed (*Polygonum hydropiper*) grow. Toadflax (*Kickxia elatine*) and goldenrods (*Solidago* spp.) like sandy soil. Field pepperweed (*Lepidium campestre*) indicates limestone soils; sagebrush (*Artemisia tridentata*) and woody asters (*Aster* spp.) thrive in alkaline soils. Sedges (*Cyperus* spp.) suggest a drainage problem (they favor wet soils).

Lots of pigweeds (*Amaranthus* spp.), lamb's-quarters (*Chenopodium album*), galinsogas (*Galinsoga* spp.), and mallows (*Malva* spp.)? Well, at least you can take heart in the knowledge that your soil is rich, well drained, and mellow. A good garden grows great weeds.

Can't Uproot 'Em? Smother 'Em

You've tilled, hoed, and got down on your hands and knees to pull weeds out—but you still have that tenacious quackgrass (*Agropyron repens*) hanging around. One way to get rid of a patch of established weeds is to cover-crop it repeatedly. Even tough quackgrass will succumb to a year of buckwheat as a cover crop. Sow the buckwheat in early summer (it likes warm weather). Each time it flowers, till it under and sow it again. You should get three stands of buckwheat during the season, and you can follow that with a winter cover crop of clover or annual rye.

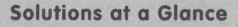

PROBLEM: These weeds stay green almost all winter and are ready to flower and set seed at the first hint of warm weather.

CULPRIT: Cool season perennials, like common chickweed (*Stellaria media*), henbit (*Lamium amplexicaule*), and sheep sorrel (*Rumex acetosella*)

SOLVE IT! Get a jump on spring cleaning by taking advantage of pleasant winter days to get those weeds out of the garden. Many are shallow-rooted, so you can pull or hoe them out with ease as long as the top inch or so of the soil isn't frozen.

PROBLEM: This mulch looks nice, but it can add too much acidity to the soil for some ornamentals.

CULPRIT: Wood chip or shredded bark mulch

SOLVE IT! A double layer of newspaper under the mulch will keep it from decomposing too quickly and adding too much acid to the soil at once.

For good measure, follow the clover the next year with a crop of pumpkins or winter squash. The large leaves will shade out any quackgrass that might remain.

EASY, WEED-FREE CARROTS I

Carrots are slow to germinate, especially in the cool soil of early spring, which means that weeds may get a jump on the crop. Here's how to make the weeds' eager-beaver tendencies work for you.

1. Prepare a seed bed and plant the carrots as usual. Water the seeds well, if the soil isn't already moist.

2. Lay a sheet of black plastic over the entire bed, weighting it down with boards or bricks.

3. After 2 weeks, start peeking under the plastic every day. You'll see lots of pale, sun-starved weeds. What you're looking for, though, are the sprouting carrots.

4. When you see the carrots start to emerge, remove the plastic. Most of the weed seeds in the soil's surface will have sprouted and died for lack of light. The carrots have the bed to themselves. Works great for parsnips, too!

Easy, Weed-Free Carrots II

Cass Peterson's gardening neighbors in Warfordsburg, Pennsylvania, use this method to save weeding work when planting carrots, parsnips, beets, or spinach.

1. Prepare a seed bed and furrow out a shallow row for the seeds of choice with the tip of a hoe (or use a push seeder with the chain that covers the seeds lifted out of the way).
2. Sprinkle the seeds in the furrow (or put them in with the push seeder, again with the chain attachment lifted out of the way). Don't cover the seeds.
3. Water the seeded furrow well.
4. Sprinkle ½ inch of dry peat moss down the furrow to cover the seeds.

Peat moss doesn't absorb moisture, so it will act as a mulch, helping to keep the seeds moist until they germinate. It's also free from weed seeds, so no weeds will sprout in the row with the carrots. And it's easy to see the planted row, so you can hoe on either side!

COVERING CARROT SEEDS WITH PEAT MOSS HELPS THE SEEDS SPROUT IN A TIDY ROW, FREE FROM WEEDS—SAVING YOU WEEDING WOES.

Pest Identification Guide

Not sure what insect is snacking on your tomatoes or nibbling on your roses? This handy guide to 31 common garden pests will help you recognize the bad guys— and then tells you how to give them the old heave-ho the organic way.

Pest	Description	Damage	Organic Control
APHID	Adults: $\frac{1}{16}$"–$\frac{3}{8}$" long; pear-shaped; have 2 tubes on rear of abdomen and long antennae. May be winged or wingless; green, pink, black, gray, or white. Nymphs: resemble adults. Common in North America.	Nymphs and adults suck sap from vegetable crops, small ornamentals, and fruit or shade trees; if severe, leaves and flowers may drop. Cause plant distortion. Secrete honeydew, which helps sooty mold to grow. Feeding may spread plant viruses.	Plant pollen and nectar plants. Release aphid midges, lady beetles, lacewings, or parasitic wasps. Spray plants with water to knock aphids off. Use garlic spray, summer oils, or insecticidal soap.
APPLE MAGGOT	Adults: $\frac{1}{4}$" long; dark-colored flies; yellow legs; transparent wings patterned with dark, crosswise bands. Larvae: $\frac{1}{4}$" long, white, develop inside fruit. Found in eastern United States and Canada; also in northern California.	Maggot larvae tunnel through apples, blueberries, and plums, leaving brown winding trails behind. Often, infested fruit will drop prematurely. Thin-skinned and early-maturing cultivars are most affected.	Plant late-ripening cultivars. Plant white clover groundcover to attract pupae predators. Hang traps in trees from mid-June until fruit colors. Pick up and destroy dropped fruit daily until September; collect fruit twice a month in fall.
ARMYWORM	Adults: pale, gray-brown moths with 1$\frac{1}{2}$"–2" wingspans. Have a white dot in the center of each forewing; active at night. Young larvae: smooth and pale green. Older larvae: reach 1$\frac{1}{2}$"; greenish brown with white side stripes and dark or light back stripes. Eggs: greenish white; on lower leaves. Found east of the Rockies, southeastern Canada, New Mexico, Arizona, and California.	Will feed on lawn grass, corn, and other field crops, especially asparagus, beans, beets, cabbage, cucumbers, lettuce, spinach, and tomatoes. Will move en masse to a new location when food supplies become limited. Larvae can consume entire plants in 1 night. First-generation larvae cause the most damage.	Attract native predators, including parasitic wasps and flies. Spray *Bacillus thuringiensis* var. *kurstaki* (BTK) to kill larvae. In July, spray superior oil to kill eggs of second generations. Cultivate the soil after harvest to expose pupae to predators.

Pest	Description	Damage	Organic Control
BLACK CHERRY APHID	Adults: $1/8$" long; winged or wingless. Nymphs: smaller than adults but are otherwise identical. Both adults and nymphs are black. Commonly found wherever black cherries are grown in North America.	Adults and nymphs feed by sucking sap from black cherry leaves and tender shoots. Feeding curls leaves and can stunt growth in leaves and stems. Heavy infestations may kill young trees. Aphid honeydew spots foliage and fruit and promotes the growth of sooty fungus.	Plant pollen- and nectar-producing flowers to attract native predators. Release purchased aphid midges, lacewings, lady beetles, or parasitic wasps. Spray insecticidal soap, though sparingly because it may damage cherry leaves.
BLACK VINE WEEVIL	Adults: up to $1/3$" long; oblong; flightless; brownish gray or black with dirty yellow back patches. Larvae: $1/2$" long, white grubs with yellowish heads. Eggs: in soil around host plants. Found in northern United States and southern Canada.	Both adults and larvae feed on broad- and narrow-leaved evergreen trees and shrubs, fruits, and ornamentals. Adults chew along leaf edges, though damage is rarely severe. Larvae can stunt plant growth by feeding on roots, potentially resulting in plant death.	At night, shake weevils onto a sheet and destroy them. Release parasitic nematodes into the soil by applying a liquid solution. Catch adult weevils on shrubs by tying a 6" band of plastic wrap around the shrub trunk and painting the plastic with Tanglefoot.
CABBAGE LOOPER	Adults: gray-brown moths with a silvery spot in the middle of each forewing; $1\frac{1}{2}$" wingspans; active in late evening. Larvae: green with two white or light yellow lines down their backs and sides. Eggs: on the undersides of leaves. Common in the United States and southern Canada.	Larvae chew large holes in leaves of cabbage-family plants, as well as beets, celery, lettuce, peas, spinach, tomatoes, carnations, nasturtiums, and mignonette. They cause the most damage during their last few days of development. May destroy entire plants.	If the infestation is small, handpick caterpillars several times weekly. Attract native predators and parasites by planting pollen and nectar plants. Bury cabbage crop residue to destroy cocoons before adults emerge in spring. Spray BTK.
CODLING MOTH	Adults: gray-brown with $3/4$" wingspans. Wings have wavy, coppery brown patterns; forewings have brown tips. Larvae: up to $3/4$" long, brown-headed, pinkish white caterpillars. Found throughout North America.	Larvae tunnel through and ruin apples, apricots, cherries, peaches, pears, and plums. Tunneling begins at the base of the fruit and usually ends at the core. Dark castings may be found at the base of the tunnel, although this may not be noticed until the fruit is cut open.	Trap caterpillars by tying sticky tree bands around trunks as they leave to pupate. Destroy all trapped larvae and pupae. Attract ground beetles. Use pheromone traps. In late winter, remove cocoons from tree bark by scraping, and spray dormant oil.

(continued)

Pest Identification
Guide—Continued

Pest	Description	Damage	Organic Control
COLORADO POTATO BEETLE	Adults: $\frac{1}{3}$" long; yellowish orange; 10 long black stripes on their wing covers; black spots on their thoraxes. Larvae: $\frac{1}{16}$"–$\frac{1}{2}$" long, humpbacked, dark orange grubs with a row of black side dots. Eggs: bright yellow ovals that stand in clusters on the undersides of leaves. Found throughout North America.	Adults and larvae feed on potatoes and other related plants. They both chew on leaves and stems, resulting in severe defoliation of older plants, or death of young plants. Mature plant yields may be reduced due to feeding.	Mulch plants with deep straw; cover plants with floating row covers. Destroy adults, eggs, and larvae on sight. Shake adults from older plants onto a sheet and destroy them. Spray *Bacillus thuringiensis* var. *san diego* when eggs are present. In fall, kill beetles by tilling the soil.
CORN EARWORM	Adults: yellowish tan moths with a wingspan of $1\frac{1}{2}$"–2". Larvae: 1"–2" long, have yellow heads, black legs, white and dark side stripes; green, pink, or brown. Eggs: round, ribbed and light green; on undersides of leaves or on corn silks. Found throughout North America.	Larvae enter corn ears from the tips, feed on corn silks and kernels, and leave excrement trails. Will chew tomato flower buds and leaves and will burrow into ripe fruit. Also known to attack peppers. Mostly affects early and late corn cultivars.	Plant corn cultivars with tight, long husks. Attract native predators by interplanting with pollen and nectar plants. Keep outdoor lights off at night. Once corn silk starts to dry, apply BTK, parasitic nematodes, or mineral oil to ear tips. Time sprays so they coincide with egg hatches.
CUCUMBER BEETLE, SPOTTED	Adults: $\frac{1}{4}$" long; greenish yellow with 12 black spots on wing covers. Larvae: up to $\frac{3}{4}$" long, white grubs with reddish brown heads; brown patches on first and last segments. Found throughout the United States and southern Canada east of the Rockies.	Larvae feed on roots of cucumber and corn plants by tunneling into the base of stems. Adults chew fruit skin, leaves, and sometimes petals of squash family plants, or other crops and flowers. Adults may transmit cucumber mosaic virus and bacterial wilt.	Plant squash family cultivars resistant to wilt and cucumber mosaic virus. Cover small and low plants with floating row covers; you may have to hand-pollinate the plants. Apply parasitic nematodes to soil around corn plants. Remove and destroy crop residue after harvest.
CUCUMBER BEETLE, STRIPED	Adults: $\frac{1}{4}$" long; yellow; have black heads and three black stripes on wing covers. Larvae: $\frac{3}{4}$" long grubs, white with reddish brown heads. Found west to Colorado and New Mexico; in Canada, west to Saskatchewan.	Larvae feed on roots of squash family plants, sometimes stunting or killing plants. Adults feed on squash, bean, corn, and pea seedling leaves and shoots; flowers of older plants; and fruit. Adults may transmit bacterial wilt and mosaic viruses.	Plant cultivars resistant to wilt and mosaic viruses. If infestation is severe, cover plants with floating row covers. Mulch plants with deep straw. Apply parasitic nematodes to soil around plants.

Pest	Description	Damage	Organic Control
CUTWORM	Adults: large, brownish gray moths with $1\frac{1}{2}$" wingspans. Larvae: 1"–2" long, fat, greasy gray or brown caterpillars with shiny heads. Most species are in soil, some climb plants. Found throughout North America.	Larvae are night feeders and will cut the stems of seedlings, shoots, and transplants of early vegetables and flowers at or below the soil line, injured plants may fall over. If plants are small, they may be eaten entirely! Adults do not damage plants.	Plant later in the season. Use cutworm collars around stems of plants. Dig around damaged plants and destroy worms. Sprinkle bran mixed with BTK and molasses a week before planting.
EUROPEAN CORN BORER	Adult females: pale yellow-brown moths with dark wing zigzags and 1" wingspans. Males: darker and smaller. Larvae: 1" long; grayish beige with brown heads and dots on segments. Found in northern and central United States, central and eastern Canada.	Larvae may attack beans, peppers, potatoes, tomatoes, and small grains. Find young larvae on corn tassels, beneath ear husks, and on the first whorl of leaves. Older larvae feed on stalks, tassels, and ears. Weakened stalks may break. Larvae overwinter in crop residue.	Plant strong-stalked and tight-husked cultivars. Attract native predators. If infestation is severe, detassel two-thirds of corn plants before pollen sheds. Apply BTK or mineral oil to ear tips. If on leaves, spray BTK. After harvest, shred and compost, or bury stalks immediately.
FLEA BEETLE	Adults: $\frac{1}{10}$" long; black, brown or bronze; large hind legs used to jump like fleas when disturbed. Larvae: up to $\frac{3}{4}$" long, white grubs with brown heads; live in soil. Found throughout North America.	Adults chew small holes in leaves of cabbage-family plants, potatoes, and spinach, with most damage in early spring. Seedlings may be killed, larger plants usually survive. Larvae feed on plant roots and may cause large losses. Adult flea beetles may spread viruses.	Delay planting to avoid population peak; cover seedlings and shoots with floating row covers or fine mesh until beetles die. Interplant crops to create shady conditions, which deter flea beetles.
GREEN FRUITWORM	Adults: Grayish pink forewings, each with two purplish gray spots. Larvae: $1\frac{1}{4}$" long; pale green with narrow white stripes. Eggs: white with grayish tinge and many ridges. Found throughout North America.	Larvae feed on leaves of deciduous fruits. They usually do not cause serious damage to leaves but later bite into fruit and may completely consume it.	Where infestations are heavy, spray BTK as soon as leaf damage is noticed.

(continued)

Pest Identification Guide—Continued

Pest	Description	Damage	Organic Control
IMPORTED CABBAGEWORM	Adults: White-winged butterflies with black wing tips and 2 or 3 spots on forewings; 1½" wingspan. Larvae: green with a light yellow back stripe. Eggs: tiny yellow cones on leaf undersides. Found throughout North America.	Larvae feed on leaf undersides of all cabbage-family plants, eventually leaving ragged holes in cabbage leaves and florets of cauliflower and broccoli. Soils leaves with dark green pellets.	Plant purple cabbage cultivars; protect and attract natural enemies, including yellow jacket wasps. Handpick caterpillars and eggs. Cover plants with floating row covers. Use yellow sticky traps. Spray BTK.
JAPANESE BEETLE	Adults: ½" long; blocky; metallic blue-green; bronze wing covers; white abdomen hair; long legs with large claws. Larvae: up to ¾" long, fat, dirty white grubs, found in soil. Found in all states east of the Mississippi River.	Adults feed on many vegetables, especially asparagus, beans, corn, okra, onions, rhubarb, and tomatoes. In warm weather, they eat flowers and cause leaves to drop by skeletonizing them. May defoliate plants completely. Larvae feed on roots of lawn turf and other grasses.	Cover small or valuable garden plants with screens or floating row covers. Handpick or vacuum beetles or shake beetles off plants and destroy. Dry out lawn between waterings and aerate the turf in late spring and early fall.
LEAFHOPPER	Adults: ⅒"–½" long; wedge-shaped; broad triangular head; brown or green; color bands on wings; use strong hind wings to jump into flight. Nymphs: similar to adults but paler and wingless; hop rapidly. Found throughout North America.	Adults and nymphs suck juice from stems and leaf undersides of flowers, fruit trees, and vegetables, especially apple trees, beans, eggplant, grapes, peanuts, potatoes, and squash-family plants. Plants may develop tipburn and yellowed, curled leaves with white spots, or warty, crinkled and rolled edges.	Encourage parasitic flies, lady beetles, lacewings, spiders, and other native predators. Spray strong streams of water to wash nymphs from plants. Spray dormant oil to kill overwintering adults. Spray neem or insecticidal soap while nymphs are small.
MEXICAN BEAN BEETLE	Adults: ¼" long; yellowish brown with 16 black spots on wing covers. Larvae: ⅓" long, yellowish grubs with spines. Eggs: bright yellow, laid in clusters on leaf undersides. Found east of Mississippi River, Texas, Arizona, Utah, Colorado, and Nebraska.	Both larvae and adults skeletonize leaves of cowpeas, lima beans, snap beans, and soybeans. They feed from underneath leaves, creating a lacy pattern. Infestations may decrease pod production or kill plants.	Plant resistant cultivars; plant early; cover young plants with floating row covers. Attract native predators with flowering weeds; plant soybeans as a trap crop—destroy them once they're infested with larvae. Handpick larvae and adults.

Pest	Description	Damage	Organic Control
PEAR PSYLLA	Adults: 1/10" long; dark red-brown; green or red marks; transparent wings (like roofs) over their backs. Nymphs: small, oval, yellow with red eyes and no wings. Eggs: yellow and oval. Found in eastern United States and Canada; also in Pacific Northwest and California.	Saliva causes pear and quince leaves to yellow. If infestation is severe, leaves will brown and drop; fruit will drop prematurely or be stunted. Honeydew supports growth of sooty mold. May spread diseases and viruses by sucking juices.	Encourage native predators. Spray dormant oils after fall leaf drop and before bud swell in spring. Spray insecticidal soap or summer oil during growing season.
PLUM CURCULIO	Adults: 1/5" long; brownish gray; warty wing covers; white hair. Larvae: 1/3" long, white grubs with brown heads. Eggs: round, white, laid singly under crescent-shaped cuts in fruit skin. Found in eastern North America.	Adult feeding and egg-laying leaves half-circle scars in fruit skin of apples, blueberries, and most tree fruits. Larvae tunnel and feed near fruit pits, causing fruit to rot or prematurely drop.	Collect and destroy fallen fruit daily. Knock curculios from trees onto a ground sheet by sharply tapping tree with a padded stick; drown the curculios in soapy water.
ROSE CHAFER	Adults: 1/3" long; reddish brown with yellow hairs on wing covers; black underside. Larvae: small white grubs in soil. Found throughout North America.	Adults chew on flowers, leaves and fruit of blackberries, grapes, raspberries, strawberries, tree fruits, garden vegetables, dahlias, hollyhocks, irises, peonies, poppies, and roses. Serious damage occurs when numbers are high. Larvae feed on grass and weed roots.	Control is usually not needed. Handpick if necessary. With severe infestations, protect plants with floating row covers. Cultivate soil to kill pupae.
SLUG	Adults: 1/8"–1" long; gray, tan, green or black with dark spot patterns; exude a slimy mucus. Eggs: clear; oval or round; found in jellylike masses under stones, twigs, logs, or other garden debris. Found throughout North America.	Feeds on decayed plant matter. Will chew large holes in bulbs, stems, and plant foliage. May completely destroy seedlings; young shoots and plants may be severely damaged. May climb trees and shrubs to feed. Will attack any vegetable; can decimate citrus and tender plants.	Encourage birds, snakes, toads, lizards, ground beetles, and fireflies. Repel slugs with copper strips on tree trunks or shrubs. Edge gardens with copper flashing. Use commercial slug tape. Spread cinders or wood ash to protect seedlings. Set out small dishes of beer to drown slugs.

(continued)

Pest Identification Guide—Continued

Pest	Description	Damage	Organic Control
SPIDER MITE	Adults: $\frac{1}{75}$"–$\frac{1}{50}$" long; eight legs; reddish, pale green or yellow with fine hairs. Nymphs: like adults; six legs. Spins fine webs on leaves and shoots. Found throughout North America.	Adults and nymphs feed by sucking juice from plant cells on leaf undersides. Will attack vegetables, ornamental trees, fruit trees, berries, herbs, annuals, perennials, shrubs, vines, and houseplants. Feeding weakens plants, causes leaf drop, and stunts fruit. Look for yellow-speckled or bronze leaves and webbing.	Maintain high humidity in greenhouses and around houseplants. Release predatory mites. Spray dormant oil on fruit trees; minimize pesticide use to protect predatory mites. Spray neem or insecticidal soap. Spray summer oil on tolerant woody shrubs and trees.
SQUASH BUG	Adults: $\frac{5}{8}$" long; oval; dark brown to black; flat abdomen with fine, dark hair. Nymphs: pale green. Older nymphs: reddish thorax and abdomen; sometimes looks like they've been rolled in gray powder. Found throughout North America.	Adults and nymphs suck plant juice from pumpkins, squash, or other squash-family plants. May cause leaves and shoots to turn black and die. Severe infestations may limit fruit production. Damage mimics wilt disease.	Plant resistant cultivars. Use floating row covers over young plants—you may have to hand pollinate. Handpick bugs from leaf undersides. Place boards on the ground next to plants; in the morning, destroy adults found under the boards.
SQUASH VINE BORER	Adults: moths with brownish olive forewings; clear hind wings; fringed hind legs; and a red abdomen with black rings; 1"–$1\frac{1}{2}$" wingspan. Larvae: 1" long, white grubs with brown heads. Found throughout most of North America.	Larvae burrow into vines of squash-family plants, but especially those with thick stems like gourds, pumpkins, and squash. While boring, the larvae chew inner vine tissue and leave slimy castings behind. Attacked vines will wilt and girdled vines will rot. May also feed on fruit.	Plant early; promote vigorous and fast growth. Cover young plants with floating row covers—you may have to hand pollinate.
STINK BUG	Adults: $\frac{1}{2}$"–$\frac{5}{8}$" long; five-sided, shield-like body; green, tan, brown or gray. May have bright red or black harlequin markings. Will emit a foul smell if disturbed. Nymphs: wingless, oval, similar to adults. Eggs: barrel-shaped, underneath leaves. Found throughout North America.	Adults and nymphs suck sap from leaves, flowers, fruit and seeds of beans, cabbage, corn, okra, peas, squash, soybeans, tomatoes, peaches, and forage crops. Leaves may wilt, turn brown, or have brown spots. Feeding on fruit causes scarring. Legume pods may drop or have deformed seeds.	Encourage native predators; control garden weeds; remove crop residue in fall. Handpick all stages; crush eggs; shake plants over a container of soapy water. Spray insecticidal soap. Till garden at end of growing season.

Pest	Description	Damage	Organic Control
TARNISHED PLANT BUG	Adults: 1/4" long; oval; light green to brownish copper, top of each wing has black-tipped triangle; back half of wings slant to the rear. Nymphs: wingless; yellow-green; five black dots on body; similar to adults. Found throughout North America.	Adults and nymphs suck juice from leaves, buds, and fruit of a wide variety of flowers, fruit, vegetables, and weeds. Toxic saliva causes plants to drop buds and pods; will also distort leaves and shoots. Sometimes plants will wilt or be stunted. Branch tips blacken and die back.	Avoid legumes as cover crops in orchards. Encourage native predators. If infestation is severe, cover small plants with floating row covers. Mow weeds and decrease crop debris. Spray summer oil on tolerant plant species.
TOMATO HORNWORM	Adults: narrow-winged, gray moths with 4"–5" wingspans. Larvae: up to 4 1/2"; green with large black horn on tail; diagonal side marks. Found throughout North America.	Larvae chew holes in leaves of tomatoes, eggplants, peppers, potatoes, and tobacco, leaving the midribs. Young plants may be completely defoliated. If infestation is severe, may chew on stems and fruit.	Handpick and destroy caterpillars. Spray BTK or neem if caterpillars are small. Till garden soil in early spring and fall.
WATER LILY BEETLE	Adults: 1/4" long; blocky wing covers; yellow legs; brown joints; long antennae; dark, rusty brown. Larvae: small white grubs. Found in North America where waterlilies and smartweed grow.	Chews holes in leaves and flowers of water lilies, smartweeds, purple loosestrife, and water chestnut. Will leave stippling on plant leaves.	Clean up dead plant foliage, especially from the water's edge. Wipe off eggs from underneath leaves. Handpick larvae from leaves. If infestation is severe, though limited to one plant, remove infested plant from garden.
WHITEFLY	Adults: 1/20" long; powdery-white. Nymphs: 1/30" long; flat; legless; translucent and scaly. Eggs: gray or yellow pinpoint-sized cones on leaf undersides. Found in North American greenhouses and in warm regions of California, Florida, the Gulf states, and West Coast areas.	Nymphs and adults suck plant juice from citrus, ornamentals, annuals, rhododendrons, azaleas, grapes, and vegetables (especially squash- and tomato-family plants), causing plants to weaken. May spread viruses; honeydew supports sooty mold.	Encourage native predators. Capture adults on yellow sticky traps. Vacuum adults from leaf undersides. Spray neem, insecticidal soap, or summer oil on oil-tolerant plants.

Resources

To help you find great plants, garden supplies, and even more ingenious gardening ideas, we've compiled the following list of plant associations, gardening organizations, mail-order nurseries, garden suppliers, and product manufacturers. When you contact associations or specialty nurseries by mail, please enclose a self-addressed, stamped envelope with your inquiry. Notes in italics indicate particular products, plants, or services offered.

ASSOCIATIONS AND ORGANIZATIONS

American Dianthus Society
Rand B. Lee
P.O. Box 22232
Santa Fe, NM 87502-2232

American Iris Society
Ada Godfrey
9 Bradford Street
Foxborough, MA 02035
Web site: www.irises.org

American Rose Society
P.O. Box 30000
Shreveport, LA 71130-0030
Phone: (318) 938-5402
Fax: (318) 938-5405
Web site: www.ars.org

Backyard Wildlife Habitat Program
National Wildlife Federation
8925 Leesburg Pike
Vienna, VA 22184-0001
Web site: www.nwf.org/habitats

Bio-Dynamic Farming and Gardening Association
Bldg. 1002B, Thoreau Center, The Presidio
P.O. Box 29135
San Francisco, CA 94129-0135
Phone: (888) 516-7797
Fax: (415) 561-7796
E-mail: biodynamic@aol.com
Web site: www.biodynamics.com

California Certified Organic Farmers
1115 Mission Street
Santa Cruz, CA 95060
Phone: (831) 423-2263
Fax: (831) 423-4528
E-mail: ccof@ccof.org
Web site: www.ccof.org

The Lady Bird Johnson Wildflower Center
4801 La Crosse Avenue
Austin, TX 78739-1702
Phone: (512) 292-4100
Fax: (512) 292-4627
E-mail: wildflower@wildflower.org
Web site: www.wildflower.org

The Maine Organic Farmers and Gardeners Association
P.O. Box 2176
Augusta, ME 04338
Phone: (207) 622-3118
Fax: (207) 622-3119
Web site: www.mofga.org

National Gardening Association
180 Flynn Avenue
Burlington, VT 05401
Phone: (802) 863-1308
Fax: (802) 863-5962
Web site: www.garden.org

North American Butterfly Association (NABA)
4 Delaware Road
Morristown, NJ 07960
Phone: (973) 285-0907
Fax: (973) 285-0936
E-mail: naba@naba.org
Web site: www.naba.org

North American Fruit Explorers (NAFEX)
1716 Apples Road
Chapin, IL 62628
Phone: (217) 245-7589
Fax: (217) 245-7844
E-mail: vorbeck@csj.net
Web site: www.nafex.org

Northeast Organic Farming Association (NOFA)
Web site: www.nofa.org
An affiliation of seven state chapters—CT, MA, NH, NJ, RI, VT. Check Web site for state contacts

Rodale Institute Experimental Farm
611 Siegfriedale Road
Kutztown, PA 19530
Phone: (610) 683-1400
Fax: (610) 683-8548
E-mail: info@rodaleinst.org
Web site: www.rodaleinstitute.org

Seed Savers Exchange
3076 N. Winn Road
Decorah, IA 52101
Phone: (319) 382-5990
Web site: www.seedsavers.org

Seeds of Diversity Canada
P.O. Box 36
Station Q
Toronto, Ontario M4T 2L7
Canada
Phone: (905) 623-0353
E-mail: sodc@interlog.com
Web site: www.seeds.ca

BENEFICIAL INSECTS
Gardens Alive!
5100 Schenley Place
Lawrenceburg, IN 47025
Phone: (812) 537-8651
Fax: (812) 537-5108
Web site: www.gardensalive.com

Gurney's Seed and Nursery Co.
110 Capital Street
Yankton, SD 57079
Phone: (605) 665-1671
Fax: (605) 665-9718
Web site: www.gurneys.com

Harmony Farm Supply and Nursery
P.O. Box 460
Graton, CA 95444
Phone: (707) 823-9125
Fax: (707) 823-1734
Web site: www.harmonyfarm.com

Peaceful Valley Farm Supply
P.O. Box 2209
Grass Valley, CA 95945
Phone: (530) 272-4769
Fax: (530) 272-4794
Web site: www.groworganic.com

Territorial Seed Co.
P.O. Box 157
Cottage Grove, OR 97424-0061
Phone: (541) 942-9547
Fax: (888) 657-3131
E-mail: tertrl@srv1.vsite.com
Web site:
    www.territorial-seed.com

BULBS
Breck's
6523 N. Galena Road
Peoria, IL 61632
Phone: (800) 804-6742
Web site: www.brecks.com

Brent and Becky's Bulbs
7463 Heath Trail
Gloucester, VA 23061
Phone: (804) 693-3966,
    (877) 661-2852
Fax: (804) 693-9436
E-mail:
    store@brentandbeckysbulbs.com
Web site:
    www.brentandbeckysbulbs.com

Dutch Gardens
P.O. Box 2105
Lakewood, NJ 08701
Phone: (800) 818-3861
Fax: (732) 780-7720
E-mail: info@dutchgardens.nl
Web site: www.dutchgardens.nl

McClure and Zimmerman
P.O. Box 368
108 W. Winnebago
Friesland, WI 53935-0368
Phone: (800) 883-6998
Fax: (800) 374-6120
E-mail: info@mzbulb.com
Web site: www.mzbulb.com

Van Bourgondien Bros.
P.O. Box 1000
Babylon, NY 11702-9004
Phone: (800) 622-9997
Fax: (800) 327-4268
E-mail: blooms@dutchbulbs.com
Web site: www.dutchbulbs.com

FLOWERS
Abundant Life Seed Foundation
P.O. Box 772
Port Townsend, WA 98368
Phone: (360) 385-5660
Fax: (360) 385-7455
E-mail: abundant@olypen.com
Web site:
    http://csf.Colorado.edu/
    perma/abundant

Kurt Bluemel, Inc.
2740 Greene Lane
Baldwin, MD 21013-9523
Phone: (800) 248-7584
Fax: (410) 557-9785
E-mail: kbi@bluemel.com
Web site: www.bluemel.com

Bluestone Perennials
7211 Middle Ridge Road
Madison, OH 44057
Phone: (800) 852-5243
Fax: (440) 428-7198
E-mail: bluestone@bluestone
   perennials.com
Web site:
   www.bluestoneperennials.com

Bountiful Gardens
18001 Shafer Ranch Road
Willits, CA 95490-9626
Phone: (707) 459-6410
Fax: (707) 459-1925
E-mail: bountiful@sonic.net
Web site:
   www.bountifulgardens.org

W. Atlee Burpee and Co.
300 Park Avenue
Warminster, PA 18974
Phone: (800) 888-1447
Fax: (215) 674-4170
Web site: www.burpee.com

Busse Gardens
17160 245th Avenue
Big Lake, MN 55309
Phone: (800) 544-3192
Fax: (320) 286-6601
E-mail: customerservice@
   bussegardens.com
Web site: www.bussegardens.com

California Carnivores
7020 Trenton-Healdsburg Road
Forestville, CA 95436
Phone: (707) 838-1630
Fax: (707) 838-9899
E-mail: califcarn@aol.com
Web site:
   www.californiacarnivores.com
*Commercially propagated pitcher
plants* (Sarracenia *ssp.*)

Ferry-Morse Seed Co.
P.O. Box 488
Fulton, KY 42041-0488
Phone: (800) 283-3400
Fax: (800) 283-2700
Web site: www.ferry-morse.com

Flowery Branch Seed Co.
P.O. Box 1330
Flowery Branch, GA 30542
Phone: (770) 536-8380
Fax: (770) 532-7825
E-mail:
   seedsman@mindspring.com
Web site: www.flowerybranch.com

Forestfarm
990 Tetherow Road
Williams, OR 97544-9599
Phone: (541) 846-7269
Fax: (541) 846-6963
E-mail: orders@forestfarm.com
Web site: www.forestfarm.com

Fragrant Farms, Inc.
413 Woods Lane
New Harmony, IN 47631
Phone: (888) 814-4665
Fax: (812) 682-4577
E-mail: mark@fragrantfarms.com
Web site: www.fragrantfarms.com

Heronswood Nursery
7530 N.E. 288th Street
Kingston, WA 98346
Phone: (360) 297-4172
Fax: (360) 297-8321
E-mail: orders@heronswood.com
Web site: www.heronswood.com

Jackson and Perkins
P.O. Box 1028
Medford, OR 97501
Phone: (800) 292-4769
Fax: (800) 242-0329
E-mail: service@jacksonand
   perkins.com
Web site: www.jacksonand
   perkins.com

Johnny's Selected Seeds
RR 1, Box 2580
Foss Hill Road
Albion, ME 04910-9731
Phone: (207) 437-9294
Fax: (207) 437-2759
E-mail:
   johnnys@johnnyseeds.com
Web site: www.johnnyseeds.com

Logee's Greenhouses, Ltd.
141 North Street
Danielson, CT 06239-1939
Phone: (860) 774-8038;
   (888) 330-8038
Fax: (888) 774-9932
E-mail: logee-info@logees.com
Web site: www.logees.com

Niche Gardens
1111 Dawson Road
Chapel Hill, NC 27516
Phone: (919) 967-0078
Fax: (919) 967-4026
E-mail: orders@nichegdn.com
Web site: www.nichegdn.com

Nichols Garden Nursery
1190 N. Pacific Highway
Albany, OR 97321-4580
Phone: (541) 928-9280
Fax: (800) 231-5306
E-mail: customersupport@
nicholsgardennursery.com
Web site:
www.nicholsgardennursery.com

Pinetree Garden Seeds
P.O. Box 300
New Gloucester, ME 04260
Phone: (207) 926-3400
Fax: (888) 527-3337
E-mail: pinetree@superseeds.com
Web site: www.superseeds.com

Plant Delights Nursery, Inc.
9241 Sauls Road
Raleigh, NC 27603
Phone: (919) 772-4794
Fax: (919) 662-0370
E-mail: office@plantdel.com
Web site: www.plantdel.com

Prairie Moon Nursery
R.R. #3, Box 163
Winona, MN 55987
Phone: (507) 452-1362
Fax: (507) 454-5238
Web site:
www.prairiemoonnursery.com

Seeds Blüm
27 Idaho City Stage Road
Boise, ID 83716
Phone: (800) 742-1423
Fax: (208) 338-5658
E-mail:
103374.167@compuserve.com
Web site: www.seedsblum.com

Seeds of Change
P.O. Box 15700
Sante Fe, NM 87506-5700
Phone: (888) 762-7333
Fax: (888) 329-4762
E-mail:
gardener@seedsofchange.com
Web site:
www.seedsofchange.com

Select Seeds Antique Flowers
180 Stickney Hill Road
Union, CT 06076
Phone: (860) 684-9310
Fax: (800) 653-3304
E-mail: info@selectseeds.com
Web site: www.selectseeds.com

Shepherd's Garden Seeds
30 Irene Street
Torrington, CT 06790-6658
Phone: (860) 482-3638
E-mail:
custsrv@shepherdseeds.com
Web site: www.shepherdseeds.com

Territorial Seed Co.
P.O. Box 157
Cottage Grove, OR 97424-0061
Phone: (541) 942-9547
Fax: (541) 942-9881
E-mail: tertrl@srv1.vsite.com
Web site:
www.territorial-seed.com

Thompson and Morgan, Inc.
P.O. Box 1308
Jackson, NJ 08527-0308
Phone: (800) 274-7333
Fax: (888) 466-4769
E-mail:
tminc@thompson-morgan.com
Web site:
www.thompson-morgan.com

Van Ness Water Gardens
2460 North Euclid Avenue
Upland, CA 91784-1199
Phone: (800) 205-2425
Fax: (909) 949-7217
E-mail: vnwg@vnwg.com
Web site: www.vnwg.com

Wayside Gardens
1 Garden Lane
Hodges, SC 29695-0001
Phone: (800) 845-1124
Fax: (800) 457-9712
E-mail:
curator@waysidegardens.com
Web site:
www.waysidegardens.com

Wildseed Farms
P.O. Box 3000
425 Wildflower Hills
Fredericksburg, TX 78624-3000
Phone: (800) 848-0078
Fax: (830) 990-8090
E-mail: wsf@fbg.net
Web site:
www.wildseedfarms.com

FRUITS AND BERRIES

Adams County Nursery, Inc.
26 Nursery Road
P.O. Box 108
Aspers, PA 17304
Phone: (717) 677-8105
Fax: (717) 677-4124
E-mail: acn@cvn.net
Web site: www.acnursery.com

Bear Creek Nursery
P.O. Box 411
Northport, WA 99157
Phone: (509) 732-6219
Fax: (509) 732-4417
E-mail:
    info@bearcreeknursery.com
Web site:
    www.BearCreekNursery.com

Edible Landscaping
361 Spirit Ridge Lane
P.O. Box 77
Afton, VA 22920-0077
Phone: (804) 361-9134
Fax: (804) 361-1916
E-mail: el@cstone.net
Web site: www.eat-it.com

Hartmann's Plant Company
P.O. Box 100
Lacota, MI 49063-0100
Phone: (616) 253-4281
Fax: (616) 253-4457
E-mail: info@harmannsplant
    company.com
Web site: www.hartmannsplant
    company.com

Indiana Berry and Plant Co.
5218 West 500 South
Huntingburg, IN 47542
Phone: (800) 295-2226
Fax: (812) 683-2004
E-mail: berryinfo@inberry.com
Web site: www.inberry.com

Raintree Nursery
391 Butts Road
Morton, WA 98356
Phone: (360) 496-6400
Fax: (888) 770-8358
E-mail: customerservice@
    raintreenursery.com
Web site:
    www.raintreenursery.com

**Rocky Meadow Orchard &
    Nursery**
360 Rocky Meadow Road NW
New Salisbury, IN 47161
Phone: (812) 347-2213
Fax: (812) 347-2488
E-mail: rockymdw@netpointe.com

Southmeadow Fruit Gardens
P.O. Box 211
10603 Cleveland Avenue
Baroda, MI 49101
Phone: (616) 422-2411
Fax: (616) 422-1464
E-mail: smfruit@aol.com

**Stark Bro's Nurseries and
    Orchards Co.**
P.O. Box 10, Dept. AB 1122 A9
Louisiana, MO 63353
Phone: (800) 478-2759
Fax: (573) 754-5290
E-mail: service@starkbros.com
Web site: www.starkbros.com

Van Well Nursery
P.O. Box 1339
Wenatchee, WA 98807
Phone: (509) 886-8189,
    (800) 572-1553
Fax: (509) 886-0294
E-mail: vanwell@vanwell.net
Web site: www.vanwell.net

GARDENING SUPPLIES AND TOOLS

Biocontrol Network
5116 Williamsburg Road
Brentwood, TN 37027
Phone: (615) 370-4301
Fax: (615) 370-0662
E-mail: info@biconet.com
Web site: www.biconet.com

BioSensory
Windham Mills Technology Center
322 Main Street, Building 1,
    2nd floor
Willimantic, CT 06226-3149
Phone: (860) 423-3009
Web site: www.biosensory.com

Bountiful Gardens
18001 Shafer Ranch Road
Willits, CA 95490-9626
Phone: (707) 459-6410
Fax: (707) 459-1925
E-mail: bountiful@sonic.net
Web site:
    www.bountifulgardens.org

W. Atlee Burpee and Co.
300 Park Avenue
Warminster, PA 18974
Phone: (800) 888-1447
Fax: (215) 674-4170
Web site: www.burpee.com

Charley's Greenhouse Supply
17979 State Route 536
Mount Vernon, WA 98273-3269
Phone: (800) 322-4707
Fax: (800) 233-3078
Web site:
    www.charleysgreenhouse.com

**Delgard Aluminum Ornamental
    Fencing**
Delair Group, Inc.
8600 River Road
Delair, NJ 08110
Phone: (800) 235-0185
Fax: (856) 663-1297
E-mail: info@delairgroup.com
Web site:
    www.delairgroup.com/delgard

Dripworks
190 Sanhedrin Circle
Willits, CA 95490
Phone: (800) 616-8321
Fax: (707) 459-9645
E-mail: dripwrks@pacific.net
Web site: www.dripworksusa.com
Drip irrigation products

Ehrlich Chemical Company
Magic Circle Deer Repellent
Donna Zerbee
500 Spring Ridge Drive
Reading, PA 19612
Phone: (610) 372-9700

Gardener's Supply Co.
128 Intervale Road
Burlington, VT 05401-2850
Phone: (888) 863-1700
Fax: (800) 551-1412
E-mail: info@gardeners.com
Web site: www.gardeners.com

Gardens Alive!
5100 Schenley Place
Lawrenceburg, IN 47025
Phone: (812) 537-8651
Fax: (812) 537-5108
E-mail:
    gardenhelp@gardens-alive.com
Web site: www.gardensalive.com

**Harmony Farm Supply and
    Nursery**
P.O. Box 460
Graton, CA 95444
Phone: (707) 823-9125
Fax: (707) 823-1734
E-mail: info@harmonyfarm.com
Web site: www.harmonyfarm.com

Johnny's Selected Seeds
RR 1, Box 2580
Foss Hill Road
Albion, ME 04910-9731
Phone: (207) 437-9294
Fax: (207) 437-2759
E-mail:
    johnnys@johnnyseeds.com
Web site: www.johnnyseeds.com

Kinsman Garden Co., Inc.
P.O. Box 357
River Road
Point Pleasant, PA 18950-0357
Phone: (800) 733-4146,
    (215) 297-0890
Fax: (215) 297-0450
E-mail: kinsmangarden@bux.com
Web site:
    www.kinsmangarden.com

Lehman's Catalog
One Lehman Circle
P.O. Box 41
Kidron, OH 44636
Phone: (888) 438-5346
Fax: (330) 857-5785
E-mail: info@lehmans.com
Web site: www.lehmans.com

A. M. Leonard, Inc.
241 Fox Drive
P.O. Box 816
Piqua, OH 45356-0816
Phone: (800) 543-8955
Fax: (800) 433-0633
E-mail: info@amleo.com
Web site: www.amleo.com

Max-Flex Fence Systems
U.S. Route 219
Lindside, WV 24951
Phone: (800) 356-5458
Fax: (304) 753-4827
E-mail: mail@maxflex.com
Web site: www.maxflex.com

The Natural Gardening Co.
P.O. Box 750776
Petaluma, CA 94975
Phone: (707) 766-9303
Fax: (707) 766-9747
E-mail:
    info@naturalgardening.com
Web site:
    www.naturalgardening.com

Natural Insect Control
RR#2
Stevensville, Ontario
L0S 1S0 Canada
Phone: (905) 382-2904
Fax: (905) 382-4418
E-mail: nic@niagara.com
Web site: www.natural-insect-
    control.com

N.I.M.B.Y.
DMX Industries
6540 Martin Luther King
St. Louis, MO 63133
Phone: (314) 385-0076
Fax: (314) 385-0062
E-mail: dmxinds@aol.com

Peaceful Valley Farm Supply
P.O. Box 2209
Grass Valley, CA 95945
Phone: (888) 784-1722,
    (530) 272-4769
Fax: (530) 272-4794
E-mail: contact@groworganic.com
Web site: www.groworganic.com

Planet Natural
1612 Gold Avenue
Bozeman, MT 59715
Phone: (406) 587-5891
Fax: (406) 587-0223
E-mail: ecostore@mcn.net
Web site: www.planetnatural.com

**Pond and Landscape
   Solutions, Inc.**
2899 E. Big Beaver, #238
Troy, MI 48083
Fax: (248) 524-9059
E-mail: sales@pondsolutions.com
Web site: www.pondsolutions.com

**Saratoga Rail Fence and
   Supply Co.**
P.O. Box 13864
Albany, NY 12212-9600
Phone: (800) 869-8703
Fax: (518) 869-8755
PVC post and rail fencing

Seeds of Change
P.O. Box 15700
Sante Fe, NM 87506-5700
Phone: (888) 762-7333
Fax: (888) 329-4762
E-mail:
   gardener@seedsofchange.com
Web site:
   www.seedsofchange.com

H. B. Sherman Traps Inc.
3731 Peddie Drive
Tallahassee, FL 32303
Phone: (850) 575-8727
Fax: (850) 575-4864
E-mail: traps@shermantraps.com
Web site: www.shermantraps.com

Smith and Hawken
2 Arbor Lane, Box 6900
Florence, KY 41022-6900
Phone: (301) 771-4542
Fax: (301) 986-4829
E-mail: smithandhawkencustomer
   service@discovery.com
Web site:
   www.smithandhawken.com

The Tanglefoot Company
314 Straight Avenue SW
Grand Rapids, MI 49504-6485
Phone: (616) 459-4139
Fax: (616) 459-4140
E-mail: tnglfoot@aol.com
Web site: www.tanglefoot.com

Territorial Seed Co.
P.O. Box 157
Cottage Grove, OR 97424-0061
Phone: (541) 942-9547
Fax: (541) 942-9881
E-mail: tertrl@srv1.vsite.com
Web site:
   www.territorial-seed.com

Unilock New York, Inc.
51 International Boulevard
Brewster, NY 10509
Phone: (800) 864-5625
Fax: (914) 278-6788
E-mail: unilock@unilock.com
Web site: www.unilock.com
*Paving stones, retaining walls,
and curbing*

Whatever Works
Earth Science Building
74 20th Street
Brooklyn, NY 11232
Phone: (800) 499-6757
Fax: (718) 499-1005
Web site:
   www.whateverworks.com

Worm's Way
7850 N. Highway 37
Bloomington, IN 47404
Phone: (800) 274-9676
Fax: (800) 316-1264
E-mail: sales@wormsway.com
Web site: www.wormsway.com

Herbs

Gaia Garden Herbal Dispensary
2672 West Broadway
Vancouver, BC V6K 2G3
Canada
Phone: (604) 734-4372
Fax: (604) 734-4376
E-mail: herbs@gaiagarden.com
Web site: www.gaiagarden.com

Goodwin Creek Gardens
P.O. Box 83
Williams, OR 97544
Phone: (800) 846-7357
Fax: (541) 846-7357
E-mail: info@goodwincreek
   gardens.com
Web site: www.goodwincreek
   gardens.com

Horizon Herbs
P.O. Box 69
Williams, OR 97544
Phone: (541) 846-6704
Fax: (541) 846-6233
E-mail: herbseed@chatlink.com
Web site:
   www.chatlink.com/~herbseed

Long Creek Herbs
Route 4, Box 730
Oak Grove, AR 72660
Phone: (417) 779-5450
Fax: (417) 779-5450
E-mail: jim@longcreekherbs.com
Web site:
   www.longcreekherbs.com

Lunar Farms Herbals
3 Highland-Greenhills
Gilmer, TX 75644
Phone: (800) 687-1052
E-mail: spritsong1@aol.com
Web site:
   www.herbworld.com/lunarfarms

Nichols Garden Nursery
1190 N. Pacific Highway
Albany, OR 97321-4580
Phone: (541) 928-9280
Fax: (800) 231-5306
E-mail: customersupport@
    nicholsgardennursery.com
Web site:
    www.nicholsgardennursery.com

Richters Herb Catalogue
357 Highway 47
Goodwood, Ontario
L0C 1A0 Canada
Phone: (905) 640-6677
Fax: (905) 640-6641
E-mail: orderdesk@richters.com
Web site: www.richters.com

Sage Mountain Herbs
P.O. Box 420
E. Barre, VT 05649
Phone: (802) 479-9825
Fax: (802) 476-3722
E-mail: SageMtnHP@aol.com
Web site:
    www.sagemountainherbs.com

The Sandy Mush Herb Nursery
Dept. OGRS
316 Surrett Cove Road
Leicester, NC 28748
Phone: (704) 683-2014

Well-Sweep Herb Farm
205 Mt. Bethel Road
Port Murray, NJ 07865
Phone: (908) 852-5390
Fax: (908) 852-1649

SOIL TESTING

Cook's Consulting
R.D. 2, Box 13
Lowville, NY 13367
Phone: (315) 376-3002
*Organic recommendations, free
soil-testing kit*

Peaceful Valley Farm Supply
P.O. Box 2209
Grass Valley, CA 95945
Phone: (888) 784-1722,
    (530) 272-4769
Fax: (530) 272-4794
E-mail: contact@groworganic.com
Web site: www.groworganic.com

Timberleaf Soil Testing Services
39648 Old Spring Road
Murrieta, CA 92563
Phone: (909) 677-7510
*Basic and trace mineral soil
tests; organic recommendations
provided*

Wallace Laboratories
365 Coral Circle
El Segundo, CA 90245
Phone: (310) 615-0116
Fax: (310) 640-6863
E-mail: contact@wallace-labs.com
Web site: www.wallace-labs.com

Woods End Research Laboratory
P.O. Box 297
Mt. Vernon, ME 04352
Phone: (800) 451-0337
Fax: (207) 293-2488
E-mail: weblink@woodsend.org
Web site: www.woodsend.org

TREES, SHRUBS, AND VINES

Carroll Gardens
444 E. Main Street
Westminster, MD 21157
Phone: (800) 638-6334
Fax: (410) 857-4112
Web site: www.carrollgardens.com

Forestfarm
990 Tetherow Road
Williams, OR 97544-9599
Phone: (541) 846-7269
Fax: (541) 846-6963
E-mail: orders@forestfarm.com
Web site: www.forestfarm.com

Greer Gardens
1280 Goodpasture Island Road
Eugene, OR 97401-1794
Phone: (541) 686-8266
Fax: (541) 686-0910
E-mail: orders@greergardens.com
Web site: www.greergardens.com

Gurney's Seed and Nursery Co.
110 Capital Street
Yankton, SD 57079
Phone: (605) 665-1671
Fax: (605) 665-9718
E-mail: info@gurneys.com
Web site: www.gurneys.com

Pickering Nurseries, Inc.
670 Kingston Road
Pickering, Ontario
L1V 1A6 Canada
Phone: (905) 839-2111
Fax: (905) 839-4807
Web site:
    www.pickeringnurseries.com

ROSES

The Roseraie at Bayfields
P.O. Box R
Waldoboro, ME 04572-0919
Phone: (207) 832-6330
Fax: (800) 933-4508
E-mail: zapus@roseraie.com
Web site: www.roseraie.com

Roslyn Nursery
211 Burrs Lane
Dix Hills, NY 11746
Phone: (631) 643-9347
Fax: (631) 427-0894
E-mail: roslyn@roslynnursery.com
Web site: www.roslynnursery.com

Wayside Gardens
1 Garden Lane
Hodges, SC 29695-0001
Phone: (800) 845-1124
Fax: (800) 457-9712
E-mail:
    curator@waysidegardens.com
Web site:
    www.waysidegardens.com

White Flower Farm
P.O. Box 50
Litchfield, CT 06759-0050
Phone: (800) 255-2852
Fax: (860) 496-1418
E-mail:
    custserv@whiteflowerfarm.com
Web site:
    www.whiteflowerfarm.com

Woodlanders, Inc.
1128 Colleton Avenue
Aiken, SC 29801
Phone/Fax: (803) 648-7522

Vegetables

Abundant Life Seed Foundation
P.O. Box 772
Port Townsend, WA 98368
Phone: (360) 385-5660
Fax: (360) 385-7455
E-mail: abundant@olypen.com
Web site: csf.Colorado.edu/
    perma/abundant

Bountiful Gardens
18001 Shafer Ranch Road
Willits, CA 95490-9626
Phone: (707) 459-6410
Fax: (707) 459-1925
E-mail: bountiful@sonic.net
Web site:
    www.bountifulgardens.org

W. Atlee Burpee and Co.
300 Park Avenue
Warminster, PA 18974
Phone: (800) 888-1447
Fax: (215) 674-4170
Web site: www.burpee.com

The Cook's Garden
P.O. Box 535
Londonderry, VT 05148
Phone: (800) 457-9703
Fax: (800) 457-9705
E-mail:
    gardener@cooksgarden.com
Web site: www.cooksgarden.com

William Dam Seeds Ltd.
P.O. Box 8400
Dundas, Ontario
L9H 6M1 Canada
Phone: (905) 627-6641
Fax: (905) 627-1729
E-mail: willdam@sympatico.ca

Ferry-Morse Seed Co.
P.O. Box 488
Fulton, KY 42041-0488
Phone: (800) 283-3400
Fax: (800) 283-2700
Web site: www.ferry-morse.com

Garden City Seeds
778 Highway 93 N
Hamilton, MT 59840
Phone: (406) 961-4837
Fax: (406) 961-4877
E-mail: seeds@montana.com
Web site:
    www.gardencityseeds.com

Gurney's Seed and Nursery Co.
110 Capital Street
Yankton, SD 57079
Phone: (605) 665-1671
Fax: (605) 665-9718
E-mail: info@gurneys.com
Web site: www.gurneys.com

Irish Eyes with a Hint of Garlic
P.O. Box 307
Thorp, WA 98926
Phone: (509) 964-7000
Fax: (800) 964-9210
E-mail: potatoes@irish-eyes.com
Web site: www.irish-eyes.com

Johnny's Selected Seeds
RR1, Box 2580
Foss Hill Road
Albion, ME 04910-9731
Phone: (207) 437-4357
Fax: (207) 437-2759
E-mail: customerservice@
    johnnyseeds.com
Web site: www.johnnyseeds.com

Native Seeds/SEARCH
2509 N. Campbell Avenue # 325
Tucson, AZ 85719
Phone: (602) 327-9123

Park Seed
1 Parkton Avenue
Greenwood, SC 29647-0001
Phone: (800) 845-3369
Fax: (800) 275-9941
E-mail: orders@parkseed.com
Web site: www.parkseed.com

Ronniger's Seed and Potato Co.
P.O. Box 1838
Orting, WA 98360
Phone: (860) 893-8782
Fax: (360) 893-3492

Seed Savers Heirloom Seeds and Gifts
3076 N. Winn Road
Decorah, IA 52101
Phone: (319) 382-5990
Fax: (319) 382-5872

Seeds Blüm
27 Idaho City Stage Road
Boise, ID 83716
Phone: (800) 742-1423
Fax: (208) 338-5658
E-mail:
103374.167@compuserve.com
Web site: www.seedsblum.com

Seeds of Change
P.O. Box 15700
Sante Fe, NM 87506-5700
Phone: (888) 762-7333
Fax: (888) 329-4762
E-mail:
gardener@seedsofchange.com
Web site:
www.seedsofchange.com

Seeds Trust, High Altitude Gardens
P.O. Box 1048
Hailey, ID 83333-1048
Phone: (208) 788-4363
Fax: (208) 788-3452
E-mail: higarden@micron.net
Web site: www.seedsave.org

Shepherd's Garden Seeds
30 Irene Street
Torrington, CT 06790-6658
Phone: (860) 482-3638
Fax: (860) 482-0532
E-mail:
custsrv@shepherdseeds.com
Web site:
www.shepherdseeds.com

Southern Exposure Seed Exchange
P.O. Box 170
Earlysville, VA 22936
Phone: (804) 973-4703
Fax: (804) 973-8717
E-mail: gardens@
southernexposure.com
Web site:
www.southernexposure.com

Tomato Growers Supply Company
P.O. Box 2237
Fort Myers, FL 33902
Phone: (941) 768-1119
Fax: (888) 768-3476
Web site:
www.tomatogrowers.com

Vermont Bean Seed Co.
Garden Lane
Fair Haven, VT 05743
Phone: (803) 663-0217
Fax: (888) 500-7333
E-mail: info@vermontbean.com
Web site: www.vermontbean.com

Wood Prairie Farm
Jim and Megan Gerritsen
49 Kinney Road
Bridgewater, ME 04735
Phone: (207) 429-9765 or
(800) 829-9765
Fax: (800) 300-6494
Web site: www.woodprairie.com

Wildflowers

Abundant Life Seed Foundation
P.O. Box 772
Port Townsend, WA 98368
Phone: (360) 385-5660
Fax: (360) 385-7455
E-mail: abundant@olypen.com
Web site: csf.colorado.edu/
perma/abundant

Clyde Robin Seed Co.
P.O. Box 2366
Castro Valley, CA 94546
Phone: (510) 785-0425
Fax: (510) 785-6463
Web site: www.clyderobin.com

Native Seeds/SEARCH
2509 N. Campbell Avenue # 325
Tucson, AZ 85719
Phone: (602) 327-9123

Plants of the Southwest
Agua Fria Road
Route 6, Box 11A
Santa Fe, NM 87501
Phone: (800) 788-7333
Fax: (505) 438-8800
E-mail: contact@plantsofthe
southwest.com
Web site: www.plantsofthe
southwest.com

Prairie Moon Nursery
Route 3, Box 163
Winona, MN 55987
Phone: (507) 452-1362
Fax: (507) 454-5238
Web site:
www.prairiemoonnursery.com

Prairie Nursery
P.O. Box 306
Westfield, WI 53964
Phone: (800) 476-9453
Fax: (608) 296-2741
Web site: www.prairienursery.com

Wildseed Farms
P.O. Box 3000
425 Wildflower Hills
Fredericksburg, TX 78624-3000
Phone: (800) 848-0078
Fax: (830) 990-8090
Web site:
www.wildseedfarms.com

Recommended Reading

COMPOSTING AND SOIL

Appelhof, Mary. *Worms Eat My Garbage.* Kalamazoo, MI: Flower Press, 1982.

Greshuny, Grace. *Start with the Soil.* Emmaus, PA: Rodale, 1993.

Hynes, Erin. *Rodale's Successful Organic Gardening: Improving the Soil.* Emmaus, PA: Rodale, 1994.

Martin, Deborah, and Grace Gershuny, eds. *The Rodale Book of Composting.* Emmaus, PA: Rodale, 1992.

Martin, Deborah, and Karen Costello Soltys, eds. *Rodale Organic Gardening Basics: Soil.* Emmaus, PA: Rodale, 2000.

GENERAL GARDENING

Benjamin, Joan, ed. *Great Garden Shortcuts.* Emmaus, PA: Rodale, 1996.

Bradley, Fern Marshall, and Barbara Ellis, eds. *Rodale's All-New Encyclopedia of Organic Gardening.* Emmaus, PA: Rodale, 1992.

Bucks, Christine, ed. *Rodale Organic Gardening Basics: Vegetables.* Emmaus, PA: Rodale, 2000.

Coleman, Eliot. *The New Organic Grower.* White River Junction, VT: Chelsea Green Publishing, 1995.

Costenbader, Carol W. *The Big Book of Preserving the Harvest.* Pownal, VT: Storey Communications, 1997.

Cunningham, Sally Jean. *Great Garden Companions.* Emmaus, PA: Rodale, 1998.

Lanza, Patricia. *Lasagna Gardening.* Emmaus, PA: Rodale, 1998.

Logsdon, Gene. *The Contrary Farmer's Invitation to Gardening.* White River Junction, VT: Chelsea Green Publishing, 1997.

Stone, Pat. *Easy Gardening 101.* Pownal, VT: Storey Communications, 1998.

Swain, Roger. *The Practical Gardener.* Boston: Little, Brown and Company, 1989. Reprint, New York: Galahad Books, 1998.

FRUITS AND BERRIES

McClure, Susan. *Rodale's Successful Organic Gardening: Fruits and Berries.* Emmaus, PA: Rodale, 1996.

Nick, Jean, and Fern Marshall Bradley. *Growing Fruits and Vegetables Organically.* Emmaus, PA: Rodale, 1994.

Reich, Lee. *Uncommon Fruits Worthy of Attention.* Reading, MA: Addison-Wesley Publishing, 1991.

Herbs

Duke, James A. *The Green Pharmacy*. Emmaus, PA: Rodale, 1997.

Gladstar, Rosemary. *Herbal Healing for Women*. New York: Simon & Schuster, 1993.

James, Tina. *The Salad Bar in Your Own Backyard*. Reisterstown, MD: Gardening from the Heart, 1996.

Kowalchik, Claire, and William H. Hylton. *Rodale's Illustrated Encyclopedia of Herbs*. Emmaus, PA: Rodale, 1987.

Long, Jim. *Herbs, Just for Fun: A Beginner's Guide to Starting an Herb Garden*. Oak Grove, AR: Long Creek Herbs, 1996.

——. *Classic Herb Blends*. Oak Grove, AR: Long Creek Herbs, 1996.

McClure, Susan. *The Herb Gardener: A Guide for All Seasons*. Pownal, VT: Storey Communication, 1995.

Oster, Maggie. *Herbal Vinegar*. Pownal, VT: Storey Communication, 1994.

Oster, Maggie, and Sal Gilbertie. *The Herbal Palate Cookbook*. Pownal, VT: Storey Communications, 1996.

Smith, Miranda. *Your Backyard Herb Garden*. Emmaus, PA: Rodale, 1997.

Sombke, Laurence. *Beautiful Easy Herbs*. Emmaus, PA: Rodale, 1997.

Tourles, Stephanie. *The Herbal Body Book*. Pownal, VT: Storey Communications, 1994.

Landscape and Flower Gardening

Bender, Steve, and Felder Rushing. *Passalong Plants*. Chapel Hill: The University of North Carolina Press, 1993.

Bradley, Fern Marshall, ed. *Gardening with Perennials*. Emmaus, PA: Rodale, 1996.

Byczynski, Lynn. *The Flower Farmer: An Organic Grower's Guide to Raising and Selling Cut Flowers*. White River Junction, VT: Chelsea Green Publishing, 1997.

Cox, Jeff. *Perennial All-Stars: The 150 Best Perennials for Great-Looking, Trouble-Free Gardens*. Emmaus, PA: Rodale, 1998.

D'Amato, Peter. *The Savage Garden: Cultivating Carnivorous Plants*. Berkeley, CA: Ten Speed Press, 1998.

DiSabato-Aust, Tracy. *The Well-Tended Perennial Garden: Planting and Pruning Techniques*. Portland, OR: Timber Press, 1998.

Ellis, Barbara. *Taylor's Guide to Growing North America's Favorite Plants*. Boston: Houghton Mifflin, 1998.

Harper, Pamela, and Frederick McGourty. *Perennials: How to Select, Grow and Enjoy*. Los Angeles: Price Stern Sloan, 1985.

McKeon, Judy. *The Encyclopedia of Roses*. Emmaus, PA: Rodale, 1995.

Phillips, Ellen, and C. Colston Burrell. *Rodale's Illustrated Encyclopedia of Perennials*. Emmaus, PA: Rodale, 1993.

Sombke, Laurence. *Beautiful Easy Flower Gardens*. Emmaus, PA: Rodale, 1995.

Taylor, Norman. *Taylor's Guide to Annuals*. Rev. ed. Boston: Houghton Mifflin, 1986.

Soltys, Karen Costello, ed. *Rodale Organic Gardening Basics: Roses*. Emmaus, PA: Rodale, 2000.

Pest Management

Ellis, Barbara W., and Fern Marshall Bradley. *The Organic Gardener's Handbook of Natural Insect and Disease Control*. Emmaus, PA: Rodale, 1992.

Gilkeson, Linda, et al. *Rodale's Pest and Disease Problem Solver*. Emmaus, PA: Rodale, 1996.

Hart, Rhonda. *Bugs, Slugs, and Other Thugs*. Pownal, VT: Storey Communications, 1991.

SEASON EXTENSION

Colebrook, Binda. *Winter Gardening in the Maritime Northwest*. Seattle, WA: Sasquatch Books, 1989.

Coleman, Eliot. *Four-Season Harvest: How to Harvest Fresh, Organic Vegetables from Your Home Garden All Year Long*. White River Junction, VT: Chelsea Green Publishing, 1992.

SEED STARTING

Bubel, Nancy. *The New Seed-Starter's Handbook*. Emmaus, PA: Rodale, 1988.

Ondra, Nancy, and Barbara Ellis. *Easy Plant Propagation*. (Taylor's Weekend Gardening Guides.) Boston: Houghton Mifflin, 1998.

Powell, Eileen. *From Seed to Bloom*. Pownal, VT: Storey Communications, 1995.

WEEDS

Hynes, Erin. *Rodale's Successful Organic Gardening: Controlling Weeds*. Emmaus, PA: Rodale, 1995.

Pleasant, Barbara. *The Gardener's Weed Book*. Pownal, VT: Storey Communications, 1996.

MAGAZINES AND NEWSLETTERS

Avant Gardener, The, P.O. Box 489, New York, NY 10028

Common Sense Pest Control Quarterly, Bio-Integral Resource Center (BIRC), P.O. Box 7414, Berkeley, CA 94707-0414

Country Living Gardener, 224 W. 57th Street, New York, NY 10019

Growing for Market, P.O. Box 3747, Lawrence, KS 66046

Homesteader's Connection, P.O. Box 5186, Cookeville, TN 38505

HortIdeas, 750 Black Lick Road, Gravel Switch, KY 40328

Organic Gardening, Rodale, 33 E. Minor Street, Emmaus, PA 18098

Index

as mulch, 183

as raccoon deterrent, 35

N.I.M.B.Y., 126, 154

No-see-ums, 79–80, *79*

Nursery beds, 75

Nutritional deficiencies

of blueberries, 15, **16**

and mulch, 109

O

Oats, and strawberries, 13

Odors

as deer repellent, 2, **2**, 35–36

and mosquitoes, 107

repellent to animals, 2, **2**

P

Paperpots, 151

Parsnips, 173, 186, 187, *187*

Paths, materials for, 77

Patios, planting pockets in, 78, *78*

Peaches

and borers, 73

cracking trunks of, 71

diseases of, **73,** 122, 123

protecting from frost, 73

pruning of, 122, 123

Peach scab, and peaches, **73**

Pears

forcing to bear young, 70

pear psylla and, **72**, 193, *193*

picking, 71, *71*

Pedios (*Pediobius foveolatus*

wasps), 104

Perennials

accidental weeding of, 74

dividing, 64, *64,* 118

for dry shade, 141

easy to grow, 67

for late-season bloom, 66

prolonging bloom of, 67

supporting, 68

Pergolas, *139*

Petroleum jelly, 62

pH, lowering, **16**

Picea species, and Cooley spruce

gall adelgid, **56**

Pinching, 8

Planters. *See also* Containers

growing vegetables in, 32

growing woody plants in,

166–67, *167*

for water gardens, 177, *177*

Plant lice, 7–8, *7, 8*

Plant selection

and disease prevention, 48–49,

50, 115

for dry conditions, 33, 67, 181

for site, 58, 163–64

Plastic bags, and pests, 3

Plastic jugs, as rabbit protection,

126, *126*

Plastic "snakes," and rabbits, 3

Plum curculio, 193, *193*

Plums, **73,** 123

Poison ivy, 110–12, *110*

Potatoes, 113–14, *114*

early blight and, 49

insect pests of, 26–27, 63

storing, 114, 173

Powdery mildew, 49, 115–16, *116*

and apples, **73**

and melons, **152**

and roses, 129, *129*

and squash, **152**

and vegetables, **171**

Propagation, 117–20, **118,** *120*

Pruning, 121–24, *121, 122, 124*

as aphid control, 8

of evergreens, 54, *54,* 57

of fruit trees, 69, *70*

of hedges, 166, *166*

of roses, 127–28, *128*

of tomatoes, 159

Pumpkins, and raccoons, 4

Purple martins, 72–73

Q

Quackgrass, 185–86

R

Rabbits, 125–26, *125*

deterring, **2,** 3, 4–5, *4,* 60, 154

droppings of as fertilizer, 128

plants disliked by, **5**

and tulips, **20**

typical damage of, 6

Raccoons, 2–3, 4, 35

Radishes, and cabbageworms,

23, 25, *25*

Raised beds

and beans, 12, *12*

of concrete blocks, 76, *76*

for herbs, 88–89, *89*

for vegetables, 169

and voles, 174–75, *174*

Raspberries, 14, 15

Recipes

for animal attractant, 4–5

aphid-repelling juice, 7, *7*

baking-soda fungicides, 51,

116, 129

castor-oil mole repellent, 98

USDA Plant Hardiness Zone Map

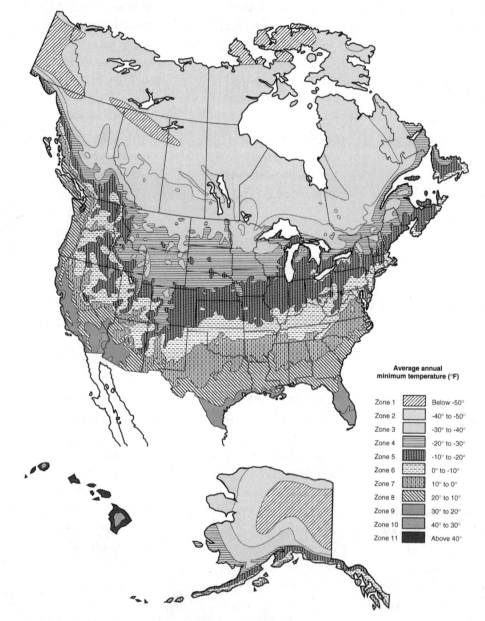

Average annual minimum temperature (°F)

Zone 1		Below -50°
Zone 2		-40° to -50°
Zone 3		-30° to -40°
Zone 4		-20° to -30°
Zone 5		-10° to -20°
Zone 6		0° to -10°
Zone 7		10° to 0°
Zone 8		20° to 10°
Zone 9		30° to 20°
Zone 10		40° to 30°
Zone 11		Above 40°

This map was revised in 1990 and is recognized as the best indicator of minimum temperatures available. Look at the map to find your area, then match its color to the key. When you've found your color, the key will tell you what hardiness zone you live in. Remember that the map is a general guide; your particular conditions may vary.